Christianity and Identity

Christianity and Identity

Public Theology, Authoritarianism, and Democracy

Faith and Public Reason, Volume 1

SCOTT RONALD PAETH

CASCADE *Books* • Eugene, Oregon

CHRISTIANITY AND IDENTITY: PUBLIC THEOLOGY, AUTHORITARIANISM, AND DEMOCRACY
Faith and Public Reason, Volume 1

Cascade Books
An Imprint of Wipf and Stock Publishers
199 W. 8th Ave., Suite 3
Eugene, OR 97401

www.wipfandstock.com

PAPERBACK ISBN: 978-1-7252-7095-4
HARDCOVER ISBN: 978-1-7252-7096-1
EBOOK ISBN: 978-1-7252-7097-8

Cataloguing-in-Publication data:

Names: Paeth, Scott, author.

Title: Christianity and identity: public theology, authoritarianism, and democracy : faith and public reason, volume 1 / Scott Ronald Paeth.

Description: Eugene, OR : Cascade Books, 2026 | Includes bibliographical references and index.

Identifiers: ISBN 978-1-7252-7095-4 (paperback) | ISBN 978-1-7252-7096-1 (hardcover) | ISBN 978-1-7252-7097-8 (ebook)

Subjects: LCSH: Public theology. | Church and state—United States. | Public theology—United States. | United States—Religion.

Classification: BT83.63 .P34 2026 (print) | BT83.63 (ebook)

Contents

Preface

Great disease was mighty
And the people were sick everywhere.
It was an epidemic,
It floated through the air.
Well, we done told you, our God's done warned you.
Jesus coming soon.

—Blind Willie Johnson, "Jesus is Coming Soon"[1]

In a very real way, we are living in the midst of the apocalypse. It's not the first, and it won't be the last. But I have entertained for some time the slightly crazy thought that, all appearances to the contrary notwithstanding, the world really did end in the year 2000, or at least a world did. All of those who were living in fear of the Y2K bug turned out to be right. The world fell apart; the center failed to hold. But rather than mere anarchy, what was unloosed upon the world was a period of unending war, economic dislocation, environmental disaster, and disease. Anarchy to be sure, but anything but mere.

In saying this, I'm not attempting to imply that I know the day or the hour of Christ's coming. As we've been warned, such speculation is foolhardy. It's also beside the point. An apocalypse is an unveiling, a revelation of that which was hidden, and the past two decades have revealed much about our world that we wished to keep hidden. As pundits praised the final years of the twentieth century as the "end of history," something was beginning to burst the seams of complacency in which many of us in the Western, so-called developed world had cocooned ourselves.

1. 1928, public domain.

Historians sometimes refer to the first fifteen years of the twentieth century as the "long nineteenth century," because in many ways those early years were simply a recapitulation of what had come before. The world of 1910 looked more like the world of 1890 than 1920. But the horrors of war, revolution, and pandemic created an abrupt ending to what many had believed was a European peace that could go on indefinitely. After World War I, the Bolshevik Revolution, and the Spanish Flu, it was no longer possible to hold to such illusions. It is no wonder Blind Willie Johnson could compose a blues anthem about these years with the refrain: "We done told you, God done warned you, Jesus is coming soon!"

This was followed by further decades of war, both hot and cold, for the rest of the century. At the same time, industrialization and economic growth led to increasing prosperity in the years following World War II. It was possible, even in a world of air raid sirens and atomic bomb drills, to envision a world that could get potentially better, even as the threat of nuclear destruction loomed.

In the end, however, the "long nineteenth century" was followed by an exceptionally short twentieth century. If in 1999 there were many who believed that the (as it turned out ephemeral) prosperity of the previous decade and the (largely illusory) peace of the post-Cold War era could continue indefinitely, September 11, 2001, proved that to be a forlorn hope.

My goal in this project is to examine what has been unveiled in our apocalyptic time. How the roots of the present moment are planted in the disordered loves around which we organized the social and political imperatives of the last century, and which have continued into the current one. Through this examination, I hope to illuminate how we might alter our current course, and move toward a more just, more peaceful, and more sustainable global society. If, as Larry Rasmussen has suggested, "there's no place to hide in the Anthropocene,"[2] then the central moral question confronting Christianity is how, in the absence of cover, we can stand forthrightly on behalf of a vision for a world beyond the paradoxes of our present age, and beyond the current apocalyptic moment.

2. Rasmussen, "There's No Place to Hide." For my part, I have my doubts about the common use of the phrase "anthropocene" to describe the present epoch. It strikes me as unnecessarily, well, anthropocentric at a point when we should be striving to become more theocentric. Yet it serves an important function in drawing attention to the impact of humanity on planet Earth.

Introduction

American national mythology typically follows one of two basic narratives: The first is that the United States is a nation of immigrants who came to America from across the world in order to forge their own way in a country that allowed them to express their unique cultural and religious identities without fear of persecution. The second is that the United States is the unique bequeathal of a particular strain of European Christianity, and all that is good about America is ultimately traceable back to that—white, Protestant—tradition.

Myths, by their nature, are stories that we tell ourselves at least in part to validate our place in the world. American mythic narratives pull our national identity in two, often opposing, directions: The first toward a celebration of difference and diversity, and the second toward a celebration of the particular heritage of a particular people. At the same time, myths of all kinds need to be distinguished from facts of history. The narratives of American origins tell us far more about the people who rely on them for their identities than they do about the real history of the United States, which has never been either as accepting of diversity, nor as monolithically grounded in one tradition, as these narratives would lead one to believe.

What these narratives *do* tell us about, however, is the America that we *want* to be, and that we wish we had always been. But again, this pulls in two contradictory directions: America as a "melting pot" of diverse peoples, or America as the "Christian nation" grounded in a story about Pilgrims coming to establish a shining city on a hill.[1] At their best, American myth-makers have combined these two narratives into a sort

1. Winthrop, *Model of Christian Charity*, 91. This sentiment was of course repurposed by Peggy Noonan for Ronald Reagan's "A Vision for America" in 1980, framing America as a great beacon of hope for the whole world in the struggle against communism.

of whole, through which the unique heritage of the Puritan colonists was the founding of a land of "freedom" and "liberty," specifically religious freedom and liberty, of which people of all nations could partake. It is this version of the myth that underlies Emma Lazarus's poem on the plaque at the foot of the Statue of Liberty, proclaiming a welcome to the "huddled masses yearning to breathe free" and Martin Luther King's description of the Declaration of Independence as a "promissory note" guaranteeing "all men, yes, Black men as well as White men" equal participation in American society.[2]

This aspirational myth—of a nation founded as a haven for those cast out for their difference—was never true. It wasn't true at our founding, and it has never been true since. But it reflects a desire on the part of many Americans for it to *become* true. The bloody American history of racism and genocide against Black and Indigenous people belies attempts to pretend that this is in any way a reflection of reality. But if it does not and cannot reflect our past, for many Americans, it might project our future.

Or at least, that was the case until fairly recently. While one would be hard pressed to select a specific date on which the tide began to turn against this unifying myth of American pluralism, one could do far worse than to pick November 8, 2016, as the date on which it finally became undeniably clear that there were many Americans who no longer subscribed to it. This was of course the date of Donald Trump's election as president of the United States.

Trump was not the cause of this demythologization. It was going on long before he ran for office. And it did not end with his presidency, or with his re-election. Rather, his presidency exposed, finally and indubitably, the rot that this unifying myth covered up. Trump, by saying out loud and explicitly what was often said quietly or in coded language, made clear that for many Americans the myth of the United States as a pluralistic haven was neither normative nor welcome. For these people, America was a white, Christian nation. Non-whites and non-Christians were—at best—to be tolerated and were far more likely to be viewed as a threat to America's white, Christian national identity.[3]

Kristen Kobes du Mez surveys the evolution of the particular constellation of white evangelical Protestantism, Americanism, and a

2. King, "I Have a Dream," 217–20.

3. See Jones, *End of White Christian America* and Jones, *White Too Long*. See also Du Mez, *Jesus and John Wayne*.

conception of rugged masculinity. As she describes it, white evangelical Christianity began to embrace this particular conflation of whiteness, Americanness, and Christianity particularly in the years following World War II.[4] Prior to this, the kind of evangelicalism now associated with Billy Graham and Jerry Falwell tended to be relegated to the cultural margins. But in making common cause with American anticommunist politics in the 1950s, it began to move closer to the political center that had previously been occupied by mainline Christian figures like Reinhold Niebuhr and Paul Tillich (both featured on the cover of *Time* during this period, with Niebuhr referred to as the "theologian of the establishment"[5]).

Yet, the evangelical ethos seemed to fit the tenor of the times in the 1950s more than its mainline cousin, grounded as it was in anxiety over the purported threats posed by communism, civil rights, and feminism:

> Fear had been at the heart of evangelical postwar politics—fear of godless communism and fear that immorality would leave Americans defenseless. What changed by the 1950s was evangelicals' sense of their own power. Between the end of World War II and the beginning of the 1960s, evangelicals had become more and more confident that they had a providential role to play in strengthening American defenses and upholding American faithfulness. . . . Among evangelicals, a rhetoric of fear would persist, though it would be aimed at internal threats as much as external ones. Instrumental to their efforts to reclaim power, this rhetoric of fear would continue to bolster the role of the heroic masculine protector. There might be a place for the softer virtues, but the perilous times necessitated ruthless power.[6]

This rhetoric of fear worked against the aspirational mythology of an America that was open and diverse even as it fed the idea of America as an exclusively Christian nation. Ethnic and ideological others posed a threat to America's Christian character, and as such, needed to be resisted with all possible force in the name of the Christian faith.

This is not to suggest that the aspirational myth of an inclusive America disappeared. But the newly empowered evangelical right, in its efforts to defend its view of what it conceived as "traditional" American values—white, patriarchal, pro-capitalist, and above all Christian—was a waxing force at the same time that mainline Christianity in the United

4. Du Mez, *Jesus and John Wayne*, 21.
5. Chambers, "Faith for a Lenten Age."
6. Du Mez, *Jesus and John Wayne*, 59.

States was beginning to decline.[7] The rise of neoconservatism in foreign policy was paralleled by the emergence of a "theoconservative" movement in religion—a collaboration between conservative Catholics and evangelicals to gain and keep political power in order to combat what they perceived as the pernicious effects of encroaching liberalism and secularism in the United States. This movement reached its apex with the election of George W. Bush in 2000.[8]

The period of time since November 2016 has only offered an increasingly stark portrait of what America looks like in the absence of this aspirational myth. It can be seen in the rise of white nationalist hate groups around the United States. It can be seen in the explicitly fascist rhetoric that motivated the "Unite the Right" rally in Charlottesville, Virginia, in 2017 and Donald Trump's Madison Square Garden rally in 2024.[9] It can be seen in the Trump-era policies of family separation at the US/Mexico border, which resulted in children, often infants, being forcibly taken from their parents, with no mechanism for them to be reunited. It can be seen in police violence against peaceful protesters. And it could be seen in every tweet that flowed forth from the phone of Donald Trump.

When, on January 6, 2021, rioters stormed the US Capitol in the name of keeping Donald Trump president despite his clear electoral loss, this was not an aberration, but rather the denouement of everything that had come before it, as well as a sign of things to come. There was no reason to believe that, with Trump out of the White House, those whose sense of nostalgia embraced the mythology of white Christian nationalism would relent. Violence against those whose identity fails to conform to this myth has continued, in sometimes more, sometimes less explicit and emphatic ways, and the prospect of ongoing violence in the name of the preservation of this mythology will continue long past the end of Trump's reign.

Again, all of this, including the tweets, pre-dated Trump's presidency. And for many Americans, particularly Americans of color, there was

7. And of course, it should be noted that mainline Protestant Christianity was seldom a bastion of resistance to these forces. Prior to the 1960s and the rise of various forms of liberation theology, Protestant Christianity was often just as accepting of racism and sexism as Evangelicalism, if sometimes more skeptical of capitalism and the use of violence.

8. Linker, *Theocons*, 5.

9. Both the setting and the rhetoric of Trump's 2024 rally echoed the pro-Nazi rally held in Madison Square Garden in 1939 organized by the German-American Bund. Bump, "Another Night at the Garden."

absolutely nothing revelatory in any of this. On the contrary, the unifying myth of American diversity had always been a thin veneer over a racist form of nationalism, and the rise of the religious right in the 1970s merely concretized the religious dimension of this nationalism.

However, the myth of a white, Christian America is no more a reflection of reality than the myth of unifying pluralism. America was never as white nor as Christian as this mythology would lead one to believe. But more significantly, this mythology was only capable of functioning by engaging in a willful erasure of the participation of non-white and non-Christian Americans in every dimension of national and cultural life. And, at least as importantly, this mythology is increasingly untenable in a nation that is both more ethnically diverse and less religious than ever.[10]

IDENTITY AND CHRISTIAN NATIONALISM

That said, this is not a book primarily about Donald Trump, even though his ongoing presence is sadly unavoidable. And it is not a book *merely* about the contradictions of American mythology, even though the reality of those contradictions will be apparent throughout. This is a book about what it means to be a Christian in America in this particular moment. More specifically, it is a book about how Christianity functions as an identity in a context in which the question of identities—racial, ethnic, national, etc.—are at the forefront of public discourse.

For many Americans, there is an indelible connection between American identity and Christian identity. While America has never been the Christian nation that some pretend that it is, many American Christians find it difficult to think of their faith apart from their national identity. We can see the markers of it in the religious symbology of many American churches, which incorporate national symbols alongside religious ones in their sanctuaries. This is particularly prevalent within certain strains of Protestantism, which may lay images of Abraham Lincoln alongside those of Jesus. It was never more explicitly illustrated to me than when, as a student minister, I was brought into the sanctuary of the church where I would be serving for the summer, only to be greeted by the enormous central stain glass window depicting, not a scene from the Bible or an image of Jesus, but a Boy Scout, arrayed in a brown shirt and shorts, holding an American flag. A few weeks later, the anthem for

10. Jones, *End of White Christian America*, 45.

the Fourth of July weekend was a karaoke version of Lee Greenwood's completely secular song, "God Bless the U.S.A."[11]

This problem of religious nationalism in the United States, intertwined as it is with Christian identity, is the primary impetus for this project. Even as the myth of white Christian Americanness has always lived within the American story, a perceptible change has taken place over the past decade—although whether it represents a new departure or a reversion to an earlier norm remains to be seen. In any event, whether emergent or resurgent, it has manifested itself in increasingly explicit and increasingly violent ways since Barack Obama's election in 2008, crystallized during Donald Trump's first term, and continues to burgeon in American political discourse through the increasingly strident rhetoric—sometimes with tragic consequences—on the American right.

Damon Linker's *The Theocons* details the means by which, over decades, the intellectual and institutional foundations for forms of right-wing Christian nationalism were laid through the work of Catholic theologians such as Richard John Neuhaus and Michael Novak, working in conjunction with evangelical movements such as the Moral Majority and the Christian Coalition. Acting as the flagship for this developing movement, the journal *First Things* shaped its ideological and policy agenda. Coalescing around issues such as abortion and the struggle over LGBTQ+ rights in the United States, the coalition of conservative/reactionary Catholics and right-wing evangelicals became a potent political force.

The theocon attitude was eloquently articulated by Richard John Neuhaus in his book *The Naked Public Square*, as he wrote:

> History is contingent. The unthinkable becomes routine, the inevitable turns out to be illusion. Nobody is an authority on the future, and those who trust alleged authorities will likely end up looking very foolish. Societies once governed by dictators become democratic and then return to dictatorship. Policies aimed at racial justice advance and then recede and then, one hopes, advance again. . . . There is no "future" to guide our

11. In recounting this story, I want to make clear that the members of this church were never anything but unfailingly kind and loving in their behavior. The stained-glass window had apparently been a gift given to the church many years before, apparently without adequate guidance about what it should, and should not, contain. And as for the song, for many otherwise faithful Christians, the phrase "God Bless the U.S.A." is apparently sufficient to baptize even the most secular sentiments, though Lee Greenwood has been happy to capitalize on its reputation, even aiding in Trump's reelection by cross-promoting his "God Bless the U.S.A." Bibles.

> present decisions. There are only possible futures that we can strive to advance or resist. More precisely, there is no "future" until it happens, and then it is fleetingly the present on the way to becoming the past. Yet we persist in trying to dismiss proposals labeled as conservative because, we confidently proclaim, they are not of the future but of the past. . . . And when our ways of ordering reality have been invalidated by speculative duties that have become specific pasts, they are still valid in our signs because they are of "the future." Thus are put into motion the ever receding horizons of utopias religious and secular, in endless flight from the perils of falsification.[12]

As Linker notes, the practical upshot of this attitude was a willingness to make common cause in the name of "a religious future in which upholding theological orthodoxy and moral traditionalism overrode doctrinal disagreements. . . . in which the most orthodox and traditionalist Christians set the public tone and policy agenda for the nation."[13] To the extent that pluralist democracy and democratic structures of governance were an impediment to this vision, so much the worse for pluralist democracy.

Yet, the contemporary brand of right-wing Christian nationalism is far less reliant on the intellectual and institutional foundations established by an earlier generation. Right-wing populists have no real interest in a set of well-grounded policy arguments. Rather, they rely on a politics of *ressentiment* and the fervor of those who experience themselves as left out of the new dispensation established by a more inclusive and pluralist polity.[14] When, in the aftermath of 2016, pundits sought a means of understanding how Trump won, they turned to analyses such as now-Vice President J. D. Vance's *Hillbilly Elegy* in an effort to understand the disaffection of white, rural and working class men and women who turned out for Trump, and yet, who seemed to have no coherent ideological basis for doing so.[15]

12. Neuhaus, *Naked Public Square*, 193.

13. Linker, *Theocons*, 86.

14. This having been said, such intellectual and institutional foundations do continue to exist. While the center of gravity has moved away from *First Things*, it has shifted to organizations like the Claremont Institute, which has provided intellectual cover for the increasingly authoritarian tone of American conservativism over the past decade.

15. Vance, *Hillbilly Elegy*. However, these retrospective analyses seemed to go out of their way to avoid grappling with the way in which these trends were grounded in white resentment of racial progress and Christian fears of religious pluralism and secularism. As such, the increasingly racially polarized language of the populist right was initially ignored or explained away, and the increasingly strident Christian nationalism

This virulent stew of Christian nationalism and right-wing populism led, through the vector of internet chatroom culture, to the development of QAnon, a perfect storm of religious devotion, right-wing ideology, and the Donald Trump cult of personality. As a perfectly self-contained political narrative, QAnon is impervious to refutation, while at the same time encouraging violence in the name of Donald Trump as the only means of defeating an apocalyptically evil cabal of political elites who subsist on the blood of infants.

QAnon is a particularly hideous manifestation of these trends, and of course there are many more examples that one could evince, but often it's far more subtle than this. It's as simple as the assumption that the Venn diagram of Christianity and American patriotism is a circle. Yet that is precisely the assumption that I want to call into question in this book. More than that, however, I want to consider some of the many ways in which Christianity and identity are parsed in contemporary culture. The central question is: What does it mean to possess an identity grounded in Christ, and how is that identity in a very real sense compatible or incompatible with the many other identities that claim us?

Considering this question requires an account of just how identities are constructed, and how identities grounded in nation, race, gender, sexuality, or political affiliation intersect with one another, as well as with our identities as Christians. Does a Christian identity require the erasure of other identities, or does it recontextualize those identities, causing us to relate to them differently than we otherwise might? As will become clear, my sympathies are toward the latter interpretation, but it is important to dwell briefly at this juncture on why that is and how it is distinct from the identification of Christianity and white nationalism that has contributed to the crisis of community faced in the United States today.

When one identifies Christianity and nationalism, one identifies Christianity with particular national or ethnic self-conceptions. This is the same with other forms of identity as well. To the extent that any identity seeks to absorb and co-opt Christian identity, it distorts the meaning of Christianity and subordinates Christianity to the imperatives of that identity. In the contemporary context, nationalism (specifically white ethno-nationalism) represents the most virulent and aggressive species of this, but the potential exists anywhere in which Christianity comes into contact with another form of self-conception.

(perversely including adoration of Donald Trump as a messianic figure), given inadequate attention.

And yet, we all have *many* forms of self-conception in addition to our Christian identity. So it cannot be the case that Christianity is simply the erasure of other forms of identity. As Kwame Anthony Appiah powerfully states: "Identities make ethical claims because—and this is just a fact about the world we human beings have created—we make our lives *as* men and *as* women, *as* gay and *as* straight people, *as* Ghanaians and *as* Americans, *as* blacks and *as* whites."[16] But the recontextualization of which I write needs to be understood as the re-articulation of those identities under the form and norm of our Christian self-conception, rather than the other way around. How this will look and what its implications may be will be articulated throughout this book.

THE FRAMEWORK: PUBLIC THEOLOGY

My approach in this text falls within the realm of what's broadly called "public theology." I say "broadly" because the realm of public theology is itself exceptionally broad, arguably too broad to offer one cohesive approach to theological method.[17] Nevertheless, I propose a particular method of public theology, as I have suggested elsewhere, and this methodology will direct my inquiry throughout this project.[18]

Public theology, in the widest sense, is simply the engagement between theology and other modes of cultural expression—whether that be art, science, economics, politics, or the institutional settings in which those forms of expression are embedded. It is, as Hal Breitenberg has stated, the realm in which theology seeks "to communicate, by means that are intelligible and assayable to all, how Christian beliefs and practices bear, both descriptively and prescriptively, on public life and the common good, and in doing so possibly persuade and move to action

16. Appiah, *Ethics of Identity*, xiv. Italics in original.

17. The most comprehensive treatment of public theology as an approach may be found in Kim and Day, *Companion to Public Theology*. See also Francis and Ziebertz, *Public Significance of Religion*. The literature on the topic continues to expand to encompass a greater variety of perspectives. For recent treatments, see Patrick, *Public Theology*; also Carbine, *Nevertheless, We Persist*; and Smallwood, *Public Theology and Violent Rhetoric*.

18. I lay out my own method of public theology most explicitly in *Exodus Church and Civil Society* and in my essay "Whose Public? Which Theology?", as well as other publications. My account in this section relies on and develops the approach I advance in those writings.

both Christians and non-Christians."[19] Of note in this definition is the double task that public theology sets for itself: It articulates Christian beliefs and practice, but it also seeks to move to action. Public theology is thus not intended to function as a passive spectator to public life, but seeks to be engaged fully in the cultural dialogue about the nature of the good and how it can be achieved.

Furthermore, as Breitenberg notes, public theology is never a purely intra-ecclesial discourse. It intentionally reaches beyond the walls of the church to engage intellectually with its wider cultural context, and to become persuasive to both Christians and non-Christians.[20] As such, it takes seriously its responsibility to both fairly engage with other disciplinary frameworks, and to articulate its own concerns in terms that those frameworks can comprehend. This requires what Eliane Graham refers to as a "dialogical sensibility," in which "public theologians face the challenge not only of articulating theologically grounded interventions in the public square, but of justifying and defending the very relevance of the Christian faith in a culture that no longer grants automatic access or credence."[21]

This dialogical sensibility is challenged, according to Graham, by the "rock" of resurgent forms of conservative religious activism and the "hard place" of increasing secularity in modern society.[22] Beyond this, within Christian theology there are schools of thought that resist attempts at dialogue as alien to the task of the church. Thinkers such as Stanley Hauerwas have long advocated the idea that the church's identity as a "contrast society" means that there is no place for dialogue with its broader cultural milieu, but only prophetic witness, or perhaps appropriation.[23] In Augustine's terminology, theology can "plunder the gold of the Egyptians" as it were, grabbing that which it finds useful for its

19. Breitenberg, "To Tell the Truth," 2, 66. Breitenberg's article is particularly notable as one of the first that attempted to clarify the conceptual apparatus of public theology, a task that he expanded in his chapter "What Is Public Theology?", 3–17.

20. To take but one recent example, see Cartledge, *Holy Spirit and Public Life*.

21. Graham, *Between a Rock and a Hard Place*, xxiii.

22. Graham, *Between a Rock and a Hard Place*, xxi.

23. Hauerwas, *In Good Company*; Hauerwas and Willamon, *Resident Aliens*. This is a consistent theme across Hauerwas's writing and can be found in almost any book of his that one would care to examine, though these two represent particularly vivid examples.

own purposes, but has no concomitant responsibility to offer anything in return except its counter-cultural witness.[24]

Public theology does not deny that the church can and ought to be a contrast society, nor that it needs to demonstrate a prophetic witness in the context of a "forensically fraught" set of social conditions.[25] However, the contrast should not be understood as negating the larger cultural context in which theology is done, but rather as revealing in and to that context its unexamined premises, unfulfilled possibilities, and unrealized potentialities. In this way, the Christian community is fully engaged in the public project of determining a wider good that extends beyond the boundaries of the church, rather than attempting to hermetically seal itself from the threat of corrupting cultural influences.

This approach also calls into question Charles Matthewes's contention that "'public theologies' are self-destructively accommodationist: they let the 'larger' secular world's self-understanding set the terms, and then ask how religious faith contributes to the purposes of public life, so understood."[26] Public life, he argues, should be considered on theological terms, rather than the other way around. His approach is "unapologetically particularistic":

> Using the first-order vernacular of Christian faith, it argues that Christians can and should be involved in public life richly as citizens—working for the common good while remaining open, conversationally and otherwise, to those who do not share their views—and thoroughly as Christians—in ways ascetically appropriate to, and invigorating of, their spiritual formation, not least by opening their own convictions to genuine transformation by that engagement.[27]

This argument, however, suggests a degree of special pleading on Matthewes's part, an insistence that a "theology of public life" (his preferred term) is meaningfully distinct from public theology. Yet nothing in his

24. Augustine, *On Christian Doctrine*, 75. In a similar vein, John Milbank cites Augustine's principle that the church may "make *usus* of the peace of this world." "Insofar as possible, the Christian ruler will make a *usus* of the earthy peace, by subordinating it to the ecclesial purposes of charity and of a 'loving discipline.'" Milbank, *Theology and Social Theory*, 406–7. Milbank goes on to note, however, the problem of "how can such a proper use not simply *negate* the earthly peace altogether" (407, italics in original).

25. Simpson, "Theologia Crucis and the Forensically Fraught World," 173–205.

26. Matthewes, *Theology of Public Life*, 1.

27. Matthewes, *Theology of Public Life*, 2.

characterization distinguishes it from public theology, at least as I am using the term—and arguably, as its most prominent exponents use it.

However, given how widely the term public theology is utilized in contemporary discourse, and without sufficient methodological clarification, it is easy to see why Matthewes can credibly make this claim. Far too often, public theology is simply a blanket term for any public engagement by Christians, regardless of its qualities, or of its quality. And yet I would argue that a well-articulated public theology is one that encompasses and absorbs the approach suggested by Matthewes.

Public theology, in its most well-developed form, is a mediating theology. As Matthewes suggests, it engages fully in civic life, and yet operates from within the framework of Christian theology in a way that both critiques and allows itself to be critiqued by other cultural forms and institutions, allowing itself to remain open to genuine transformation in the midst of discourse. It is a form of "mutual critical correlation" between theology and culture, to use David Tracy's terminology, that takes place in the context of multiple modalities, including the church's internal discourse, the discourse of academic theology, and the multiple fields of public and cultural discourse that take place beyond the walls of church and academy.[28] It is not beholden to the terms and categories of secular discourse, but creatively engages those categories through a theological lens.[29]

How public theology goes about this engagement requires a threefold methodology, in which it offers an analytic account of the context within which it is operating, an interpretive account of the ways in which theological categories can address, respond to, and critique that context, and a constructive account of what it understands God to be calling human beings to do and to be in the midst of their context.[30] Contra Matthewes, this is not a matter of allowing the secular realm to set the terms of the discourse, but of understanding, in theological terms, the

28. Tracy, *Analogical Imagination.*

29. It is also worth noting that a dialogical stance with regard to the wider cultural context in which theology operates does not per se mean allowing the agenda to be set by secular categories. Indeed, insofar as public theology has as part of its project the drawing out of the implicit theology in cultural forms that are not directly theological, its project is precisely calling into question the secularity of even the most secular disciplines.

30. Gustafson, *Ethics from a Theocentric Perspective*, 327.

contextual situation within which Christianity is called upon to discern God's call to do and to be as an intellectual, moral, and spiritual field of action.[31]

In its analytic mode, public theology offers an account of its context in light of the concerns of Christian theology. Contrary to the idea that this allows the secular world to "set the terms" of discourse, the description that public theology offers emerges from the internal demand of theology to understand the situation in which it functions. The descriptive task of public theology takes advantage of the resources of other disciplines while respecting the internal integrity of those disciplines with respect to their fields of study. It does not seek to refashion those disciplines in its own image, but rather to dialogically engage them on their own terms within a theological framework. This can certainly involve "using the first order vernacular" of Christian theology, though it can also involve a redescription of theological language in light of contemporary terminology, clarifying the meaning of that vernacular in the contextual setting within which it dwells.[32]

In its interpretive mode, public theology goes beyond the mere description of its context in order to draw out the significance of the context for theology, and of theology for the context, responding to the demand of the present moment from within institutional, doctrinal, and moral terms of the Christian community. It is the mediating moment of public theology. It seeks to take the understanding developed through its analytic task in order to articulate its own theological response, while also drawing on those aspects of the tradition that can cast light on the significance of the subject of discussion. It is here that public theology draws out the implicit theological dimensions of the broader cultural forms with which it engages.

31. At the same time, there is little to be gained in caviling over labels. Whether or not what Matthewes understands to be a "theology of public life" is just a redescription of what I understand to be public theology, our projects, at least as I understand the matter, are commensurable with one another and tread much of the same terrain. And Matthewes's rearticulation of an Augustinian foundation for such a theology is a vital contribution to the discourse. Though I will still insist on calling it "public theology."

32. Here Paul Tillich's *Systematic Theology* offers an example of how such terminological redescription might take place. Throughout the three volumes of this work, Tillich utilizes the philosophical and psychological terminology that was current at the time of its writing in order to frame Christian theology in a way that was relevant to his contextual setting. At the same time, he insisted, rightly in my estimation, that his theology remained true to, and grounded in, the Christian theological tradition. See Tillich, *Systematic Theology*.

In its constructive mode public theology offers a synthesis through which it displays its relevance within its contemporary setting. It is here that public theology articulates, in James Gustafson's language, "what God is enabling and requiring us to do and be in this time and place."[33] It moves beyond simply drawing out the implicit theology within cultural forms and addresses itself to discerning precisely how God is acting within the world and what the proper response to that divine action should be. In particular, it answers the question of what Christianity's public responsibility is in the midst of the demands raised within the larger social and cultural setting in which it dwells.[34]

Public theology in this modality allows Christianity to act with integrity alongside the wider public within which it dwells, not in a way that is beholden to the categories of society, but which is capable of engaging society on its own terms but within Christianity's own modality for the sake of articulating a Christian theological response to matters of public concern and the common good.[35]

Public theology is also in this way distinguished from political theology, even as the two cover much of the same territory, though as a term, "political theology" may be even more capacious than "public theology."[36] As with Matthewes's "theology of public life," the main characteristics of political theology can be understood to be encompassed by public

33. Gustafson, *Ethics from a Theocentric Perspective*, 306.

34. I have offered a more detailed account of these three tasks in *Exodus Church and Civil Society* as well as "Whose Public? Which Theology?", 461–85.

35. It should be noted that the methodological question in public theology is a matter of perennial discussion. Much of the best work on public theology in the past two decades has been done in South Africa. See, in particular, Hansen, *Christian in Public.* Much excellent work has been done by the Byers Naude Center for Public Theology at Stellenbosch University.

36. There are certainly a plethora of different uses of the term, some of which, as in its usage by Carl Schmitt, are not even in any obvious way theological. Schmitt seems to understand the term in a purely political sense in his *Political Theology*. Similarly, Ernst Kantorowicz uses the phrase historically in the subtitle of *The King's Two Bodies*. Even in the field of the "new" political theology as advocated by Jürgen Moltmann and J. B. Metz, which was explicitly intended as theological, the applications and implications can differ widely by author. In a more recent treatment, Luke Bretherton in *Christ and the Common Life* defines political theology as "an interpretive art for discovering faithful, hopeful, and loving judgements about how to act together in response to shared problems" (6). Adam Kostko, by contrast, in *What Is Theology?* argues that "the name serves fundamentally as an emblem for the field's rejection of the modern secular truism that politics and theology are supposed to be kept rigorously separate. . . . political theology asserts that politics and theology are inextricably intertwined, always and everywhere" (17).

theology.[37] Insofar as various forms of liberation theology are understood as cousins of political theology (yet another contentious claim), they do possess a characteristic distinction that is relevant to the current project, as liberation theologies emerge from concrete experiences of oppression. Thus Latin American liberation theology is related to and yet distinct from Black liberation theology, which is in turn related to and distinct from feminist, womanist, and mujuerista theologies. As such, they bring their own claims, grounded in particular understandings of identity, to the theological discourse which cannot be swallowed up by a more general category, whether that be "public" or "political" theology. Even so, the concerns foregrounded by the various theologies of liberation are shared within both political and public theologies. To the extent that there is a promise of fruitful mutual discourse in addressing both the similarities and differences, I hope to do so within the larger scope of this project.

OVERVIEW

To close, I would like to offer a brief outline and summary of the general argument I will be making. The first two chapters fall into the descriptive category of public theology and will diagnose the current social and political conditions surrounding the rise of Christian religious nationalism in the United States. The question of identity will be a constant reference point throughout. However, it will be important from the outset to distinguish between different ways in which the concept of "identity" is politically deployed. There are authentic and valid ways of conceiving of identity, and there are inauthentic and invalid ways. How we distinguish these approaches is going to be important going forward in analyzing the resurgence of right-wing political movements in the United States, as well as globally. A shorthand way of framing the distinction that I am seeking to make here is that authentic conceptions of identity open up new ways of conceiving of our relationships with one another in a pluralistic context, while inauthentic ones foreclose those conceptions. The one approach recognizes the validity and importance of cultural pluralism, while the other seeks to deny the significance, or even the existence, of that pluralistic framework.

37. I offer a more detailed account of this argument in "Jürgen Moltmann's Public Theology," and more recently in "Jürgen Moltmann and the 'New Political Theology.'"

Thus, in chapter 1, I will examine the historical background of the issue. There are of course many places to begin such an analysis; however, I will start with the fall of the Berlin Wall in 1989, not because these conceptions of identity began there, but because it represents a symbolic inflection point for an understanding of how American identity began to fragment in the years following. Using Francis Fukuyama's flawed appropriation of the idea of the "End of History" to frame the conversation, I will examine the way that the hoped-for age of liberal capitalism and prosperity actually opened up the rifts that had been covered up in Western society by the Cold War conflict. I will then turn to some of the ways in which forms of ethno-nationalist identity politics manifest themselves in the larger context of American political thought today. In particular, I will examine the breakdown on the political right of the so-called "fusionist consensus" that motivated the American right during the years of the Cold War, and the rise of neo-reaction and Integralism as alternatives gaining traction on the American right. What is particularly notable about these alternatives, apart from their strongly anti-democratic rhetoric, is their focus, once again, on particular conceptions of identity as drivers for political and social action.

The second chapter addresses Donald Trump as a cultural and political figure, looking at the 2016 and 2024 Trump victories and their aftermaths and the way in which his framing of political discourse in terms of conflict, struggle, and violence has created a fraught and dangerous context for a politics of discourse and pluralism that has outlasted Trump's presidency. Trump is not the creator of this framework. He is its creature. But he has so thoroughly embodied it in the American context that it is now understood in terms of him, rather than he in terms of it. What Donald Trump's influence on American culture illustrates is the way in which conceptions of identity can be turned into destructive forms of authoritarianism. Trump's political influence illustrates the connection between particular ways of framing the concept of identity and the burgeoning influence of anti-democratic ideology in political culture. It also illustrates the many ironies of the contemporary political moment, as seemingly contradictory moral and ideological stances transform in the face of a powerfully demagogic figure or movement.

The third chapter moves into the analytic category and will examine the idea of identity more broadly, in terms of its political, social, and philosophical dimensions. Drawing on the work of figures such as Kwame Anthony Appiah, Amartya Sen, and others, I will examine what it means to claim and be claimed by a particular identity, the multifaceted nature of the concept of identity, and how those conceptions function in contemporary American culture in both constructive and divisive ways. I will examine some of the critical conversation around the meaning of terms such as "identity politics" and attempt to distinguish between ways of conceiving of identity that provide the framework for a more hopeful and cosmopolitan understanding of how the particular and the universal interact with one another in our use of the term, and the ways in which the term can serve to separate and divide.

The final two chapters fall into the constructive category of public theology. In the fourth chapter, I will offer a different way of conceiving of identity, one rooted not in ethno-nationalism but in Jesus Christ. This conception of identity is intended to lead us away from anti-liberal and anti-democratic frameworks and toward a more universal conception of identity, one that does not deny the pluralism of our self-conceptions but reframes them in terms of the identity of Jesus Christ. Similarly, in terms of its political implications, this does not undermine or erode democratic pluralism within a multi-cultural society, but rather offers Christians a way of conceiving of their own multiple identities in conversation with the multiple identities of those with whom they share a diverse polity.

The final chapter will offer the symbol of the kingdom of God and the eschatological vision of the new Jerusalem as ways of understanding the kind of multicultural and multi-ethnic polity toward which Christians ought to strive, one in which the gates of the city are never shut, but in which all are welcome, and in which people will come from every nation to share community together.

As will become clear in the latter half of this volume, my thinking has been and remains deeply indebted to the work of Jürgen Moltmann. From my first experience encountering *Theology of Hope* and *The Crucified God* in a discount bookstore in Connecticut during my college years, through my deepening appreciation for his work throughout seminary, to my decision to focus on his thought as the subject of my doctoral dissertation, Moltmann has been the predominant theological figure in my own development. While he would undoubtedly disagree with me at a number of points both in my overall argument in this volume, and in my interpretation and application of his thought, I return over and over to his writings as the fullest expression of ideas that I am continually struggling to articulate in my own way and in my own voice. While I mourn his recent death, I also celebrate his life as one that was fully lived in the light and love of God.

Finally, I want to be clear on my own perspective entering into this project. I am a Christian theologian, and this is a work of Christian theology. It is primarily intended as a means of helping Christians think theologically about how we might move past the present moment of social and moral crisis in our country.

Furthermore, I am a white man writing about identity at an historical moment when the normativity of white male identity is being justly called into question. It is by no means my objective to undermine those efforts to open up space in public discourse to those who have been historically marginalized. On the contrary, I hope through my efforts here to demonstrate the vacuousness of the kind of white Christian nationalism that has been exploited by the right to attempt to keep those on the margins where they are.

I am also writing as an American. Most of the analysis in this book will be specific to the American context. However, this is not to suggest that these issues are only relevant to the United States, or that a similar analysis could not be applied to the kinds of nationalism experienced in other parts of the world, even when they are grounded in other forms of ethnic and religious identity. I hope that what I write here will be useful to Christians elsewhere who struggle in their own context as American Christians seek to struggle in ours.

ACKNOWLEDGMENTS

To conclude this introduction, I want to offer my thanks to the many people who have been instrumental in the completion of this volume. First, I want to thank DePaul University and my colleagues for their support and feedback over the protracted period of time it took to complete this book. I was able to make substantial progress on bringing it to conclusion thanks to a research leave during the 2022–2023 academic year and I am grateful for the willingness of DePaul to give me the necessary time to think and write.

I also wish to thank the University of Chicago Divinity School's Martin Marty Center for the Public Understanding of Religion for accepting me as the Senior Martin Marty Fellow during that same time period. I particularly want to thank Willemien Otten and Emily Crews for aiding me during my time as a fellow. In addition, I wish to thank Laurie Zoloth and William Schweiker for their time and insight during my tenure. Their influence on this project is substantial, as they each gave me much to consider on questions of theology, morality, and identity in our conversations. I must also thank the Junior Marty Fellows, who engaged me in vigorous conversation and whose own projects inspired me in many ways. Finally, I thank James Robinson, the Dean of the University of Chicago Divinity School, for extending the school's hospitality to me during my time there.

I would also like to thank a number of friends and colleagues whose thoughts and feedback on various drafts of this project aided in its completion. In particular, I would like to thank Ruben Rosario Rodriguez, Joseph Scrivener, Sarah Brown, and Beth Potterveld. To the degree that this work makes a worthwhile contribution to the field, it is owed in large part to them. Of course, the flaws in this work remain mine alone.

Finally, I would like to thank my family, whose constant support and encouragement are an ongoing source of strength and inspiration for me. I hope that this work contributes in a small way to making the world a better place for them to live in.

April 4, 2025

1

After the End of History
Mythology, Identity, And Religious Nationalism

The mastery of historical destiny is a tortuous process in which powerful forces may be beguiled, deflected, and transmuted but never simply annulled or defied.

—Reinhold Niebuhr[1]

INTRODUCTION

The choice of a starting point for this story is necessarily arbitrary. Religious nationalism has been a reality of American life in one form or another since its inception. The creation of an American identity grounded in a particular conception of Christianity has been coupled since the first colonists landed on American shores with a Christian identity grounded in a particular conception of what it means to be American.

One could thus easily tell this story with a particular emphasis on that colonial history, or on the way in which Christianity and national identity coalesced around the Civil War in the mid-nineteenth century. One could also look at the relationship between Christianity and

1. Niebuhr, *Irony of American History*, 143.

nationalism as it manifested itself in the periods of World Wars I and II, or in the Cold War era.

My choice to begin the tale at the end of the Cold War is grounded in the way that our particular historical moment is in many ways the outgrowth of the fall of the Berlin Wall, the subsequent collapse of the Soviet Union, and the crisis of national identity that this caused for many Americans. When the Cold War myth of national unity in opposition to communism no longer motivated the American sense of identity, many of the contradictions within that identity rose to the fore in ways that we are only now beginning to understand and see manifested in full.

NOVEMBER 1989 AND THE END OF HISTORY

When the Berlin Wall fell on November 9, 1989, it was an event that few would have anticipated even a few months earlier. And indeed, it seems to have happened almost by accident, the result of a garbled communication from an East German government official.[2] The absurdity of it was almost comical, but the resultant watershed was unstoppable. Within months, the move toward a unified and democratic Germany was well underway, and it was a mere two years later, in December 1991, that the Soviet Union was formally dissolved and the Cold War, for all intents and purposes, came to its official end.

To the degree that the Cold War had given meaning and direction to what it meant to be American during the decades prior, its ending called on the United States to find new sources of meaning and direction. What's more, the Cold War had papered over deep divisions within American society that began to become more apparent in its aftermath. The civil rights and anti-war movements in the 1960s had already exposed some of those fissures, but the deeper unity, grounded in an America mythology of democratic optimism and civic republican virtue, remained. With the end of the Cold War, America faced a situation not unlike Robert Redford's character in *The Candidate*,[3] looking at an unexpected victory and asking, "What do we do now?"

Political scientist Francis Fukuyama famously declared this period "the end of history."[4] Capitalism and liberal democracy had at long

2. Hasic, "'Gates of the Wall Stand Open Wide.'"

3. Ritchie, *Candidate*.

4. Fukuyama, *End of History*.

last won the twilight struggle against tyranny, and all that was left was to expand the circle of its influence to encompass the whole world. For the optimistic apologists for this neoliberal consensus, it was a time of enormous potential—internationalism, globalization, open markets, and the expansion of individual liberty. On the leftward end of the spectrum, there was also an increased faith in the power of international institutions, the regime of international law, and the Universal Declaration of Human Rights as the moral backbone of a more humane world order.

For Fukuyama however, the end of history was far from an unvarnished good. With the end of history came also the end of struggle, the end of those conflicts with which we endow our lives with meaning, the end of the myth of progress, because, after all, no progress is possible when you've arrived at the eschaton. He writes:

> There will be plenty of metaphorical wars—corporate lawyers specializing in hostile takeovers who will think of themselves as sharks or gunslingers, and bond traders who imagine, as in Tom Wolfe's novel *The Bonfire of the Vanities*, that they are "masters of the universe." (They will believe this, however, only in bull markets.) But as they sink into the soft leather of their BMWs, they will know somewhere in the back of their minds that there have been real gunslingers and masters in the world, who would feel contempt for the petty virtues required to become rich or famous in modern America. How long megalothymia will be satisfied with metaphorical wars and symbolic victories is an open question. One suspects that some people will not be satisfied until they prove themselves by that very act that constituted their humanness at the beginning of history: they will want to risk their lives in a violent battle, and thereby prove beyond any shadow of a doubt to themselves and to their fellows that they are free. They will deliberately seek discomfort and sacrifice, because the pain will be the only way they have of proving definitively that they can think well of themselves, that they remain human beings.[5]

To the degree that our conception of virtue is entangled with a conception of "manliness" grounded in conflict and war, Fukuyama recognizes that the end of history strips us of an important signifier of identity. The eschaton that he envisions is ultimately not one of fulfillment, but disappointment. It is not a completion, but merely a continuation. And since

5. Fukuyama, *End of History*, 329.

life and society continue to march on even after the end of history, they do so in the absence of a frame that gives that march significance.

Of course, there were many even at the time who viewed Fukuyama's diagnosis as painfully naïve and optimistic. While it was certainly the case that globalization and free trade were assumed as economic norms even within center-left governments—Clinton's New Democrats and Blair's New Labour are two obvious examples—the rise of human rights and international institutions of order failed to come about. Instead, we got conflict in Serbia and Kosovo, the failure of the United Nations to exercise meaningful global leadership, and the willingness of putative democracies to do business with regimes for which human rights were a bad joke, as long as they were willing to open their borders to free trade.

The flip side of Fukuyama's diagnosis was reflected in Samuel Huntington's *The Clash of Civilizations*, which argued that, far from ending, historical conflict would reconfigure itself around cultural and religious discord. In particular, and famously, he identified a clash between "Western Civilization" and Islam.[6] And while Huntington's gross caricatures of the civilizations he describes were rightly criticized, after the events of September 11, 2001, his diagnosis seemed prescient, and certainly more acute than Fukuyama's.[7]

Indeed, 9/11 represents another inflection point in the story of who we are now. If, following the fall of the Berlin Wall, the 1990s seemed to promise, albeit hollowly, a future of meaningless prosperity and hedonic excess, 9/11 promised a renewal of the warrior spirit that Fukuyama saw withering on the vine. It was a chance once again for the United States to show its mettle to the world.

It also once again papered over the deep fissures that continued to develop in American society. The years prior to the terrorist attacks had been marked by a long run of dot-com inspired prosperity, but they were

6. Huntington, *Clash of Civilizations*. The clash between Islam and the West was not the only clash Huntington envisioned. He also envisioned a clash between the West and emerging Asian powers, particularly China. However, in the wake of the 9/11 attacks, it was the Muslim connection that drew the most attention.

7. That said, Huntington came in for much justified criticism of his thesis, and the broad strokes with which he drew his conclusions. See, for example, Sen, "Democracy as a Universal Value"; Said, "Clash of Ignorance"; Berman, *Terror and Liberalism*; Bottici and Challand, *Myth of the Clash of Civilizations*. In brief, most critics argued that Huntington took a deterministic view of culture, which failed to recognize the diversity within various cultures and as a result reduced those cultures to monolithic entities destined to "clash" rather than complex and multifarious societies with diverse interests and goals, which are capable of change, modification, and negotiation.

also accompanied by the emergence of right-wing militias. The anti-government ideology of these militias had been intensified by the raids on the Branch Davidian compound in Waco, Texas, and Ruby Ridge, Idaho. These events catalyzed a narrative in which "jack-booted thugs" from government agencies were poised to deprive God-fearing Americans of their guns, and to impose a "New World Order" of secular tyranny.[8]

Meanwhile, anti-globalization activists mobilized in 1999 to protest the World Trade Organization meeting in Seattle.[9] While there were some facile similarities between these protests and the actions of the right-wing militias, the differences went deeper. The Seattle protestors' agenda was anti-corporate and anti-capitalist, while opposition to capitalism was not part of the right-wing agenda. And while there was some vandalism associated with the protests, they were largely non-violent, whereas the militia movement was grounded in the expectation of violent confrontation between "citizen soldiers" and the government. However, what these movements shared was a deep suspicion of the American government and of the international institutions which were emerging from the Cold War.

While the anti-globalization protestors were actually in many cases internationalist and secular in terms of their philosophical outlook, the militias were strongly nationalist and grounded in a particular conception of Christian identity. They were quintessentially "white nationalist Christians" even when they didn't explicitly identify with neo-Nazi or fascist movements. Thus, despite surface similarities, the two movements were oceans apart ideologically. This same dynamic would recur during the Great Recession of 2008, when Tea Party protestors and the Occupy movement would echo one another's rhetoric while standing in opposition to one another ideologically.[10]

While 9/11 temporarily masked the breakdown in the Cold War consensus that accompanied the fall of the Berlin Wall, it reemerged quickly during the Iraq war. The period between 2001 and 2004 is in some ways a lacuna in the narrative of increasing American division, in part because dissent was harshly criticized. To take just one example, comedian Bill Maher was fired from his popular late night talk show after criticizing the rhetoric describing the 9/11 attackers as "cowards."[11]

8. See Toobin, *Homegrown*.

9. Bayne, "Why Did Seattle Fail"; Levi, "Coalitions of Contention."

10. See Paeth, "Great Recession."

11. Carter, "ABC to End 'Politically Incorrect.'"

While most Americans supported the invasion of Afghanistan, the Bush administration's immediate pivot to planning an invasion of Iraq began to draw increased criticism. This was magnified in the aftermath of the war when the much-vaunted weapons of mass destruction that Iraq was alleged to have failed to materialize. Once again, the fissures of mistrust began to appear on the surface of American unity. The multiple scandals that afflicted the second Bush administration, including revelations of government torture of prisoners, continued that erosion of trust.

The 2008 financial crisis and the Great Recession that followed represent a third inflection point in this narrative, or perhaps it was the election of Barack Obama as the first black president of the United States that was the real inflection point. The instability accompanying the recession undermined many Americans' sense of self, while the Obama presidency encouraged forms of racist obstinacy and resistance to authority exemplified by Congressman Joe Wilson's outburst of "You lie!" at Obama during a Congressional address in 2009. The Tea Party movement similarly reflected both a crisis of identity among many, largely white, Americans and a willingness to deploy racist tropes against Obama.

Donald Trump played into these dynamics, first in his embrace of "birther" conspiracy theories to attack Obama, and subsequently, during both his presidential campaigns, in attacking immigrants. At core, his political appeal was precisely in driving home the divisions among Americans, primarily on racial and ethnic lines. His explicit embrace of white ethnic nationalism was an appeal to a particular vision of American identity grounded in the pre-civil rights era in which white power and privilege predominated.

This particular sense of American identity was one that many white Americans lost with the racial advances of the 1950s and 1960s, partial though even these advances were. With his election in 2016 and his subsequent four years in office, Trump hammered home this vision repeatedly, refusing to denounce explicit racism among his followers, while going out of his way to attack athletes, such as Colin Kapernick, for kneeling in protest of police violence, and the Black Lives Matter movement. During his 2020 re-election campaign, he once again leaned into this racist rhetoric with appeals to suburban voters, arguing that Joe Biden would rezone their suburbs (with the unspoken implication that this would allow more blacks to move in), and destroy their "suburban way of life."[12]

12. Karni et al., "Trump Plays on Racist Fears."

This trend continued throughout his postpresidency, spawning a legion of imitators, for whom the fomenting of racial and ethnic enmity are viewed as a pathway to power, and during his 2024 campaign he once again invoked racist tropes against Haitians and Puerto Ricans.

The emerging picture of America over the past thirty years is one in which a unifying mythology of American identity—one that was never wholly credible, and never really held together with any degree of integrity—finally ceased to exercise a hold on the American imagination.[13] This mythology originally took hold in the era around World War II, and was grounded in a picture of American power and virtue, rooted in the heroism and self-sacrifice of America's "Greatest Generation"[14] (This moniker was always a bit silly and ultimately self-defeating. When you begin with "the Greatest Generation," how can your story be anything but a narrative of decline?). At core, this story depicted the American role in the world as one of struggle in defense of global democracy against the tyranny, first of Nazi Germany and then of Soviet Communism.

Even at its inception, this mythology was troubled by reality. As Reinhold Niebuhr noted in *The Irony of American History*, the narrative of American virtue in the world, and its singular capacity to take responsibility for world security, was grounded in a combination of naïve self-confidence and willful blindness toward America's own capacity for injustice and imperialism. He writes:

> We were not only innocent half a century ago with the innocency of irresponsibility; but we had a religious version of our national destiny which interpreted the meaning of our nationhood as God's effort to make a new beginning in the history of mankind. Now we are immersed in worldwide responsibilities; and our weakness has grown into strength. Our culture knows little of the abuse of power, but we have to use power in global

13. Ann Applebaum notes in *Twilight of Democracy*, regarding many of the conservative figures she was acquainted with during this era: "Some were Cold Warriors because, as realpolitik diplomats or thinkers, they feared the traditional Russian aggression lurking beneath Soviet propaganda, they worried about nuclear war, and they cared about American influence around the world. Others—and I include myself in this category—thought that we were fighting against totalitarianism and dictatorship, and for political freedom and human rights. Still others, it turns out, fought the Soviet Union because Soviet ideology was explicitly atheist and because they believed that America stood on the side of God. When the Soviet Union fell apart, the links that had held these different anti-Communists together broke as well" (160).

14. This moniker was conferred on the World War II generation by the Baby Boomers, and specifically by Tom Brokaw in his book *The Greatest Generation*.

> terms. Our idealists are divided between those who renounce the responsibilities of power for the sake of preserving the purity of our soul and those who are ready to cover every ambiguity of good and evil in our actions by the frantic insistence that any measure taken in a good cause must be unequivocally virtuous. We have taken, and must continue to take, morally hazardous actions to preserve our civilization. We must exercise our power. But we ought neither to believe that a nation is capable of perfect disinterestedness in its exercise, or become complacent about the particular degrees of interest and passion which corrupt the justice by which the exercise of power is legitimized.[15]

For Niebuhr the rising American hegemony of the postwar era confronted it with the responsibility for leading the world in a conflict in which moral ambiguity was at its core. Yet our self-conception as an "innocent" nation deluded us with the idea that we could accomplish this leadership virtuously, avoiding the pitfalls that had corrupted other pretenders to global leadership.

Niebuhr recognized that this self-conception was both false on its face and bound to fail in the face of the pressures of international politics. However, he also believed that the Cold War threat of the Soviet Union justified American leadership, because at least we were capable of grappling with the moral ambiguities of our role in a way that the Soviet Union was not.

This paradox of naïve idealism coupled with destructive self-righteousness was well-illustrated in Graham Greene's novel *The Quiet American*. In the novel, Alden Pyle, a young American agent in Vietnam, believes sincerely and enthusiastically in the promise of bringing democracy to the Vietnamese people, on the basis of books he read by people who had never been to Vietnam. He tries to cultivate a "third force" to stand between the French and the Communists, one controlled by the United States. But his innocence and naïvety only result in bloodshed and destruction.[16]

Greene's English skepticism toward the myth of American virtue notwithstanding, this postwar idealism provided a unifying vision for the United States in the second half of the twentieth century. While the

15. Niebuhr, *Irony of American History*, 4–5.

16. Greene, *Quiet American*. The themes of Greene's novel became newly relevant in the years after our invasion of Iraq in 2003, as the United States deployed many diplomats with an Alden Pyle enthusiasm to "rebuild Iraq" with little to no actual knowledge of the country or its history.

upheavals of the civil rights movement and the counterculture exposed some of the disunity behind that myth, it proved to be remarkably stable. While we refer to "the 1960s" as an era of social upheaval, it really only lasted from about 1963 to 1968, and the counterculture was never as countercultural as it pretended. By the 1970s most were perfectly happy to resume their place in the American mythic portrait, waving their flags during the bicentennial celebrations of 1976. Many of those who had been plotting revolution in 1968 (at least in their minds) were happily voting for Ronald Reagan in 1980.

Meanwhile, the civil rights movement had accomplished its most significant legislative victories by 1965, and the racial backlash of the late 1960s and the 1970s deprioritized civil rights in favor of agendas of "welfare reform." Richard Nixon's now-notorious racist rants on the Watergate tapes echoed the sentiments of many white Americans, and progress toward inclusion for African Americans in many cases stalled.[17]

However, at the same time, the United States was becoming more ethnically and religiously diverse. The Immigration and Nationality Act of 1965 had opened the door to new migrants from all over the world, including many from countries where Christianity was not the predominant religion. As a result, Hinduism and Islam began to become more apparent in American life, to the dismay of many for whom the myth of American unity was founded on a specifically Christian worldview.

Because the myth of American virtue and unity was so closely aligned with the Cold War, its end meant the end of a narrative that gave American life coherence. Anne Applebaum describes a similar experience in the UK, writing:

> The conflict with communism had offered British conservatives, in concert with their American allies, the chance to take part in a very successful moral crusade; in 1989, when the Berlin Wall fell and Communist regimes rapidly crumbled, they felt vindicated. . . . Now they had proof that Thatcher was right. Together they had fought against those who had been fascinated by Communism—and they had won.

But once it was over there was a vacuum. All other causes suddenly seemed less important, less glamorous.[18]

17. Coates, "Case for Reparations."

18. Applebaum, *Twilight of Democracy*, 77–78.

Thus in the years that followed, the key question, again, was "what do we do now?" As Applebaum notes, the problem with the triumph of liberal capitalism and democracy is how little they serve to inspire and motivate:

> The principles of competition, even when they encourage talent and create upward mobility, don't answer deeper questions about national or personal identity. They don't satisfy the desire for unity and harmony. Above all, they do not satisfy the desire of some to belong to a special community, a unique community, a *superior* community.[19]

It is that desire for uniqueness, for the sense of a special calling, a privileged place in the universe, that was lost with the end of the Cold War—Fukuyama's lost *megalothymia*. What has taken its place is not a single unifying myth, but a breakdown in the mythic narrative that governs American life, to be replaced by many, often competing mythologies, some of which are hopeful and optimistic, but many of which are virulent and destructive. In the end though, this multiplicity of myths ultimately bespeaks a search for a unifying identity.

MYTHOLOGY AND IDENTITY

In discussing the idea of "myth" in relation to identity, I am referring not to the common conception of mythology as stories of gods and heroes. Mythology clearly has a religious valance, which I will touch upon, but mythology in the sense that I am using it is broader than that. It refers to the set of narratives and symbols through which we frame and give meaning to our experiences.[20] The Greek word *mythos* simply means "story," and a myth is a story that we tell about ourselves, our origins, our struggles, and our destiny.

The kind of story we tell affects the kind of people we become. But within our mythologies, there are symbols—figures, events, images, moments—that can cut in multiple directions. There is never only one myth, or one interpretation of a common myth, that defines our mythology. Rather than foreclose introspection and critique of who we are, mythologies should ideally open us to reflection on the correspondence, or lack thereof, between who we are and significant elements of that mythology.

19. Applebaum, *Twilight of Democracy*, 59. Italics in original.

20. Tillich, *Systematic Theology*, 1:80–81.

Our identity is thus defined both by which symbols we draw from our mythology and how those symbols motivate us to live and act.[21]

Crucially for my purposes here, I want to emphasize that the word "myth" does not imply falsehood. Myths are not false stories of who we are. On the contrary, myths are often more profoundly true than a mere recounting of events may allow. Myths do not merely offer factual accounts, but point us to deeper questions of meaning. Why are we who we are? What does it mean for us to be this people, this community, with this story? And how should we live and act in light of our stories. Myths are also potentially aspirational, providing exemplars to guide moral development and action.

At the same time, mythology can offer us an unwarranted sense of our collective accomplishment, both by associating our own personal stories with stories of national victory and greatness and by shading, eliding, or outright distorting the unsavory dimensions of our history. When Reinhold Niebuhr refers to the United States as an "innocent nation," he is referring precisely to this[22]—the degree to which the United States has allowed itself to believe, Alden Pyle–like, in its own naïve virtue, and the capacity for righteous victory that this virtue gives us. And of course, it is precisely the fact that we were never so innocent nor so virtuous that is the irony of which he writes.

In the United States, that mythology has undergone numerous transformations over the course of more than two centuries, and contrasting versions of these myths have at times almost pulled the country apart. Are we a nation of yeoman farmers or cosmopolitan urbanites? Are we a nation of rugged individuals who don't need any government to tell us what to do or a collectivity of citizens who join together for the general welfare? Are we a loose confederation of states or do we need a strong central government? There is no single, "true" answer to these questions, because the various answers draw from legitimate strains in American national mythology.

More sinisterly, this dynamic plays out in the conflicts surrounding the Civil War and the abolition of slavery. Northern and Southern mythologies diverge over the meaning of the war and its causes, and create distinct accounts of the very meaning of the United States as a nation. This divergence has allowed for versions of American identity

21. Tillich, *Systematic Theology*, 1:110.

22. Niebuhr, *Irony of American History*, 19.

that celebrate racism and authoritarianism alongside versions that view the United States as a multicultural democracy. And again, neither of these is *more* true than the other. Those who argue in favor of racism and authoritarianism can draw on wells of history, tradition, and narrative at least as deep as those who argue for pluralism and democracy.

The fight isn't over whose version of the myth is "true," but over the morality of adhering to one mythology in preference to the other. In this sense, one's moral commitments are prior to one's worldview. Or perhaps it would be better to say that worldview and morality coalesce simultaneously in the formation of identity. In either case, the choice of what's true is entangled within the choice of what's good, and thus our epistemological and moral choices are intertwined.

Mythology, morality, and identity are related in such a way that they mutually reinforce one another as aspects of persons. They are also mutually at risk. To the degree that identity is reliant on a coherent, "true" myth and a set of justificatory moral principles, whatever puts those first two at risk threatens the very nature of the self. Thus, a pathological mythology that infects one's self-conception can become deeply embedded in one's psyche precisely because its loss would mean a loss of self. Furthermore, to the degree that one's moral principles are grounded in those myths, it places one's very ability to function socially in jeopardy, unless replaced with some other framework or orientation. Thus, narratives of white supremacy continue to survive in the United States both because they justify the pathological dimensions of our mythology, but also because the collective introspection necessary to address the moral failure of the United States would require a questioning of the very moral core of American identity.

But not every aspect of American national mythology is pathological, and in its aspirational call for equality and human dignity, this mythology has offered justification for an increasingly open and pluralistic society. This can provide precisely the antidote to mythologies of white supremacy, through the reaffirmation, rather than the repudiation, of the myth. This was at the heart of Martin Luther King Jr.'s appeal in his "I Have a Dream" speech to those aspects of the American narrative that resonated with the civil rights movement, citing the Emancipation Proclamation and the Declaration of Independence in support of the idea that their promises were for *all* Americans. King was no less eager to lay claim to the American myth for its entanglement with white supremacy, but rather sought to turn the anticipatory dimensions of that myth against its pathological dimensions, drawing on it to seek to be more of what it could become than what it had been.[23]

In the United States the pathological dimensions of our mythology are tied not only to white supremacy, but to the way in which white supremacy and religious nationalism have combined to provide theological sanction for a particular conception of what "American" means. And this religious nationalist portion of the American narrative is intertwined with the recent reemergence of right-wing identity politics.

MYTHOLOGY, MASCULINITY, AND NATIONALISM

Several recent studies have documented the history of American Christian nationalism along with its contemporary appeal.[24] In particular, Robert P. Jones has offered an account of how white supremacism flourished within American Christianity, and its role in the ongoing decline of Christian belief in the United States.[25] As he notes, "White Christian America had its golden age in the 1950s, after the hardships and victories of World War II and before the cultural upheavals of the 1960s."[26] Evoking images of June Cleaver, church dinners, and prayers before football games, Jones writes that "it was a world of shared rhythms that punctuated the week," with Christianity at the center of cultural life.[27]

At the same time, he notes, this image out of Rockwell (whether Norman or Lincoln might be worth discussing) belied the actual division and diversity within American Christianity. "It always operated parallel to the rich religious and cultural domain of African American Protestants."[28] Yet the decline of this predominating vision has contributed to the rise of

23. King, "I Have a Dream," 217.

24. See Seidel, *Founding Myth*; Stewart, *Power Worshipers*; Cooper-White, *Psychology of Christian Nationalism*. Also of recent note are FitzGerald, *Evangelicals*, which is not about Christian nationalism per se, but which, as the subtitle suggests, traces the recent history of evangelical political influence in the United States, which intersects with the questions raised by Christian nationalism.

25. Jones is primarily interested in the currents of white *Protestant* Christianity, though certainly much of what he says can also apply to how Christianity was perceived and practiced within white Catholic communities. However, for much of American history, Catholicism was relegated to the social margins even in contexts where Catholics were prominent. Jones, *End of White Christian America*, 31.

26. Jones, *End of White Christian America*, 38.

27. Jones, *End of White Christian America*, 38.

28. Jones, *End of White Christian America*, 38.

Christian nationalism as a form of nostalgic backstop, standing athwart history and yelling "Stop!" in William F. Buckley's famous turn of phrase.

The image that Jones evokes to declare the death of a particular form of Christianity is precisely the image that contemporary American Christian nationalism is seeking to resurrect. This image of the Christian nation—unified, at peace, sharing a common faith and a common set of cultural practices—is threatened by the increasing diversity of a secular and multi-religious nation, in which many cultural practices abound. As Andrew Whitehead and Samuel Perry note, "more and more Americans collectively agree that the United States should not favor Christianity formally. Consequently, the sizable portion of Americans who pine for Christianity's former prominence in American civic life feel threatened and marginalized."[29]

That nostalgia for Christianity's former prominence is coupled with a particular set of values and social priorities. It is not simply motivated by a benign desire to recapture a lost era of comity and community, but rather the desire to impose a particular social order: "with boundaries and hierarchies among natives and foreigners, whites and nonwhites, men and women, heterosexuals and others—an order they recognize is also being threatened."[30]

Another way of framing this is that, for those American Christians who pine for the nostalgic mythic past, their sense of identity is bound up with those same boundaries and hierarchies. In their absence, their very sense of self is threatened and placed at risk. For them, the dissolution of that myth is an existential crisis. Thus it becomes ever more urgent for them to police those boundaries and preserve those hierarchies lest "all that is solid melt into air."[31]

Of course, policing those borders means that all who do not conform to the conditions of this preferred social order are at best suspect,

29. Whitehead and Perry, *Taking America Back for God*, 4–5.

30. Whitehead and Perry, *Taking America Back for God*, 5.

31. The full quote from Karl Marx and Friedrich Engels is instructive here: "All that is solid melts into air, all that is holy is profaned, and man is at last compelled to face with sober senses, his real conditions of life, and his relations with his kind" (*Marx-Engels Reader*, 476). Marx and Engels are describing the way in which the constantly revolutionizing character of capitalism displaces traditional forms of life and reduces workers to their mere economic status. One could easily read the same anxiety in the conservative reaction to the rise of secularism, religious pluralism, and racial and ethnic diversity. See also Berman, *All That Is Solid Melts into Air*. American Christian nationalists have an air of Berman's "unaccommodated man" about them.

perhaps tolerated, and more commonly treated as an enemy, the expulsion or control of whom is necessary for the preservation of this myth-bound identity.

It is in this context that Kristen Kobes Du Mez's analysis of the connection between white evangelical Christianity and a particular understanding of the links between religion, nationalism, and masculinity can be understood. Du Mez identifies the years immediately following World War II as the era in which evangelicalism fully embraced a conception of manhood not grounded in earlier virtues such as restraint and self-denial, but one rooted instead in aggression and dominance. At the turn of the twentieth century, those earlier understandings of what it meant to be a Christian man seemed to lack credibility at precisely the same moment that a young American president embodied a new way of conceiving masculinity:

> When Roosevelt became president in 1901, the embodiment of heroic manhood became the undisputed leader of the American nation. By fashioning a violent, fantasized masculinity, and then injecting that sensibility into national politics, Roosevelt offered ordinary men the sense that they were participating in a larger cause. Roosevelt's hypermasculinity appealed to men anxious about their own status, and the nation's. For many, these anxieties would become inseparable.[32]

But if the Christian conception of masculinity was to change, then Christianity itself needed to change alongside it. "Virile, aggressive men could hardly be expected to submit themselves to such an emasculating faith."[33] Thus within the evangelical movement, Christianity itself became redefined as a warlike faith, and men were understood to be protectors and defenders of their families, their communities, and their country: "Southern evangelicals found a way to define Christian manhood in a manner that sanctified aggression: to maintain order and fulfill their role as protectors, there were times when Christian men must resort to violence."[34] Thus, the Christian ethic of servanthood was transformed into an ethos of mastery, and a morality grounded in humility and self-sacrifice was transformed into one obsessed with the trappings of honor,

32. Du Mez, *Jesus and John Wayne*, 16–17.

33. Du Mez, *Jesus and John Wayne*, 17.

34. Du Mez, *Jesus and John Wayne*, 17.

once more evoking the concept of *megalothymia*. This was the era in which the phrase "muscular Christianity" came to prominence.

And yet, this transformation of Christian piety into aggressive Christian nationalism did not begin to flourish until the founding of the National Association of Evangelicals in 1942.[35] At a time when self-identified evangelicals represented a small minority of American Christians, it was only through an intensive strategy of evangelization, spearheaded by Billy Graham and including the first ventures into Christian mass media, that evangelicalism began to overtake mainline Protestantism as the publicly predominant form of American Christianity. Throughout the 1950s and 1960s, Graham and other evangelical stars promoted the mythology of muscular white American Christianity as the normative model for Christian faith. Graham himself was virtually an avatar for this myth. As Kobes Du Mez describes him: "Standing six feet two inches tall, he was the 'All-American Male' with 'Scottish genes and Nordic looks,' a 'craggy face, blue eyes, square jaw.'"[36] And Graham bought into the role thoroughly: "Graham took pains to bolster his masculine credentials. He jogged, lifted weights, and otherwise kept up a rigorous exercise regime; in preparation for his crusades he trained 'like a prizefighter.'"[37]

> In this way, militant masculinity linked religious and secular conservatism. In time, the two would become difficult to distinguish. As red-blooded American manhood became infused with God-and-country virtues, otherwise secular models would come to exemplify an ideal Christian manhood. This conflation of religious and secular can be see in the cult like status John Wayne enjoyed among American conservatives in the 1960s and 1970s.[38]

John Wayne exemplified in the secular realm everything that Graham preached in the religious. He was the embodiment of masculine patriotism, which was inseparable from his conservative advocacy. Leveraging his iconic status on behalf of anticommunism and in support of the Vietnam War, Wayne's performance of manhood became the standard by which Christian and secular conservatives measured moral worth, and this was inextricably tied to nationalism.

35. Du Mez, *Jesus and John Wayne*, 21.
36. Du Mez, *Jesus and John Wayne*, 23.
37. Du Mez, *Jesus and John Wayne*, 23.
38. Du Mez, *Jesus and John Wayne*, 54.

There is a certain irony here that Du Mez does not flag, but which is worth pointing out. *The Searchers*, arguably Wayne's best movie, calls into question everything that Wayne's mythic status embraced.[39] In the movie, Wayne's character is a battle-scarred Civil War veteran. Hunting for Debbie, his kidnapped niece, among the Native Americans, he decides to kill her when he discovers her among the wives of a Comanche chieftain. Yet, when he has the opportunity to do so at the end of the film, he instead restores her to the white community from which she was taken. The movie concludes with Wayne's character framed outside the doorway to the ranch house, isolated and separate from the community, alienated and alone.

While it is possible to watch *The Searchers* and read it as a confirmation of American mythic identity—Wayne the masculine loner fighting to preserve the sanctity of white identity and community—it can also be read as a challenge to these very ideas. After all, Wayne's character fought in the Civil War, but on the side of the Confederacy—a traitor, not a patriot. Furthermore, his pursuit of his niece is largely pointless, motivated solely by his hatred of the Native Americans and his belief that it is better for her to be dead than to live among them. His actions drive him farther and farther from the community he seeks to preserve, and in the end, when he delivers his niece back to the community of which she is no longer a part, she is given no voice and no choice in the decision. He simply sweeps her into his arms, pronouncing "Debbie, let's go home!"[40] The climax of the film depicts the wholesale slaughter of a Native American community. Rather than a celebration of white American mythic identity, everything in the movie's narrative, and in Wayne's portrayal, seems to undermine it and put its flaws on full display.[41]

39. Du Mez does mention *The Searchers*, noting the explicit racism of Wayne's protagonist, Ethan, in the context of discussing Wayne's own racism. As she quotes, Wayne once stated that "I believe in white supremacy until the blacks are educated to a point of responsibility." Du Mez, *Jesus and John Wayne*, 57.

40. This reading of *The Searchers* underlies Paul Schrader and Martin Scorsese's retelling of the narrative in *Taxi Driver*, in which the protagonist, Travis Bickle, is clearly a deranged psychopath, whose murder spree at the end of the movie is depicted as an explosion of rage rather than a justified rescue of Jodie Foster's Iris, a teenage prostitute.

41. As with any criticism, the question of the intent of the creators is of questionable value when analyzing and assessing what constitutes a valid interpretation. There are many ways in which the film continues to lean upon traditional tropes of mid-century Westerns. And yet, what John Ford does in *The Searchers* is to turn those tropes against themselves, acknowledging the racism of the white settlers and elevating the Native characters, rather than collapsing the narrative into the standard "good white man/bad

In some ways, Wayne's character exemplifies the "policing of the borders of identity" discussed above, as he arrogates to himself the right to decide others' worth, and even their right to live, on the basis of whether they violate his conception of racial purity. His character fights to preserve slavery, fights to subject Mexico, fights to murder Native Americans, fights to preserve a sense of racial purity. To the extent that Wayne became an icon to both secular and Christian forms of American nationalism during this period, it is in large measure because he embodied both their fears and their preferred responses to those fears.

CHRISTIAN NATIONALISM AND THE RELIGION OF FEAR

Jason Bivins discusses the connection between conservative Christian anxiety and politics in *The Religion of Fear*. He notes that this "religion of fear" is grounded in a number of sociopolitical shifts that took place in the decades after World War II. Some of these shifts were socioeconomic, reflecting the decline in working class power. Some shifts were political, as formerly marginalized groups began to move toward the center of discourse, displacing the once-dominant white male hegemony in political life.[42] And some were cultural as the increasingly pluralistic and diverse nature of American cultural life supplanted the formerly normative modes of cultural expression that were distinctively rooted in white experience.

In *The Case for Christian Nationalism* Stephen Wolfe offers a defense of Christian society grounded in the kind of values outlined in the previous section. It is useful in understanding what the positive case for the Christian nationalist vision is from the perspective of its defenders—is there a way of conceiving of this approach to religion and politics that doesn't fall victim to the image of it as a "religion of fear" grounded in evangelical anxiety over order and masculinity?

Contrary to the criticisms that Christian nationalism as a form of "civic religion" with no clear grounding in the teachings of Christ or the traditions of the Christian church, Wolfe argues that it offers a coherent and morally compelling vision of a rightly ordered social life.

Native American" approach of many Westerns. Yet it cannot be denied that for all that, it is by no means the kind of deconstruction of Westerns that later movies like Arthur Penn's *Little Big Man* attempted.

42. Bivins, *Religion of Fear*, 10–11.

"In addition to justifying the institutionalization of Christianity, I offer reasons and exhortations for Christians to act in confidence for that institutionalization."[43] The particular form of institutionalized Christianity that Wolfe argues for is grounded in "reformed Christian political theory,"[44] and even more particularly, the reformed scholasticism of the sixteenth and seventeenth centuries. That said, Wolfe argues that his work is grounded in natural theology: "Christian political theory treats natural principles as the foundation, origin, and source of political life, even *Christian* political life."[45] Nevertheless, as *Christian* political theory, it relies as well on revelation to make the case for a particularly Christian form of nationalism. This implies, for example, "assuming that *civil leaders ought to order the people to the true God* (a natural principle), we can conclude that *civil leaders ought to order the people to the Triune God*."[46]

The general definition that Wolfe offers of Christian nationalism is "*a totality of national action, consisting of civil laws and social customs, conducted by a Christian nation as a Christian nation, in order to procure for itself both earthly and heavenly good in Christ*."[47] He goes on to state that, based on this definition, "Christian nationalism . . . is just, the real arrangement for Christians, and something worth pursuing with determination and resolve."[48]

The enemies of this Christian nationalist project, in Wolfe's estimation, are what he refers to as a "gynocratic" "Global American Empire"—"the governing virtues of America are feminine vices, associated with certain feminine virtues, such as empathy, fairness and equality . . . gynocracy pacifies men by eliminating independent agency and suppressing competitive, spontaneous coordination."[49] The drive to fairness and equality, he argues, undermines masculine virtue: "men are naturally animated by rugged individualism and natural hierarchy formation . . . they are capable of agonistic self-organization that often disregards or demotes women."[50] (Note that this demotion is not, in Wolfe's estimation,

43. Wolfe, *Case for Christian Nationalism*, 5.
44. Wolfe, *Case for Christian Nationalism*, 17.
45. Wolfe, *Case for Christian Nationalism*, 18. Italics in original.
46. Wolfe, *Case for Christian Nationalism*, 19. Italics in original.
47. Wolfe, *Case for Christian Nationalism*, 9. Italics in original.
48. Wolfe, *Case for Christian Nationalism*, 9. Italics in original.
49. Wolfe, *Case for Christian Nationalism*, 448.
50. Wolfe, *Case for Christian Nationalism*, 448.

a failure on the part of "natural male rugged individualism," but is rather a necessary, and missing, component of American public life.)

This "gynocracy," by rendering men weak and compliant, and orienting them away from individual excellence and toward social and communal concern, makes them easier to subjugate in the name of the "Global American Empire" (which Wolfe abbreviates as "GAE"). He continues:

> A masculine society is preferred because it harmonizes the individual and hierarchy for the common good. Masculine societies are not threatened by the feminine virtues but complement them, neither eliminating nor suppressing them to the common good. Without masculine leadership, feminine virtues will inevitably become disordered and self-destructive. Masculine virtues are ordered not directly by the feminine virtues but in the leadership of them. To be sure a masculine society is not a male-only society but rather a society whose principal institutions embody masculine virtues, and the feminine virtues operate through them.[51]

To the undoubted relief of women everywhere, Wolfe continues that "Women are necessary and vital for the common good." However, he continues, "the pursuit of gender equality will produce more harm than good."[52]

One of the harms that results from this "gynocracy," according to Wolfe, is the abandonment of Christian nationalist values in the name of a "globalist American empire," the purpose of which is to "advance

51. Wolfe, *Case for Christian Nationalism*, 453–54.

52. Wolfe, *Case for Christian Nationalism*, 454. And of course, Wolfe is particularly concerned for the harm that will accrue to *men* as a result: "If you are a white, heterosexual, cisgendered male, then the world will not offer you any favors. Indeed, your career advancement depends on sacrificing your self-respect by praising and pandering to your inferiors who rule over you. Even the CEOs, in the end, are dominated by the woke scolds. Ponder well the demeaning demands of 'greatness' in our time. Imaging spending forty years of your life in the military to become a general only to learn about 'white rage' and oversee, by the order of some ditsy and lecturing congresswoman, a program to integrate transgenderism into the military. How many of us conservatives have entered these timeless professions and strove for greatness in them only to find ourselves in the middle of a clown show and enforcing policies that lead to the destruction of the military, or worse: seeing it set its sights on Old America" (464). One almost gets the sense, in reading this passage, that Wolfe is a seething cauldron of resentment over his thwarted desire for "greatness," and rather than take responsibility for himself, has decided that it's the fault of women and "the gays."

modern liberal ideology across the globe."[53] He continues: "All Western nations are in the GAE to one degree or another, and together they advance international liberalism."[54] Holding up the war in Ukraine as an example of the corrosive effects of the GAE, and offering up examples of the alleged decadence being imposed upon Ukraine by the GAE, he argues that as a result "Ukraine will become just another mass of restlessness, full of consumers of GAE products, talking about GAE entertainment, and orienting their lives around GAE fandom."[55] All of which is, apparently, inferior to a the hierarchically ordered form of Christian nationalism in which men are men and women know their place. "When it is too late . . . Ukrainians of the older sort—after waking from a drunken slumber induced by GAE consumption—will learn that they chose not a new identity but a sort of liberal, soft occupation."[56]

One might wonder, reading all of this, how the form of Christian nationalism advocated by Wolfe can be squared with ideas such as religious pluralism or political dissensus. Wolf reassures his readers, it cannot be: "proponents of religious liberty have asserted a *non sequitur* for centuries, arguing that since true inward religion cannot be forced but is a matter of persuasion, the magistrate cannot use coercive power to suppress external false religion."[57] In other words, while the state can't force anyone to *believe* Christianity, it can, and should, compel them to *practice* it. He offers up the following summary:

> The question is whether a Christian magistrate, having civil rule over a civil society of Christians, may punish (with civil power) false teachers, heretics, blasphemers, and idolaters for their external expressions of such things in order to prevent (1) any injury to the souls of the people of God, (2) the subversion of Christian government, Christian culture, or spiritual discipline, or (3) civil disruption or unrest.[58]

He concludes by declaring: "Modern religious liberty advocates deny this and I affirm it."[59] He does note that "Christian Nationalism does not deny

53. Wolfe, *Case for Christian Nationalism*, 440.

54. Wolfe, *Case for Christian Nationalism*, 440.

55. Wolfe, *Case for Christian Nationalism*, 441.

56. Wolfe, *Case for Christian Nationalism*, 441.

57. Wolfe, *Case for Christian Nationalism*, 354.

58. Wolfe, *Case for Christian Nationalism*, 359.

59. Wolfe, *Case for Christian Nationalism*, 359. It is worth considering Wolfe's footnote in this section, in which he writes, "The civil regulation of religion assumes

the good of viewpoint diversity." However, he insists that this diversity cannot include "(1) political atheism, (2) subversion of public Christianity, (3) opposition to Christian morality, (4) heretical teaching, and (5) the political and social influence of non-Christian religion and its adherents."[60] He assures his readers, however, that "the purpose here is not to stifle public debate, but to maintain conditions for public debate to serve a Christian people."[61]

In summary, Wolfe's argument throughout *The Case for Christian Nationalism* is that only by the imposition of Christianity as the normative basis for American civil law can the United States overcome its enslavement to the "gynocratic" GAE and instill a genuine sense of hierarchically ordered liberty grounded in manly virtues at the center of American life. It is difficult to read Wolfe's argument as other than a confirmation of precisely the criticism offered by Du Mez and others—Christian nationalism is in the end grounded in the dislocation of white male identity at the center of American civic life. While Wolfe's argument focuses on gender rather than race, it falls easily into the kind of anxiety of which Du Mez writes.

What should be clear by now is that Christian nationalism is not merely a set of ideas, ideologies, or policy positions, but an identity. What's more, it is an identity that is, in a strange way, separable from Christianity itself. While Wolfe strives to ground his argument in an (idiosyncratic) reading of Christian history and theology, for many of those who identify

both that the civil rulers are Christians (at least with regard to profession and church membership) and that the principal part of the people are Christian. Thus the question is not whether civil rulers are required to regulate religion in all demographical circumstances. The regulation of religion is in the service of Christians, not absolute duty that the civil ruler fulfills in every set of circumstances" (Wolfe, *Case for Christian Nationalism*, 359). Of course, Wolfe's argument is that the United States *should* be (or even already is given its "demographic circumstances") just such a Christian nation, and thus should engage in just such action.

60. Wolfe, *Case for Christian Nationalism*, 384–85.

61. Wolfe, *Case for Christian Nationalism*, 359. Wolfe offers an extensive defense of punishment for "Arch-heretics" who "are publicly persistent in their damnable error and actively seek to convince others of this error," though he generously allows that "this is not to say that capital punishment is the necessary, sole, or desired punishment" for such people (391). "Banishment and long-term imprisonment may suffice as well." He continues, "Those who do not profess Christianity and yet actively proselytize their non-Christian religion or belief system or actively seek to refute the Christian religion are subject to the same principles outlined above" (392). It will no doubt be a relief to the many Jews, Muslims, Hindus, Buddhists, atheists, and adherents to the many other religions present in the United States that they risk, perhaps, mere banishment or long-term imprisonment for their publicly stated beliefs.

as Christian nationalists, such concerns are at best ancillary. As a study by the Public Religion Research Institute notes, barely half of those who identify as "Christian nationalists" attend church regularly.[62] What this suggests is that it is the nationalism that is the primary component of identity, rather than the Christianity. Christianity modifies nationalism only grammatically. It does not bring any distinct philosophy or value to the nationalist project. More broadly, perhaps, one could say that this is a problem that affects a wide array of religious nationalisms—Hindu nationalism in India, Jewish nationalism in Israel, Islamic nationalism in a variety of settings.[63] The purpose of religion becomes primarily functional. To the degree that the core values and commitments of the religion conflict with the nationalist agenda, they are reinterpreted or disregarded, in the sense that they are *literally* treated as though they do not exist.

Because this problem seems to transcend Christianity as a particular religion, Christianity *qua* Christianity does not seem to be the central problem that needs to be addressed in criticizing Christian nationalism, nor is Christian nationalism responding to a problem generated from within Christianity itself. Rather, just as other religious nationalisms co-opt particular religious forms for the sake of parochial agendas, so too does Christian nationalism. So while there are self-described Christian nationalists of color, the operative term in the phrase "white Christian nationalism" is not "Christian," but "white."[64] What it is seeking to preserve is not Christian power or identity, but *white* power and identity.[65] Christianity is, in Robert Jones's words, simply the "conductor" through which white supremacy flows, like a current on a wire. "Whatever else it has been . . . [Christianity] has also been the primary institution legitimizing and propagating white power and dominance."[66] There is evidence to suggest that actual church attendance might actually diminish the attractiveness of Christian nationalism. As Daniel K. Williams suggests,

62. Public Religion Research Institute, *Christian Nation?* As Williams notes in *The Atlantic*, this is substantially higher than the overall rate of regular church attendance in the United States, but it still remains a strange fact of Christian nationalism in the United States that it is disconnected from what is often perceived as a central facet of Christian spiritual life ("What Really Happens").

63. See Kaplan, *Jewish Radical Right*; Hazoni, *Jewish State*; Van Der Veer, *Religious Nationalism*; Hate Ali, *Nationalism, Transnationalism, and Political Islam*.

64. Shin and Benfield, *Crisis of Christian Nationalism*, 11.

65. See also Anderson, *White Rage*.

66. Jones, *White Too Long*, 71.

"people become even more entrenched in their political views when they stop attending services."[67]

The kind of white Christian nationalism that confronts the United States today emerges directly from that version of the founding myth of America as a uniquely Christian country—the "shining city on a hill" of John Winthrop, Peggy Noonan, and Ronald Reagan. However, the transformations of that mythology that have taken place over the last century have intensified the white supremacist and misogynist hierarchies inherent in them. Indeed, it is those hierarchies, and their potential loss, that are the defining feature of American Christian nationalism today, rather than any doctrinal commitment, grounded in precisely the religion of fear of which Bivins writes.

And yet, while this explains much of the specifically American form of contemporary religious nationalism, it is far from an adequate explanation for the rise of similar movements around the world. Once again, the erosion of the Cold War dispensation can serve to explain how it is that nationalism has become so closely associated with religious movements internationally. In order to understand this, we need to examine the way in which globalization emerged following the Cold War as a potent force around which (and against which) nations, economies, and religions organized.

GODS THAT FAILED: GLOBALIZATION, NEOLIBERALISM, AND THE RISE OF THE GLOBAL RIGHT

Given the international character of increasing religious and ethnic nationalism, understanding the broader context in which American white Christian nationalism exists requires an examination of the contributions made over the past half century by the political and economic dimensions of globalization, and particularly the role that so-called neoliberalism has played in shifting the discourse on the subject.[68]

67. Williams, "What Really Happens," para. 4.

68. Both the term "globalization" and the term "neoliberalism" are of course highly contested and heavily freighted. In the present discussion, my goal is not to provide a comprehensive discussion of every dimension of these terms, but to examine the role that they play specifically in the rise of religious and ethnic nationalism. For a more general discussion of globalization as a topic, see Paeth, "Public Theology in the Context of Globalization" and "Globalization, Global Ethics, and the Common Good."

By "globalization" here I mean "the expanding scale, growing magnitude, speeding up and deepening impact of transcontinental transformation in the scale of human organization that links distant communities and expands the reach of power relations across the world's regions and continents."[69] It consists in what Thomas Friedman defined as the "flattening" of relations of time and space, not only in economic terms, but in cultural and interpersonal terms as well.[70]

There are both positive and negative dimensions of globalization as a phenomenon. On the one hand, it allows for free and easy communication and collaboration across national and cultural boundaries, and creates the potential for organization around principles such as international law and global human rights. On the other hand, it risks eroding both national sovereignty and the integrity of local cultures. Furthermore, under the rubric of neoliberalism, the economic regime imposed by global financial institutions has arguably increased poverty and social dislocation where it has been allowed to have an impact.

Pankaj Ghemawat refers to the state of globalization as it emerged in the second half of the twentieth century as "World 2.0," in which increasing financial deregulation accompanied increasing cross-border international integration. As he puts it: "As the conservatism of Ronald Reagan and Margaret Thatcher took hold in the 1980s, the role of government began to narrow, reinforcing the conviction that galloping globalization would flatten national, not to mention tribal structures." This set of circumstances, he continues, "supposes competition over everything from everywhere."[71] He notes that globalization, understood in this way, "worries antiglobalizers a lot but warms the hearts of most proglobalizers,

69. Held and McGrew, *Globalization/Anti-Globalization*, 1.

70. Friedman, *World Is Flat*. He writes: "I am convinced that the flattening of the world, if it continues, will be seen in time as one of those fundamental shifts or inflection points, like Gutenberg's invention of the printing press, the rise of the nation state, or the Industrial Revolution—each of which, in its day . . . produced changes in the role of individuals, the role and form of governments, the ways business was done and wars were fought, the role of women, the forms religion and art took, and the way science and research were conducted, not to mention the political labels that we as a civilization have assigned to ourselves and to our enemies" (49). Whatever one may think of Friedman's overall analysis of the phenomenon of globalization, this quote illustrates well why, as a phenomenon, it might be likely to produce a backlash in the form of new kinds of ethnocentrism, nationalism, and religious conservatism.

71. Ghemawat, *World 3.0*, 11.

regardless of their other political leanings."[72] He specifically notes the agreement of "the two Friedmans" (Milton and Thomas) on the matter.[73]

This phenomenon, through which local cultures are threatened by the ongoing commodification of every dimension of life, was once described by African philosopher John Mbiti as akin to a bulldozer threatening to bury everything in its path.[74] Emerging from the international aid regime established by the World Bank and the International Monetary Fund (IMF), what Ghemawat and Mbiti are describing is the outcome of a neoliberal realignment of international economic priorities that took root after the 1973 global financial crisis. In its aftermath, and picking up steam in the 1980s, this new aid model was dubbed "The Washington Consensus," through which IMF and World Bank aid to developing countries was made contingent on the opening of financial markets and public sector disinvestment.[75] The outcome, in many places, was an erosion in national infrastructure, public education, and general welfare programs in emerging nations at the same time that foreign companies engaged in extractive or exploitative practices that left the affected nations and their citizens poorer.[76] According to Joseph Stiglitz:

> Those who labored in the developing countries knew something was wrong when they saw financial crises becoming more commonplace and the numbers of poor increasing. But they had no way to change the rules or to influence the international financial institutions that wrote them. Those who valued democratic processes saw how "conditionality"—the conditions that international lenders imposed in return for their assistance—undermined national sovereignty.[77]

Naomi Klein, a critic of globalization, argues that what she terms "free-market fundamentalism" is a heavy contributor to climate change. Whatever the rhetoric advanced at climate conferences in Kyoto or Paris, she

72. Ghemawat, *World 3.0*, 11.

73. Ghemawat, *World 3.0*, 11.

74. Stackhouse et al., *Local Church in a Global Era*, 3. Stackhouse picked up on this image and dubbed it "the bulldozer effect."

75. Stigliz, *Globalization and Its Discontents Revisited*. Stigliz's analysis is ultimately still grounded in a version of the liberal (if not "neo") capitalist approach to international development, for better or for worse. In his *Fair Trade for All*, written with Andrew Charlton, he proposes what he perceives to be a fairer international trade regime.

76. Stigliz, *Globalization and Its Discontents Revisited*.

77. Stigliz, *Globalization and Its Discontents Revisited*, 9.

argues, it is ultimately undermined or ignored when it conflicts with the power of global markets since the World Trade Organization, established in order to mediate trade disputes between nations, frequently restricts local climate legislation when it conflicts with free trade priorities.[78]

These effects of the neoliberal economic model have produced a global backlash in defense of forms of national sovereignty and local traditions and ways of life. This backlash was explicitly manifested in the form of the attacks on the World Trade Center and the Pentagon in September of 2001.[79] At the time, this event was seen in many corners as a confirmation of Samuel Huntington's "clash of civilizations" thesis. Yet there were others who saw the event, as well as similar attacks in Madrid on March 11, 2004, and in London on July 7, 2005, as the expression of a reaction against encroaching globalization. These were not attacks on the West per se or on its values, but rather responses to the dislocation caused by globalization and the neoliberal economic regime.[80] The economic, political, and cultural dimensions of this reaction were intertwined with one another, making it easy to lay the blame on Islam rather than seeing the reaction within the Muslim world as a response (whether legitimate or not) to a perceived threat.[81]

Benjamin Barber lays a version of this argument out in his book *Jihad vs. McWorld*, originally published before the 9/11 attacks, but given new life in their wake.[82] As the title suggests, Barber views the key point of tension as resting between the "McWorld" of globalization and neoliberal economic order and the "Jihad" of traditional cultural and religious

78. Klein, *This Changes Everything*, 69–73.

79. Johnson, *Blowback*.

80. In Johnson's estimation, they were also deeply rooted in the American imperial adventures of the second half of the twentieth century, through which the United States sought to exercise hegemony over emerging nations in the global competition against communism.

81. Reza Aslan makes a crucial distinction between "Jihadism" on the one hand, and "Islamism" on the other, arguing that "Islamism" is a way of speaking of Islamically rooted religious nationalism (in distinction to secular Arab nationalisms that rose to prominence in the second half of the twentieth century), while "Jihadism" refers to the trans-national, and often anti-nationalist, terrorist groups who are not interested in the creation of specific Muslim polities on the basis of nationality, but of undermining and destroying Western influence across the Muslim world. See Aslan, *How to Win a Cosmic War*. In either case, however, Aslan makes clear that neither of these terms is a reflection of the attitudes of Muslims generally, nor, in his estimation, an adequate reflection of the teachings of Islam.

82. Barber, *Jihad vs. McWorld*.

practices.[83] Barber contrasts his analysis with that of Huntington, arguing that "the struggle of Jihad against McWorld is not a clash of civilizations but a dialectical expression of tensions built into a single global civilization as it emerges against a backdrop of traditional ethnic and religious divisions, many of which are actually created by McWorld and its infotainment industries and technological innovations."[84] He notes that modern terrorist movements such as al-Qaeda are as dependent on the technological and economic "flatteners" of globalization as are the major nation states and economies: "Imagine terrorism without its reliance on credit cards, global financial systems, modern technology and the Internet. Terrorists would be reduced to throwing stones at local sheiks."[85] In this respect, terrorism in the name of the preservation of local and traditional culture is itself an expression of the very globalization it opposes. Barber continues:

> What we face is not a war between civilizations but a war within civilization, a struggle that expresses the ambivalence within each culture as it faces a global, networked, material future and wonders whether cultural and national autonomy can be retained, and the ambivalence within each individual juggling the obvious benefits of modernity with its equally obvious costs.[86]

If this conflict is an expression of the dialectic that Barber describes, the question then becomes how it might be possible to surpass the tension in order to establish a new set of conditions through which those tensions can be resolved.[87] If the very expression of resistance to globalization is

83. The title, I would note, is regrettable in light of the rise of Islamophobia that took place in the wake of the 9/11 attacks and the subsequent wars in Afghanistan and Iraq. Barber does attempt to nuance his use of the term, stating "*Jihad* is, I recognize, a strong term. In its mildest form, it betokens religious struggle on behalf of faith, a kind of Islamic Zeal. In its strongest political manifestation, it means bloody holy war on behalf of partisan identity that is metaphysically defined and fanatically defended. . . . I use the term in its militant construction to suggest dogmatic and violent particularism of a kind known to Christians no less than Muslims, to Germans and Hindis [*sic*] as well as Arabs" (Barber, *Jihad vs. McWorld*, 9).

84. Barber, *Jihad vs. McWorld*, xvi.

85. Barber, *Jihad vs. McWorld*, xvi.

86. Barber, *Jihad vs. McWorld*, xvi.

87. Barber's invocation of dialectics obviously lends itself to a Hegelian interpretation, through which the conflict between the moment and its negation (globalization and local resistance respectively), require a transcending *aufhebung*, through which a new moment incorporates the elements of the prior conflict into itself in a new way.

itself a manifestation of globalization, how can globalization itself be transcended?

Barber proposes global civil society as the vehicle for local democratic action to manifest itself across national boundaries. Nation-states are ultimately insufficient actors in a global context: "The challenges of global McWorld and regional Jihad are not susceptible to its interventions; and the ideology of laissez-fair that accompanies McWorld and has become the mantra of its proponents within national government undermines whatever residual capacity it might have for action in the name of public good."[88] What this model offers, he claims, is a means by which both the narrowness of local concerns and the anesthetic decadence of globalization can be overcome.

Yet, as an antidote, the idea of global civil society seems inadequate. While it offers the advantage of not being bound to specific political or governmental formations, and has the potential to magnify local issues on a global level, there is a real question as to whether, absent large-scale governmental action across national boundaries, it can do more than simply contribute to the ongoing discourse about neoliberalism vs. locality, McWorld vs. Jihad.

The lessons of the past two decades have shown how misplaced the hope was that the neoliberal economic consensus and the emerging global economy were sufficient to replace the conflicts of the previous generation. The return of the local is itself a global phenomenon, as the reactionary movements emerging around the world attest. As was said of communism after the first half of the twentieth century, in the twenty-first century, neoliberalism and globalization are themselves "gods that failed."[89]

At the same time that globalization was producing transnational backlash in the form of terrorism, it was also producing backlash within nation-states, as religious and ethnic minorities became targets of increasingly strident forms of religious nationalism. In the European context, the rightward turn in Hungary under Viktor Orbán offers one example of the knock-on effects of the conflict between globalization

88. Barber, *Jihad vs. McWorld*, 276.

89. Crossman and Engerman, *God that Failed*. On the other hand, Hans-Hermann Hoppe takes the other side of the argument in arguing that it is democracy rather than capitalism, that has failed. Thus rather than critiquing the anti-democratic trends within capitalism, Hoppe critiques the anti-capitalist dimensions of democracy (Hoppe, *Democracy—the God that Failed*).

and locality.[90] Orbán's rise was aided by the refugee crisis in Syria, which was itself an expression of the ongoing conflicts originating in that same tension. Similar dynamics can be seen in the Hindu nationalism of Narendra Modi's BJP in India, in which on the one hand globalization and neoliberalism have opened the country up to a multiplicity of influences, at the very same time pluralism on the local level is being diminished and repressed, often violently.[91] This parallels the increasing Islamic nationalism seen in many parts of the Arab world, but certainly in Pakistan and Bangladesh.[92]

In the United States, one casualty of neoliberalism's failure was the consensus that had unified the political right for much of the second half of the twentieth century—through which libertarian commitment to free markets and minimal legislation was accompanied by socially conservative morality on subjects such as sexuality and the separation of church and state. This always-uneasy alliance was justified and supported by the struggle against communism, which was perceived as a threat to both capitalism and religiously grounded morality. What the decades following the fall of the Berlin Wall demonstrated was the fractiousness of that coalition, and the limits of what such an alliance could sustain in the absence of a world-historical threat.

THE DEAD CONSENSUS

According to John Ganz, 1992 was "the year the clock broke."[93] In that year, he argues, Pat Buchanan's insurgent candidacy for the Republican nomination placed into stark relief the tensions that existed on the American right, tensions that had been papered over by the Cold War

90. Szelényi, *Tainted Democracy*. Orbán has argued that Hungary should be an "illiberal democracy" the goal of which is "to harmonize [the] relationship between the interests and achievements of individuals . . . with the interests and achievements of the community, and the nation" (Orbán, "Full Text"). Functionally, this has meant an increasing intolerance for ethnic and religious minorities, an authoritarian approach to governance, and an increasing reliance on the rhetoric of Christian nationalism to justify repressive policies.

91. Ghosh, *BJP and the Evolution of Hindu Nationalism*; Tore Flåten, *Hindu Nationalism, History and Identity in India*; Menon, *Everyday Nationalism*.

92. Toor, *State of Islam*; Devi, *Muslim Zion*; Ahmed, *Jinnah, Pakistan, and Islamic Identity*; Uddin, *Constructing Bangladesh*.

93. Ganz, "Year the Clock Broke." This article was subsequently expanded into a book, *When the Clock Broke*.

consensus that united the pro-business, libertarian end of the conservative spectrum with the racially freighted religious nationalism of figures like Buchanan.

Ganz focuses on the relationship between Buchanan and other emerging "paleo-conservatives," such as political staffer Sam Francis and the *National Review*'s Joe Sobran. These figures saw the white-supremacist gubernatorial candidacy of David Duke in Louisiana as a model to be emulated on the national level—a populism grounded in more or less explicitly racist appeals to a lost white national heritage and charges of a "culture war" between liberalism and "traditional American values."

> Sensing that America as they knew it was in peril, they hoped to recast American democracy around the "negative solidarity" of knowing who you hated or wanted to destroy: this system would be based on domination and exclusion, a restricted sense of community that jealously guarded its boundaries and policed its members, and the direction of a charismatic leader who would use his power to punish and persecute for the sake of restoring lost national greatness. In a period when some said that ideological struggle was irrelevant and that even history itself had ended, they looked for inspiration among the ideological ruins of earlier times: nationalism, populism, racism, antisemitism, and even fascism. In the words of one, they wanted to "break the clock" of progress—returning American to a previous dispensation while also creating an entirely new country of their own devising.[94]

It was in this context that Buchanan offered his incendiary speech at the 1992 Republican National Convention, saying: "There is a religious war going on in this country. It is a cultural war, as critical to the kind of nation we shall be as was the Cold War itself, for this war is for the soul of America. And in that struggle for the soul of America, Clinton and Clinton are on the other side, and George Bush is on our side."[95] This rhetoric of religious and cultural warfare was an indication of both how far the divisions on the American right had developed in the three

94. Ganz, *When the Clock Broke*, 4.

95. Buchanan, "Culture War Speech." It is notable that even this early, Hillary Clinton is held up for demonization on the American right. Ordinarily, a speech such as this would have referred to "Clinton and Gore," as the running mates in the election, but from the start, the right promoted the idea that the *real* running mates in the 1992 election were Bill and Hillary Clinton. And of course, this demonization would follow Hillary Clinton throughout her subsequent terms in the Senate and as Secretary of State and to her own 2016 presidential bid.

years since the fall of the Berlin Wall, and a sign of things to come in the decades to follow.

As Ganz notes, a feature of this emerging paleoconservative movement was its not terribly well-hidden anti-Semitism. The very term paleoconservative was meant to contrast with the—largely Jewish—neoconservative movement,[96] which rankled the paleo-right with its aggressive approach to foreign policy, as well as its rhetoric of American responsibility to promote democracy on a global scale.[97] Democracy itself was suspect from the paleo perspective. As Sobren would write: "Now that democracy has overthrown communism, we can turn to the problem of how to overthrow democracy."[98] This sentiment was echoed by Francis: "The first thing we have to learn about fighting and winning a cultural war is that we are not fighting to conserve something; we are fighting to overthrow something."[99]

Whatever the paleo-conservative discontent with the reigning paradigm in Republican politics, the election of George W. Bush in 2000, followed quickly by the 9/11 terrorist attacks and the wars in Afghanistan and Iraq, temporarily marginalized those voices. Neoconservatism

96. Neoconservatism was by no means monolithically Jewish, of course. However, many of its most prominent members were Jewish converts from the political left, such as Irving Kristol and Norman Podhoretz. For the first generation of neocons, it was precisely the idea that democracy could best be preserved under forms of capitalist imperialism, which they viewed as threatened by the New Left of the 1960s, that pushed them to the political right.

97. That this rhetoric was often hollow is somewhat beside the point. Neoconservative figures such as Jeanne Kirkpatrick were more than happy to speak publicly on behalf of authoritarian governments in Central America, arguing speciously that such governments had the potential to develop into democracies, unlike what she termed "totalitarian" governments such as the Soviet Union. See Kirkpatrick, *Dictatorships and Double Standards.*

98. Ganz, *When the Clock Broke*, 79. See also Hoppe, *Democracy—The God That Failed.*

99. Ganz, *When the Clock Broke*, 370. As Ganz argues, "what made Francis stand out from his fellow New Rightists was his abandonment of the idea of 'conservatism' altogether. 'Viewed in this sociopolitical perspective,' he wrote, 'the New Right is not a conservative force but a radical or revolutionary one.' While the New Right's 'social and cultural values are indeed conservative and traditionalist . . . unlike almost any other conservative group in history, it finds itself not only out of power in a formal sense but also excluded from the informal centers of real power. Consequently, the political style, tactics, and organizational forms of the New Right should find a radical, antiestablishment approach better adapted to the achievement of its goals'" (64–65). Returning to this theme later, Ganz notes that, for Francis, the Italian communist theoretician Antonio Gramsci offered a model for radical political organization that corresponded to the kind of approach Francis favored (370–72).

predominated in discussions of American foreign policy even as the rhetoric of the religious right predominated in the administration's domestic policy. This was the era when theoconservatives such as Richard John Neuhaus, Michael Novak, and George Weigel looked to the Bush administration as a conduit through which their vision of a restoration of traditional values to American life could be achieved.[100]

In the aftermath of Donald Trump's election in 2016 however, the earlier paleoconservative culture war themes, largely (though not entirely) stripped of anti-Semitic rhetoric, reemerged as a form of internal critique on the American right. In 2019, *First Things* published a statement signed by a number of prominent conservative intellectuals, most notably Sohrab Ahmari. This statement, titled "Against the Dead Consensus," argued that Trump's election represented a watershed on the American right. "*There is no returning to the pre-Trump conservative consensus that collapsed in 2016*," the statement declared.[101] This former consensus, which emphasized "prosperity at home and the expansion of a rules-based international order," was nevertheless fatally flawed insofar as it "tracked the same lodestar liberalism did—namely individual autonomy."[102] The authors continued:

> Yes, the old conservative consensus paid lip service to traditional values. But it failed to retard, much less reverse, the eclipse of permanent truths, family stability, communal solidarity, and much else. It surrendered to the pornographization of daily life, to the culture of death, to the cult of competitiveness. It too often bowed to a poisonous and censorious multiculturalism.[103]

The "consensus conservative" dogmas of prudential judgment, they argue, include "free trade on every front, free movement through every boundary, small government as an end in itself, [and] technological advancement as a cure all."[104] In other words, precisely the components

100. Neuhaus and Novak themselves could properly be labeled neoconservative, as Catholic (or in the case of Neuhaus, Lutheran-to-Catholic convert) leftists who shared with other neocons a disillusionment with the project of the New Left, an embrace of capitalism in economics, and aggressive anti-communism in foreign policy. See Linker, *Theocons*.

101. Ahmari et al., "Against the Dead Consensus." Italics in original.

102. Ahmari et al., "Against the Dead Consensus."

103. Ahmari et al., "Against the Dead Consensus."

104. Ahmari et al., "Against the Dead Consensus."

of globalization that alarmed left-wing anti-globalizers and provoked myriad forms of resistance on the level of local cultures.

In the face of these dogmas, the authors reject what they see as a dehumanizing culture of affluence, which embraces pornography, surrogate motherhood, and gender nonconformity.[105] At the same time that they declare that "our society must not prioritize the needs of the childless, the healthy, and the intellectually competitive," they also declared that "as Americans we owe one another a distinct allegiance and must put each other first." Thus, appeals to universal human dignity notwithstanding, they oppose immigration on the grounds that it "attempts to displace American citizens" and creates a "borderless world," grounded in cosmopolitan values, writing:

> For those who enjoy the upsides, a borderless world brings intoxicating new liberties. They can go anywhere, work anywhere. They can call themselves "citizens" of the world. But the jetsetters' vision clashes with the human need for a common life. And it has bred resentments that are only beginning to surface. We embrace the new nationalism insofar as it stands against the utopian ideal of a borderless world that, in practice, leads to universal tyranny.[106]

Needless to say, the authors do not explain *how* it leads to universal tyranny. It just does. Indeed "tyranny" is one of their favorite words. They "resist a tyrannical liberalism." They declare that "When an ideological liberalism"—also undescribed and unarticulated—"seeks to dictate our foreign policy and dominate our religious and charitable institutions, tyranny is the result, at home and abroad."[107] By tyranny, they seem to mean that, in a democratic polity in which they do not represent the majority, they often do not get their way. Failing to be persuaded by their arguments is, apparently, the essence of "tyranny."[108]

105. This is, it must be said, a strange way to go about critiquing a "culture of affluence"—there is no mention of income inequality or environmental destruction, the dissolution of local communities by large corporations, or the general problem of industrial decline. The concern with affluence is entirely confined to concerns about what the affluent might do with their genitalia.

106. Ahmari et al., "Against the Dead Consensus."

107. Ahmari et al., "Against the Dead Consensus."

108. Ahmari went on to write *Tyranny, Inc.*, in which to his credit he addresses the role of corporate power in the creation of what he addresses as "private tyranny," the role that collaboration between government and business has played in the dislocation of middle-class workers and local communities. This is in the interest of putting

This line of thought is laid out more explicitly in a subsequent article by Ahmari, also in *First Things*, titled "Against David-French-ism." French, a *New York Times* columnist and himself former writer for *First Things*, is the target of Ahmari's ire precisely because, as Ahmari argues, he is too *nice*: "It is in part that earnest and insistently polite quality of his that I find unsuitable to the depth of the present crisis facing religious conservatives."[109] By contrast, Ahmari embraces, with almost Conan the Barbarian–esque enthusiasm, the idea that religious conservatives must "fight the culture war with the aim of defeating the enemy and enjoying the spoils in the form of a public square reordered to the common good and ultimately the Highest Good."[110]

Doing so, however, requires abandoning French's commitment to pluralism and democratic discourse.[111] Arguing against the idea that the protection of individual autonomy is and should be a central political value, an idea that French shares with the "enemies" that Ahmari is seeking to defeat, he writes:

> Such talk—of politics as war and enmity—is thoroughly alien to French, I think because he believes that the institutions of a technocratic market society are neutral zones that should, in theory, accommodate both traditional Christianity and the libertine ways and pagan ideology of the other side. Even if the latter—that is the libertine and the pagan—predominate in elite institutions, French figures, then at least the former, traditional Christians, should be granted spaces in which to practice and preach what they sincerely believe.[112]

Ultimately, however, Ahmari argues, this desire for maximal autonomy is unsustainable for those who subscribe to the purportedly traditional

---

another nail in the coffin of the "dead consensus" and striking a further blow against the liberal individualist emphasis on personal autonomy.

109. Ahmari, "Against David-French-ism."

110. Ahmari, "Against David-French-ism."

111. This is the element that is concerning in Ahmari's ideology-crossing appeal to left-wing critics of corporate power. In *Tyranny, Inc.* he offers a trenchant critique of corporate power in the context of American capitalism. Much of his critique could be echoed by left-wing critics of capitalism. Indeed his involvement with the journal *Compact*, which seeks to bring together left- and right-wing critics of American capitalism, demonstrates the appeal of this rhetoric. However, one ignores Ahmari's preferred end-state of social conditions to their peril. The "highest good" to which he appeals is not one that would allow for many of the individual liberties that are conditions for a democratic society.

112. Ahmari, "Against David-French-ism."

values that both he and French embrace. Because "individual experiments in living" require a social space in which to be freely exercised (Ahmari says that they require "some level of moral approval by the community"), it becomes impossible—all recent evidence to the contrary notwithstanding—to offer any kind of public critique grounded in traditional values. Identifying those on the other side of the debate as "bullies," Ahmari argues for government action on behalf of his preferred traditionalism—countering the cultural bullies, apparently, with bigger bullies, bullies with guns and a monopoly on the use of force.

Ahmari then turns, bizarrely, to Donald Trump as a champion of the traditionalism he espouses, arguing that "with a kind of animal instinct, Trump understood what was missing from mainstream (more or less French-ian) conservatism":

> [Trump's] instinct has been to shift the cultural and political mix, ever so slightly, away from autonomy-above-all toward order, continuity, and social cohesion. He believes that the political community—and not just the church, family, and individual, has its own legitimate scope for action. He believes that it can help protect the citizen from transnational forces beyond his control.[113]

Leaving aside the rather dubious claim that Donald Trump can be said to actually "believe" anything, it is strange to hold him up as an avatar of "order, continuity, and social cohesion," let alone one who has opinions about the role of church and family in the political order.

At core, however, what Ahmari is advocating is precisely the kind of Christian nationalism we examined above—though this time clothed in the robes of Catholicism rather than the austere Presbyterian black of Stephen Wolfe.[114] Under the Catholic moniker, this position is known as "Integralism," defined as the idea that:

> Societies are bound to worship God according to the truth He has revealed, and this is done principally by recognizing and supporting the Church He has founded. Thus the two powers—the temporal power of earthly rulers and the spiritual power of

113. Ahmari, "Against David-French-ism."

114. Indeed, Bradford Littlejohn suggests as much, writing, "Given that few of the Catholic anti-liberals are prepared to reduce their political program to the command to 'Repent and submit to the Pope!,' one suspects that what many of them are really after is not a political Catholicism, but a renewed political Protestantism." "Ahmari Among the Protestants," para. 8.

> the Apostles and their successors—are meant to enter into an ordered relation. Each has its own proper concern. The temporal society is concerned with the common good of a "temporal" society, a society belonging to the present order of time, that is destined to pass away. The spiritual power is concerned with the common good of an eternal city not of this world, although it is already present in mystery in this world. Yet . . . since both of these powers are from God and both rule over the same subjects, there must be an order between them.[115]

Thus, the "integral" relationship between church and state, society and religion, is one in which both are oriented toward securing the common good as understood and defined according to the teaching of the church. Societies are "principally" required to recognize and support the church. And, lest the point be obscured, "church" here means the Roman Catholic Church, rather than Christianity in general or even a broadly ecumenical religious ethos. Integralists affirm that it is *only* through the Roman Catholic Church that the true *telos* of society can be attained. Or, as Sohrab Ahmari would have it, the public square should promote both the common good and the *Highest Good*. As Thomas Crean and Alan Fimister put it:

> Hence only the Catholic Church is properly speaking and intrinsically a perfect society. For her end is beatitude: the vision of God in union with Christ and the saints. When attained, this brings complete fulfillment and a happiness experienced as wholly satisfying: first for the soul alone, and then, after resurrection, for the whole man. . . . Since grace presupposes and perfects nature, the Church is also entitled to possess the natural resources necessary to sustain us in this mortal life as we seek for beatitude: hence her official organs have an indefeasible right, belonging to her by her constitution and not by the grant of any human government, to possess property, to educate her baptised children, to try by her own judges offenses against her common good, and punish such offenses either by her own officers or by calling on the assistance of civil officers who recognize her authority. *This implies that she has the right to temporal power itself.* Not as if her ordained ministers were to wield the material sword or to judge on temporal matters, but in the sense that *this temporal power must be held by baptised Catholics and put at the service of the highest common good.* Rather than speak of "Church and State" as two perfect societies, it is thus more

115. Waldsten, *Integralism and the Common Good*, xii.

> exact to say that there is but one perfect society, the Church or city of God, in which two powers, spiritual and temporal, are hierarchically arranged. The very word "State," suggesting as it does a complete society corresponding adequately to man's natural end, appears in fact fatally misleading.[116]

Whether under the crypto-dominionist rubric of Stephen Wolfe or the Integralist approach of Sohrab Ahmari, these forms of Christian nationalism are explicitly anti-liberal (in the broadest sense of the word "liberalism"), anti-pluralist, and anti-democratic. Echoing John Henry Newman, they proclaim that the state must either accept or deny the church's claim to supremacy, but it cannot stand neutral before it.[117] To which the liberal, the pluralist, and the democrat might rightly reply, "Well, why not? The truth claims on offer aren't ours to accept or deny, or even acknowledge. And if within the space of a free public discourse, your ideas cannot win support of their own accord, how is it the role of the state to impose them on the rest of us?"

Christian nationalists of whatever stripe do not have an answer to that question. While they may well be right that the Cold War era consensus on the American right is no longer capable of sustaining itself, it is not at all clear why the imposition of one specific set of values then becomes the responsibility of the state, particularly when it has consistently failed to win the support of the electorate. However, it does become increasingly clear why, under those circumstances, religious nationalists would begin to look toward authoritarianism as a solution. If the role of society is to seek, not just the self-perceived good of each, but the divinely ordained good of *all*, then to the degree that democracy fails to achieve that, it must be overcome. Having failed to win the democratic debate, both Integralists and Christian nationalists, to return to the words of Joe Sobren, "turn to the problem of how to overthrow democracy."

THE POST-CHRISTIAN MOMENT: LIVING IN THE END TIMES

What Francis Fukuyama predicted to be the end of history may just as easily be understood as the "end times"—an eschatological vision of a transformed world. The world did not, however, transform in quite the

116. Crean and Fimister, *Integralism*, 20–21. Italics added.

117. Waldsten, *Integralism and the Common Good*, xi.

way he envisioned it, and the past two decades have offered plenty of grist for the idea that history's end is not something to be lightly predicted or sought. This was something the prophet Amos understood well, when he excoriated Israel, declaring, "Woe to you who desire the day of the LORD! . . . It is darkness, not light, as if someone fled from a lion, and was met by a bear" (Amos 5:18–19). And while Fukuyama may have understood that the end of the Cold War was not nearly as happy a prospect as it may have appeared at the time, few could have foreseen the direction the years to follow would take.

The rise of Christian nationalism, Catholic integralism, and the reactionary and authoritarian politics that accompany them are grounded in the loss of meaning and purpose that accompanied the historical transition to a post-Cold War world. The lack of an arena in which to display the "muscular Christianity" that had become such a part of conservative Christianity in those decades, in which to demonstrate their *megalothymia*, left cold warriors and the faith militant bereft precisely at their moment of triumph.

At the same time, the decline of religious observance, the secularization of the public sphere, and the "rise of the nones" demonstrated that the social importance of religion generally, and Christianity in particular, no longer possessed the potency it had in the aftermath of World War II. The intersection of evangelical Christianity with particular forms of masculinity made it increasingly unpalatable to women who were finally free to determine their own destinies apart from the need to be tied to a spouse, and its intersection with white supremacy made it unpalatable to those who believed in racial and ethnic equality in a democratic society. These contributing factors to religious decline also contributed to the growing sense among religious conservatives that their values and ideology could not succeed in the context of a democratic and pluralistic America. Thus democracy itself, alongside political liberalism and social pluralism, became suspect.

The moment in which we currently live is defined just as much by the post-Christian ethos in which we dwell as it is by the threats to democracy posed by right-wing revanchists and Christian reactionaries. Those who value liberalism and pluralism are disillusioned by the idea of religion as innately repressive and authoritarian, and suspicious of the institutional forms it takes. Religious decline is grounded in both the lack of credibility that religious ideas themselves are perceived to possess and the lack of credibility that the traditions through which those ideas are conveyed possess.

2

Identity and Authoritarianism

Plutocracy, Technology, and Conspiracism

Surrounded by madness, surrounded by hunger, surrounded by everything but death, I knew death was our only way out.

—Harlan Ellison, "I Have No Mouth, And I Must Scream"[1]

TRUMP AGONISTES: OR THE CRISIS OF THE MANUFACTURED PLUTOCRAT

In his own inimitable way, David Bentley Hart once wrote an essay on Donald Trump, which, in meandering through a series of illustrations and images, recalled a friend's observation that most literary depictions of Satan portray the Prince of Darkness as a kind of suave sophisticate, whereas in reality, the devil is more properly depicted as "a thug, . . . a merciless real estate developer whose largest projects are all casinos."[2] His friend continues:

> [T]o the extent that the devil has any personality to speak of at all—even if the story is true and he was once an archangel or something of that sort—he must by now be a pretty sordid, unimaginative, and dreary little fellow. He would have to be so

1 Ellison, *Greatest Hits*, 19.

2. Hart, "Person You Flee at Parties," para. 17.

> monstrously self-absorbed: not a brilliant conversationalist, not a philosopher and wit, not a bon-vivant or perverted aesthete, but just some tedious little troll, full of spite and resentment. He's probably a monomaniac who talks about nothing but his personal grievances and aims, and in the bluntest, most unrefined language imaginable—the sort of person you try your best to get away from at a party.[3]

Modern literature, in glamorizing the diabolical, in either naturalistic or supernatural forms, has obscured, as Hart would argue, the fundamental boringness, the tediousness of evil. Far from being exciting or enticing, at its core, evil is epitomized by utter self-absorption and contemptibility.

In one sense then, the comparison of Donald Trump to the devil—"a merciless real estate developer"—may seem to elevate Trump to a height of evil that fails to reflect his fundamental dullness. On the other hand, as Hart would argue, it reflects precisely the tediousness that is the real character of evil. To truly understand the nature of evil, Hart wishes to say, is to understand it as something so wretched that one cannot even stand to be in its presence. Thus, regarding Trump himself, Hart concludes:

> How obvious it seems to me now. Cold, grasping, bleak, graceless, and dull; unctuous, sleek, pitiless, and crass; a pallid vulgarian floating through life on clouds of acrid cologne and trailed by a vanguard of fawning divorce lawyers, the devil is probably eerily similar to Donald Trump—though perhaps just a little nicer.[4]

This may seem to be an uncharitable way to begin a reflection on Donald Trump as one of the most significant American political figures of the past twenty years. Yet, it is hard to divorce his personal loathsomeness from the impact he has had on the American character.

And indeed, one can trace the damage Trump has done to the American body politic back to his earliest appearance on the public scene in the 1980s. His public persona has never really been other than that of a grasping, narcissistic, greedy plutocrat. This is the self-image that he embraced from the beginning, the self-image that he celebrated as he touted his own alleged successes, his own brilliance, his own superior

3. Hart, "Person You Flee at Parties," para. 11.

4. Hart, "Person You Flee at Parties," para. 21.

sense of taste and style, even as he reflected the vulgarest manifestations of capitalist acquisitiveness.

Yet, if this is the case, the mystery becomes how it is that he has exercised such a "dark charisma" on such a large portion of the American public, not only since 2016, but for decades.[5] His utter charmlessness seems belied by the capacity he has to draw masses of people into his orbit. In this sense as well, he seems to share something in common with the Prince of Darkness—he offers trash, but has convinced us that it's treasure.

Trump can perhaps usefully be compared to the antagonist of Dennis Potter's *Brimstone and Treacle*. The play is about a young man named Martin (who may actually be the devil) who ingratiates himself into the life of a family under the pretext of being the former fiancé of their disabled daughter, Patricia. Martin is a blandly handsome young man,[6] soft-spoken and polite, who offers to put himself in their service, to ease the burden of caring for their daughter, solely out of his love for her. They are taken in out of a combination of their own real need and their willingness to allow Martin to flatter their egos. Yet, bit by bit, the mask slips and Martin's genuinely diabolical character is revealed.

In one scene, Martin and the family share drinks, as the father, Tom, attempts to liven the mood with an anti-Irish joke. Martin takes the occasion to intensify Tom's sense of racial resentment, luring him into declarations such as "England for the English!" And wishing that foreigners would just "go back where they came from." Eventually Martin takes things too far even for Tom, has he begins to declare: "They won't want to go, so we'll have to cage them! And shoot them! And VX gas them!"[7] At which point Tom recoils in horror as his own sentiments are reflected back to him in all of their malice. This, he insists to Martin, was not what he wanted, only a return to the nostalgic England of his youth. What Martin's speech reveals though is that this backward-looking desire can only be fulfilled through the willingness to unleash hideous violence.

At another point in the play, Tom's wife Amy asks Martin to offer a prayer over her daughter, who is immobilized and unable to communicate due to an accident several years earlier. Martin obliges, offering

5. Byrd, *Dark Charisma of Donald Trump*.

6. This aspect of the character is somewhat undermined in the movie version, in which Martin is played by a young and dashing Sting, still at the height of his fame with the Police.

7. Potter, *Brimstone and Treacle*, 33.

an ironic and contemptuous prayer for healing, the tone of which renders the prayer itself simultaneously sincere and blasphemous, as Amy reaches out to the God whom Martin mocks. And yet, despite Martin's satanic intent, in the end his prayer is answered and Patricia awakens. Potter has commented:

> Even if you set out to do an evil act, or if you set out to do a good one, you cannot predict with certainty the consequences of such action, but more interesting than the fact that it's because of his diabolical actions that good results, there is another force going on which is the very laughably "simple" faith of the mother, and of the characters on stage it's the mother who wins.
>
> It's the mother who asks for the prayer. It's the devil who mocks the act of prayer, the prayer itself is mocked, the act of praying is mocked, and yet the prayer is answered.[8]

Even here, however, the blessing is mixed, as Patrica's revival is accompanied by her revelation that she was injured fleeing from catching her father in an act of infidelity.[9]

Trump, like Martin, appeals to the nostalgic impulse in the national psyche. He encourages us in our worst impulses, goads us toward violence in the name of our mythic imagined past. He is not an attractive figure, yet he is nevertheless somehow magnetic. Like Martin, he gives voice to our inner ugliness, and gives permission for us to accept unacceptable ideas.

In this respect, Potter's misanthropic view in *Brimstone and Treacle* is perhaps more optimistic than reality. Tom is a flawed, racist, venal, selfish, resentful, and abusive figure. But he also has limits. He can recognize in Martin's speech that there are boundaries that should not be crossed, and in his rejection of Martin's violent fantasy he draws a moral line, albeit a feeble one.

By contrast, once Trump gave voice to the racism that lay encoded in much of the political rhetoric of the American right, and did so in a way that revealed what that encoded language had hidden, rather than turn away, many Americans embraced it. When white nationalists marched in Charlottesville, Virginia chanting "Jews will not replace us!", they were declaring an enthusiastic "yes" to the permission that Trump gave to

8. Billington, "Dennis Potter."

9. This is actually unclear from the text of the play itself, though the movie version, which differs in some ways substantially from the play, makes this element apparent.

engage in violent rhetoric and action. While Tom rejects Martin's call to violence, the American right has chosen to embrace Trump's similar call.

In *Nixon Agonistes*, Gary Wills offers a portrait of Richard Nixon in the period before the Watergate scandal that seeks to understand what Nixon's presidency revealed about the United States in the 1960s. It was a profile, not only of Nixon as a politician, but of Nixon as a political symbol. In particular, Wills reveals how Nixon's utter mediocrity in every respect was an image of America in that moment. Explaining his title, Wills recalls Milton's play *Samson Agonistes*:

> The Samson of the early scenes in that play is trudging around his millstone, chained to his sweaty task as others mock him, a man dreaming of revenge after being done in by the glamorous Delilah. John Kennedy was Nixon's glamorous Delilah. Milton's words, as usual, had several layers of meaning. An *agonistes*, in Greek, is a contestant. (Samuel Johnson's dictionary defined an agonist as a "prize fighter."). Since Milton was writing a play, he remembered that the actor-contestants in Greek tragedies were the first contestant (*prot-agonist*), the second contestant (*deuter-agonist*), and the third contestant (*trip-agonist*). So he kept his characters to three, with Samson as protagonist. Nixon was actor and contender, protagonist in his own ongoing psychodrama, always the sweaty striver who felt his strivings were unappreciated.[10]

Wills subtitled his book *The Crisis of the Self-Made Man*. It was precisely Nixon's constant striving to overcome, to prove something, to climb to the top of the heap, that renders him, in Wills's assessment, "self-made." He did come from humble beginnings to achieve the presidency, after years of being discounted and underestimated. At the same time, rather than Nixon being elevated by the presidency, the presidency was diminished by Nixon.

There is no sense in which Donald Trump could be considered a "self-made man." Much like his Republican predecessor George W. Bush, he was a classic case of what Molly Ivans once described as someone "born on third, thought he hit a triple."[11] Trump never possessed anything that was not either given to him or stolen by him. He is the farthest thing

10. Wills, *Nixon Agonistes*, xv.

11. The attribution of this quote is somewhat disputed. I have seen it ascribed to Molly Ivans on Bush Jr., Ann Richards on Bush Sr., and football coach Barry Switzer. Like success, it seems to have a thousand parents.

from the "sweaty striver" Wills depicts Nixon to be. And yet his entire self-image is wrapped up in the need to be perceived as a winner, as one who has overcome adversity. In this sense, he imagines himself as, and portrays himself to be, self-made. And he shares with Nixon the same need to prove something, whether to himself, his father, or the country.

For Trump, it was Obama, rather than Kennedy, who represented his glamorous Delilah, though in almost every respect, the positions of Nixon and Kennedy were reversed in their relationship—while Nixon started with little and rose up from humble beginnings, Trump was a child of privilege, a manufactured plutocrat whose successes were all ephemeral or illusory, whose image as an incredibly successful businessman was a wholesale media creation. John F. Kennedy was a child of privilege not dissimilar to Donald Trump. Kennedy was also born on third, though was perhaps gracious enough to recognize that he had not in fact hit a triple. Obama, on the other hand, was in background far more similar to Nixon. Yet it was precisely in his striving and overcoming, not sweatily, but with grace, that seemed to provoke Trump to ever greater degrees of apoplexy. In the end, what set the stage for his presidential run was that Trump could not tolerate being upstaged and humiliated by Obama in a public forum.

Yet, in terms of his character and rhetoric, Trump bears more in common with another character from Wills's account, George Wallace. Wallace embodied the same populist racism that Trump does, appealing to white resentment over social change. Both draw characters like Tom in *Brimstone and Treacle*, who see a world in which they are no longer at the center of things, in which their nostalgic mythology no longer commands credibility, and who wish to go back to an imagined idyllic past. While Nixon was of the establishment, Wallace, like Trump, consciously stood outside of it. In the end, Nixon's path to the presidency came from courting and winning Wallace voters, bending the knee to segregationists like Strom Thurmond, and churning white resentment against urban (that is to say, "ethnic") elites and intellectuals.

When Wills labels Nixon "the last liberal," it is not because his politics are of the left, but because he encapsulates the mentality of the liberal market—a realm of pure competition.[12] In this respect, Trump and Nixon have more in common, as both offered lip service to the power of

12. Wills, *Nixon Agonistes*, 589.

markets—economic, intellectual, or political—even as they sought ways to manipulate those markets to their advantage.

Yet, perhaps the most surprising thing about Donald Trump's rise to political prominence is the way in which he has been able to suborn the vast majority of white American evangelicals to his cause. Possibly the most irreligious figure ever to stand for president, and certainly vastly ignorant of even the rudiments of the religious tradition that he claims, Trump has nevertheless been able to convince many Christians that he is not merely a person of faith, but the instrument of God's will on earth, perhaps even a messianic figure. Like Martin, his attempts at prayer read not as sincere, but as blasphemous—the words of someone who does not only not believe his own words, but believes their precise opposite. Biblically, theologically, and morally illiterate, he can stand shamelessly at a Christian university and flaunt his inability to even read, let alone understand the meaning of, a biblical text. And yet white evangelicals have flocked to him in droves. It is as though, after a century of warning about the coming of the antichrist, when he arrived, conservative American Christians welcomed him with open arms.

In the end, of course, Trump is not the devil. He's not even the guy who gets the devil's cigarettes. But he shares the qualities with Satan that Hart's friend articulated—petty, resentful, self-absorbed, narcissistic. Trump's importance is ultimately not in the man himself, but what he tells us about ourselves. Trump could never have been able to rise to leadership were it not that America is also petty, resentful, self-absorbed, and narcissistic—those on the political left no less than those on the right. If Nixon was the president American deserved in 1968, Trump was the president we deserved in 2016 and 2024. And it will only be by becoming a country that deserves better that we will get better. As it stands, however, the great risk to American democracy is that as a country we've decided that we don't want better. What we, or at least many of us, want is a strongman, who will diabolically flatter our egos while mocking the values to which we claim to adhere. This is the recipe for authoritarianism.

AUTHORITARIAN DISPOSITIONS

In 1967, critical theorist Theodor Adorno gave a lecture at the University of Vienna titled *Aspects of the New Right-Wing Extremism.*[13] In this talk,

13. Adorno, *Aspects of the New Right-Wing Extremism.*

Adorno set himself to analyzing the rise of reactionary movements in Germany, and in particular the electoral victories of the neofascist National Democratic Party in 1964.[14] Why, after the defeat of fascism in 1945, did anyone grant credibility to an avowedly Nazi Party? Had fascism not been definitively discredited?

The answer, Adorno suggests, was that it had not. Far from being relegated to the dustbin of history, fascism was an ongoing threat to democracy.[15] Indeed, it had never really gone away, but simply retreated underground. He notes that Nazi rule in Germany had never been systemically discredited as Mussolini's fascism had been in Italy: "Identification with the system was never really radically destroyed in Germany."[16] Thus the seeds of a right-wing resurgence were planted within German democracy from the beginning.[17] What was needed was a set of favorable conditions to set up its comeback.[18] Those conditions, he insists, could not be reduced to a crudely Marxist economic analysis, but also needed to take account of the social psychological dimensions that lead to authoritarian dispositions. Adorno had already argued in 1959 that "National Socialism increased beyond measure the collective narcissism."[19]

> The individual's narcissistic instinctual drives, which are promised less and less satisfaction by a callous world and which nonetheless persist undiminished as long as civilization denies them so much, find substitute satisfaction in the identification with the whole. This collective narcissism was severely damaged by the collapse of Hitler's regime, but the damage occurred at the level of mere factuality, without individuals making themselves conscious of it and thereby coping with it. . . secretly, smoldering unconsciously and therefore all the more powerfully, these identifications and the collective narcissism were not destroyed at all, but continue to exist.[20]

In this respect, Adorno's explanation for the continuing attraction of authoritarianism parallels Reinhold Niebuhr's argument in *Moral Man and Immoral Society* that groups, unlike individuals, are not motivated

14. Weiss, "Afterword," 42.
15. Adorno, *Aspects of the New Right-Wing Extremism*, 2.
16. Adorno, *Aspects of the New Right-Wing Extremism*, 8.
17. Adorno, "Meaning of Working Through the Past," 90.
18. Adorno, "Meaning of Working Through the Past," 90.
19. Adorno, "Meaning of Working Through the Past," 96.
20. Adorno, "Meaning of Working Through the Past," 96.

by morality, but manifest a form of collective egoism.[21] For Adorno, however, the elements of authoritarian personalities manifest themselves not only on the level of groups, but also on the individual level, as certain personality traits tended to support right-wing movements.[22]

Adorno and his collaborators attempted to quantify the components that contribute to what he names "the authoritarian personality" in the book of that name, arguing that "the political, economic, and social convictions of an individual often form a broad and coherent pattern, as if bound together by a 'mentality' or 'spirit,' and that this pattern is an expression of deep-lying trends in his personality."[23] He goes on to pose the question: "If a potentially fascistic individual exists, what, precisely, is he like?"[24]

Anti-democratic dispositions, he and his fellow authors argued, are a complex interplay of social-psychological and political-economic factors. Anti-democratic ideologies exist beyond, but are idiosyncratically expressed within, the lives and actions of individuals. Ideology generally, as Adorno describes it, is "an organization of opinions, attitudes, and values—a way of thinking about man and society."[25] It can apply to the whole of a person's worldview or more narrowly to particular elements, such as one's political or economic point of view, or one's attitudes toward religious or ethnic minorities.[26] Particular ideological patterns may vary widely among individuals, but in any particular case serve the function of orienting individuals with regard to their overall social attitudes.[27]

What distinguishes a particularly anti-democratic or authoritarian disposition then? For Adorno and his collaborators, it is at least in part attributable to a "susceptibility" to anti-democratic rhetoric and propaganda and a "readiness" to act on the basis of that rhetoric:

> There seems little reason to doubt that ideology-in-readiness (ideological receptivity) and ideology-in-words and in action

21. Niebuhr, *Moral Man and Immoral Society.*

22. Adorno et al., *Authoritarian Personality.*

23. Adorno et al., *Authoritarian Personality*, 1.

24. Adorno et al., *Authoritarian Personality*, 2.

25. Adorno et al., *Authoritarian Personality*, 2.

26. Adorno et al., *Authoritarian Personality*, 2.

27. More recent analysis by Jonathan Haidt and others seeks to define political differences across a number of categories. One particular point of division that they find between those on the political left and those on the right is a greater concern on the right for values of sanctity, purity, and authority. See Haidt, *Righteous Mind.*

> are essentially the same stuff. The description of an individual's total ideology must portray not only the organization on each level but organization among levels. What the individual consistently says in public, what he says when he feels safe from criticism, what he thinks but will not say at all, what he thinks but will not admit to himself, what he is disposed to think or to do when various kinds of appeal are made to him—all these phenomena may be conceived of as constituting a single structure. The structure may not be integrated, it may contain contradictions as well as consistencies, but it is organized in the sense that the constituent parts are related in psychologically meaningful ways.[28]

For Adorno, there is little meaningful distinction between the overt action of the authoritarian street thug and the relatively passive willingness of others to allow them to act without objection. The same pathologies are at play in either case—the willingness to be led ideologically toward the conclusion that democratic institutions and practices are insufficient to deal with the perceived "threat" of outsiders and aliens.

This helps to explain the apparent ubiquity of anti-Semitism in authoritarian movements. This is a point that Hannah Arendt notes as well is *The Origins of Totalitarianism*—to some degree, anti-democratic movements tend to rely on appeals to anti-Semitism as a means of gaining and securing power.[29] As Adorno notes, the apparent ubiquity of anti-Semitism has nothing to do with Jews *qua* Jews, but rather has to do with the way that anti-Semitism functions ideologically and psychologically for the anti-Semite.[30] As Slavoj Žižek writes: "anti-Semitism is not just one among ideologies; it is ideology as such, *kat'exoben*. It embodies the zero-level (the pure form) of ideology, providing its elementary coordinates: social antagonism ('class struggle' is mystified/displaced so that its cause is projected onto the external intruder."[31]

Arendt, more broadly, notes the emergence of anti-Semitism as a formal ideology (as distinct from anti-Judaism) alongside the rise of the modern nation-state. Nationalism and anti-Semitism are apparently intertwined with one another, as Arendt notes, in ways that are replete with paradoxes:

28. Adorno et al., *Authoritarian Personality*, 5.
29. Arendt, *Origins of Totalitarianism*.
30. This is a point that Jean Paul Sartre makes as well in *Antisemite and Jew*.
31. Žižek, *Living in the End Times*, 136.

> Thus, at the same time and in the same countries, emancipation meant equality *and* privileges, the destruction of the old Jewish community autonomy *and* the conscious preservation of the Jews as a separate group in society, the abolition of special restrictions and special rights *and* the extension of such rights to a growing group of individuals. Equality of condition for all nationals had become the premise of the new body politic, and while this equality had actually been carried out at least to the extent of depriving the old ruling classes of their privilege to govern and the old oppressed classes of their right to be protected, the process coincided with the birth of the class society which again separated the nationals, economically and socially, as efficiently as the old regime. Equity of condition, as the Jacobins had understood it in the French Revolution, became a reality only in America, whereas on the European continent it was at once replaced by a mere formal equality before the law.[32]

In effect, the social assimilation of Jews within the context of emergent nation-states also gave rise to a new set of fears specifically surrounding the Jews, who "did not form a class of their own and . . . did not belong to any of the classes in their countries. As a group, they were neither workers, middle-class people, landholders, nor peasants."[33]

In a class-stratified society, Jews remained an inveterate Other, even as many Jews struggled to assimilate within nation-states defined within the emergent class system of capitalism. This status as inveterate Other was not accidental, but was at least in part the result of policy decisions by governments for whom the continuing marginalization of Jews within society was politically useful: "to a Europe with no sense of balance of power between its nations and of inter-European solidarity, the non-national, inter-European Jewish element became an object of universal hatred because of its useless wealth, and of contempt because of its lack of power."[34]

Jews are thus the perfect objects of paranoid projection in this context—what Stanley Cohen terms "folk devils"—who embody cultural fears and anxieties precisely because of the their marginal status.[35] They, along with other marginalized groups, become a blank slate for the presentation of stereotypical angst: "Thus Jews are intrusive, but also exclusive;

32. Arendt, *Origins of Totalitarianism*, 12. Italics in original.
33. Arendt, *Origins of Totalitarianism*, 13.
34. Arendt, *Origins of Totalitarianism*, 15.
35. Cohen, *Folk Devils and Moral Panics.*

Negroes are lazy and inert, but also aggressive and pushing; Mods are dirty and scruffy, but also slickly dressed; they are aggressive and inflated with their own strength and importance, but they are also cowardly."[36] The contradictions are glaring, and yet irrelevant in the context of the role anti-Semitism plays—in reassuring the insecure majority that their fears, whatever they may be, are justified, because the designated Other embodies every possible threat to decency and good order.

Yet, the template set by anti-Semitism simply provides the paradigm case for such projection. For the purposes of authoritarian ideologies, the target is less important than the moral panic created by the identification and isolation of the Other as a threat. In the United States, various ethnic minorities have at one time or another filled that role, as Donald Trump's invocation of Mexicans as rapists and drug dealers at the very outset of his 2016 presidential campaign demonstrates. And often room is made for exceptions. For Trump, while *most* Mexican migrants were rapists and drug dealers, he was quick to qualify the abject racism of this claim by noting that "some, I assume, are good people."[37] He utilized a similar tactic in 2024, accusing Haitians in Ohio of stealing and eating dogs and cats in the community.

At heart this is the dynamic that Carl Schmitt recognized in *The Concept of the Political*, in which he argued that politics was grounded precisely in the identification of the enemy:

> The specific political distinction to which political actions and motives can be reduced is that between friend and enemy. . . . Insofar as it is not derived from other criteria, the antithesis of friend and enemy corresponds to the relatively independent criteria of other antithesis: good and evil in the moral sphere, beautiful and ugly in the aesthetic sphere, and so on. . . . If the antithesis good and evil is not simply identical with that

36. Cohen, *Folk Devils and Moral Panics*, 56. Cohen's analysis centers particularly on the moral panic around conflict between "mods" and "rockers" in the 1960s UK, thus the reference here. As Adrian Daub notes, "both of these groups [mods and rockers] were perfectly real. But what became of them in the media was something quite different. The young had lost the authority to interpret their own culture. The moral panic broke away from 'particular disapproved forms of behavior (such as drug-taking or violence)' and instead attached itself to 'distinguishable social types.' Soon the British public was no longer told to be afraid of specific actions of the mods or rockers, but of mods and rockers themselves." This is a core characteristic of how folk devils of all kinds are portrayed, and has been an historic element of anti-Semitism. See Daub, *Cancel Culture Panic*, 15.

37. See Reilly, "Here Are All the Times Donald Trump Insulted Mexico," para. 1.

> of beautiful and ugly, profitable and unprofitable, and cannot be directly reduced to the other, then the antithesis of friend and enemy must even less be confused with or mistaken for the others. The distinction of friend and enemy denotes the utmost degree of intensity of a union or separation, of an association or dissociation. It can exist theoretically and practically, without having simultaneously to draw upon all those moral, aesthetic, economic, or other distinctions. The political enemy need not be morally evil or aesthetically ugly; he need not appear as an economic competitor, and it may even be advantageous to engage with him in business transactions. But he is, nevertheless, the other, the stranger; and it is sufficient for his nature that he is, in a specially intense way, existentially something different and alien, so that in the extreme case conflicts with him are possible. These can neither be decided by a previously determined general norm nor by the judgement of a disinterested and therefore neutral third party.[38]

The identification of the enemy is a crucial component in the creation of authoritarian political systems. As Umberto Eco notes, it becomes a component of identity-formation. "Having an enemy is important not only to define our identity but also to provide us with an obstacle against which to measure our system of values and, in seeking to overcome it, to demonstrate our own worth."[39] The enemy, as he notes, is not discovered but *created*, and there is no necessary connection between what we imagine the characteristics of the enemy to be and how they actually are, as was made clear in Donald Trump's wholly fictional invocation of Haitian immigrants in Ohio eating cats and dogs. It didn't have to be true. It only had to provide a convenient rhetorical location in which they could be included among the enemy, along with (non-white) immigrants generally. Eco, citing Tacitus, ties this back to the reality of anti-Semitism:

> The Jews are "strange" because they abstain from eating pork, do not put yeast in bread, rest on the seventh day, marry only among themselves, are circumcised—not (of course) for hygienic or religious reasons but "to show they are different from others"—bury their dead, and do not venerate our caesars. Having demonstrated how certain real customs are different (circumcision, Sabbbath rest), the writer can further emphasize his point by adding legendary customs to the picture (they make

38. Schmitt, *Concept of the Political*, 26–27.

39. Eco, *Inventing the Enemy*, 2.

> sacred images of a donkey and despise their parents, children, brothers, their country, and the gods).[40]

From there, smears and scurrilous accusations can be multiplied as needed. The blood-libel lodged against Jews is echoed in any setting in which an enemy is needed. The characteristics are common regardless of the target, though the details may vary.[41] "We do not have to reach the excesses of *Nineteen Eighty-Four* to recognize ourselves as beings who need an enemy. We are witnessing the fear that can be caused by new influxes of migrants. In Italy today, Romanians are being portrayed as the enemy by extending to the whole ethnic culture the characteristics of a few of its marginalized members, thus providing an ideal scapegoat for a society that, caught up in change—including ethnic change—is no longer able to recognize itself."[42]

Yet, in saying that society "needs" an enemy, Eco is not endorsing this need, but describing it as a cultural pathology that emerges most powerfully during periods of social dislocation, when, as he says, "society . . . is no longer able to recognize itself."[43] It is the same characteristic that Dennis Potter illustrates in the character of Tom: alienated and in need of someone to blame in order to "prove his worth."

Authoritarian dispositions, however, are not simply the product of individual pathologies co-opted by ideologies for political purposes. Rather, Adorno argues, "the appeal to the unconscious desire for disaster, for catastrophe, is by no means the least significant in these movements."[44] In the midst of social and political anomie, a lack of control over one's own destiny, nihilism begins to appear to be a reasonable option: "This person, from the perspective of their own social situation, longs for demise—though not the demise of their own group, as far as possible, the demise of all."[45] The identification of folk devils, in whatever form, serves to externalize the nihilistic impulse, creating a threat that can then be blamed for the perceived state of powerlessness.[46]

40. Eco, *Inventing the Enemy*, 3–4.

41. Eco goes on to describe how the same dynamic of enemy-identification is applied not only to Jews, but to blacks, "witches," and anyone who can be marked, as Schmitt notes, on the basis of their "otherness."

42. Eco, *Inventing the Enemy*, 20–21.

43. Eco, *Inventing the Enemy*, 21.

44. Adorno, *Aspects of the New Right-Wing Extremism*, 10.

45. Adorno, *Aspects of the New Right-Wing Extremism*, 11.

46. See also Stern, *Politics of Cultural Despair*.

Through the use of propaganda, authoritarian movements are able to mobilize "the masses" (in Arendt's terminology), for the purposes of social, cultural, and political self-destruction.[47] It is the "constellation of rational means and irrational ends" through which the technological equipment of self-destruction is perfected even as a larger sense of common purpose is abandoned.[48] "When the means increasingly become substitute for aims, one can almost say that, in these extreme right-wing movements, propaganda actually constitutes the substance of politics."[49]

This is why anti-Semitism lurks so close to the surface of authoritarian movements—Jews represent the easiest and most common target for propaganda precisely because of the lack of substance behind those attacks. Jews were for much of European history the ever-present, unassimilated Other. There, but not there, and thus a ready tool for propaganda purposes. But the template that has proven so effective against the Jews is no less effective against any unassimilated Other—Black, trans, Mexican, Haitian—by being both present and yet not present, visible, yet incomprehensible, they channel the nihilistic impulse of authoritarianism away from self-destruction and onto the victimization of an Other. For those wishing to transform authoritarian dispositions into political power, these others provide an irresistible temptation to demagoguery. What Donald Trump pioneered through an untamed and disorganized instinctive bigotry, others, more calculating, can more effectively put to political use.

Reactionary movements are often said to be grounded in appeals to tradition and a glorified imagined past. Yet, as John Ganz has argued, the reactionary instinct is grounded less in a yearning for a bygone era than in a nostalgia for lost hierarchy. What the wish to return to a former time reveals is a desire for a time when "we" were at the top of the hierarchy and "they" knew their place. It is significant that, when conservatives talk about the time to which they would like to return, they often invoke the 1950s. But it was not the relative economic equality or the strong labor protections of the postwar era that they miss (even conservative union members can be paradoxically anti-union, even while acknowledging the benefits won for them by their unions). Rather it is often the racial, class, and gender hierarchies of the time that really lie behind that nostalgia.[50]

47. Arendt, *Origins of Totalitarianism*, 305.

48. Adorno, *Aspects of the New Right-Wing Extremism*, 13.

49. Adorno, *Aspects of the New Right-Wing Extremism*, 13.

50. See Ganz and Klein, "Serious Man."

A deep irony embedded within contemporary forms of authoritarianism is their professed attachment to principles of liberty and freedom. While past forms of authoritarianism have often appealed to forms of organic social integration, in which individual freedom is relinquished to the larger social body, there is often an insidious connection between modern authoritarian politics and purported libertarian economic theory. What this reveals, however, is less a commitment to economic freedom within anti-democratic ideologies than a thin veneer of freedom that is painted over fundamentally anti-democratic political ideology.

ROYKO'S BASILISK: NEO-REACTION AND LIBERTARIANISM

Consider Peter Thiel.[51] If there is a figure who most clearly represents in the American context the seemingly paradoxical connection between libertarian economic ideology and political authoritarianism, it is he. Were he merely an ideologue or theoretician, he would be unremarkable. However, as has become clear in recent years, Thiel has dedicated himself and his considerable fortune to promoting and supporting candidates for elective office who share, overtly or covertly, his ideological agenda. J. D. Vance, a Thiel disciple and recipient of his largesse, not only became a senator, but vice president in large part with Thiel's support. So he is not simply a case of one figure among others advocating an apparently crank political theory. He is committed to putting that theory into action. So we do well to become acquainted with the theory.

Thiel's perspective can be helpfully summarized by a line from an essay he wrote in 2009, titled "The Education of a Libertarian." He states his thesis succinctly: "I no longer believe that freedom and democracy are compatible."[52] At first, this seems to be a contradictory statement, at least for most readers, as a core assumption underlying liberal democratic societies is that freedom and democracy are intertwined with one

51. An author with more foresight than I might have led this section with an extensive discussion of Elon Musk rather than Thiel. Yet, while Musk's rightward drift over the past several years was there for those with eyes to see, his deep involvement in the late stages of Trump's 2024 campaign, and his even deeper involvement in the early days of the second Trump administration were possibilities that escaped me at the time this chapter was being drafted. Nevertheless, the relationship between Thiel, Musk, Yarvin, and other Silicon Valley ideologues and entrepreneurs can be seen in the common threads that tie them together politically.

52. Thiel, "Education of a Libertarian," para. 2.

another, such that authentic freedom in the absence of democracy is a contradiction in terms.[53]

Thiel's pessimism about the compatibility of freedom and democracy is grounded in his belief that "the 1920s were the last decade in American history during which one could be genuinely optimistic about politics."[54] Since then, the burgeoning of social welfare programs and the extension of voting rights to women "have rendered the notion of 'capitalist democracy' into an oxymoron."[55] Here we see the nostalgia for hierarchy in action—what these policies accomplished was precisely the flattening of the economic and sexual hierarchies of a past era, threatening the freedom of those at the top of the hierarchy. What freedom? The freedom to dominate! Thus, the ineluctable conclusion presents itself: If the choice is between democracy or capitalism, Thiel would opt to jettison democracy.

The flattening of these hierarchies has endangered the viability of "capitalist democracy," as those who had not "earned" their right to rule were granted greater access to the reins of governance. While in a subsequent addendum he insisted that he was not seeking to disenfranchise women, his argument is strangely hollow. Though he states that "I don't think any class of people should be disenfranchised," it seems to be less because he values the equal rights of women to full participation in society, and more that "it would be absurd to suggest that women's votes will be taken away or that this would solve the political problems that vex us."[56] One wonders whether his position would change if he came to believe that it would. As it stands, in Thiel's estimation, since political society is irredeemably saddled with welfare recipients and voting women, who will see it as in their interest to constrain capitalist economic freedom, the only solution is to escape politics entirely.

What Thiel envisions in this essay is an idea of "freedom beyond politics," the idea that a genuine libertarian form of life would be found, not by fully engaging with the body politic and advocating for a set of policies that libertarians would prefer, but rather an escape from the constraints placed upon individuals by participation in public life entirely.

53. And, as many on the political left would argue, with substantial justification, democracy without genuine freedom from economic compulsion is equally a contradiction in terms.

54. Thiel, "Education of a Libertarian," para. 6.

55. Thiel, "Education of a Libertarian," para. 6.

56. Thiel, "Education of a Libertarian," para. 17.

Or, said differently, to the extent that individual (economic) liberty is subject to any form of democratic regulation, it is (echoing Sam Francis) democracy that must be overcome: "In our time, the great task for libertarians is to find an escape from politics in all its forms—from the totalitarian and fundamentalist catastrophes to the unthinking demos that guides so-called 'social democracy.'"[57]

Thiel imagines three possible means of escape from the constraints of democracy. The first, as befits an internet entrepreneur, is through cyberspace—the creation of "new worlds" in his words, that "will impact and force change on the existing social and political order."[58] This includes, he suggests, the "end of monetary sovereignty." Insofar as the creation of money is a task allocated to the state, a genuinely libertarian political economy would only be achievable when economic exchange is fully privatized. This is, of course, precisely that for which the ongoing boom-and-bust cycle of cryptocurrency is striving, without much success. But Thiel has other options.

His second prospect is outer space—"We must redouble the efforts to commercialize space."[59] And it is perhaps not for nothing that Thiel's erstwhile business partner (and fellow Trump supporter), Elon Musk, has devoted so much of his own fortune in recent years to the development of SpaceX, or that Jeffrey Bezos is devoting his own billions to the task. How better, after all, to escape all constraints of earthly government than to set up shop in orbit or on Mars? However, Thiel notes that libertarians should be "realistic" about the prospects for colonizing space, stating that "the libertarian future of classic science fiction, à la Heinlein, will not happen before the second half of the 21st century."[60]

57. Thiel, "Education of a Libertarian." Thiel's conception of what politics means is itself instructive. He states: "Politics gets people angry, destroys relationships, and polarizes peoples' vision: the world is us versus them; good people versus the other. *Politics is about interfering with other people's lives without their consent*" (italics added).

58. Thiel, "Education of a Libertarian."

59. Thiel, "Education of a Libertarian."

60. Thiel, "Education of a Libertarian." This affinity between right-wing political dispositions and science fiction is far from new, as Jordan S. Carroll argues in *Speculative Whiteness*. He writes: "Science fiction thinking turns out to be surprisingly prevalent in the alt-right and antecedent white nationalist movements. Fascists often speculate about zombies, supermen, and space explorers while envisioning the founding of a Cosmic Reich. . . . Science fiction serves as more than just a pop culture reference in fascist discourse. While the field of science fiction studies has long argued that speculative genres help promote radical change, the alt-right has interpreted science fiction to say that a fascist world is possible" (5). This theme will become even clearer when we turn to the work of Curtis Yarvin.

His third option, which he views as existing between the more immediate but limited prospects offered within cyberspace and the potentially limitless options posed by outer space, is "sea-steading"—colonizing the oceans away from the scrutiny of national governments. The technology for successfully creating an offshore libertarian paradise is much closer, he argues, than that which would be necessary for colonizing space, though still more distant than that offered by the exploitation of the resources of cyberspace.

In sum, what Thiel envisions is some combination of Ayn Rand's Galt's Gulch combined with the undersea city of Rapture from the video game "Bioshock" (itself a version of Galt's Gulch), though without the associated dystopian horror story. But such a vision is a nightmare under any circumstances. Far from an escape from politics, it is simply a vision of an unaccountable plutocracy not bound by any constraints other than what the wealthy and powerful few are willing and able to impose. The logical outcome of Thiel's libertarianism turns out to be authoritarianism.[61]

What Thiel's libertarian-authoritarian ideology reveals is the way in which Silicon Valley tech-bro culture creates a set of presuppositions that leads inexorably toward fascistic conclusions. This is well-illustrated through the metaphor of "Royko's Basilisk." As described by Elizabeth Sandifer, Royko's Basilisk is a thought experiment that has become a "lethal meme," an idea followed to a logical conclusion that is both intolerable and inescapable.[62]

Originating in Elizer Yudkowski's theories of "friendly artificial intelligence," Royko's Basilisk postulates a future artificial intelligence that becomes both omniscient and functionally omnipotent, and through its godlike offices chooses to "condemn to eternal torture everyone from the present who had ever imagined it if they subsequently failed to do whatever they could to bring about its existence."[63] The implication is

61. One might ask why I selected Thiel as a representative figure to critique libertarianism in this section, rather than a more philosophically sophisticated thinker such as Robert Nozick, or even someone with putative philosophical street cred, such as Ayn Rand. In Nozick's case, my answer is simply that, outside of philosophy, he's just not that representative of ground-level libertarian thought. Rand is certainly more representative in that regard, but has also been dead for decades. Thiel (and Curtis Yarvin, more about whom anon), represent current libertarian thought much more adequately than either Nozick or Rand.

62. Sandifer, *Neo-Reaction a Basilisk*, 13.

63. Sandifer, *Neo-Reaction a Basilisk*, 13.

that, once you become aware of Royko's Basilisk, you have no choice but to dedicate all of your resources to bringing it about, lest you risk eternal torment at the hands of the evil computer from Harlan Ellison's "I Have No Mouth And I Must Scream."[64]

Sandifer describes this idea as a version of Pascal's Wager, insofar as it is based on the premise that, if such an AI could even potentially come to exist, the only safe recourse is to dedicate yourself to bringing it into existence. The community around which this idea initially coalesced was based at Yudkowski's Machine Intelligence Research Institute (MIRI) and on the online forum *Less Wrong*. Sandifer continues:

> The result was a frankly hilarious community meltdown in which people lost their shit as ideas they'd studiously internalized threatened to torture them for all eternity if they didn't hand all of their money over to MIRI, culminating in Yudkowsky himself stepping in to ban all further discussion of the dread beast. This went more or less exactly how anyone who has ever used the Internet would guess, which is to say that it quickly became the thing Yudkowsky and his followers were best known for.[65]

Sandifer notes the explicit connection between Yudkowski and Thiel, in that Thiel was an early investor in MIRI. But in a more abstract sense, what Royko's Basilisk illustrates is the nest of internal contradictions that can develop from consistently following a set of first principals to their logical conclusions. One begins with "friendly AI" and ends up with a science fiction horror novel. One begins with a commitment to liberty and ends up advocating authoritarianism.

But Thiel isn't a theoretician, and one can only determine so much on the basis of his quips about the incompatibility of freedom and democracy. More influential on the development of right-wing neo-reactionary thought is Curtis Yarvin, aka Mencius Moldbug.[66] Yarvin argues explicitly that liberal democratic social forms are inescapably corrupt.

> The problem, Moldbug concludes, is one of chaos. Democracy is endlessly compromised by progressivism, which moves it

64. Ellison, *Greatest Hits*, 19.

65. Sandifer, *Neo-Reaction a Basilisk*, 14.

66. See Tait, "Mencius Goldbug and Neoreaction." Most of Yarvin's most notable writing occurred under the Mencius Moldbug pseudonym, but he has become more publicly known in the last few years under his own name. When a source refers to him by his pseudonym, I will leave that unchanged, though I will refer to him by his given name in most cases.

> eternally leftwards with its eternal mantra of change. This is chaotic; Moldbug prefers order. Indeed, he values order for its own sake.[67]

There is no particular form of order that Yarvin prefers. He appeals to no moral foundation for a theory of order. It is, he explicitly claims, *arbitrary*.[68] "It is good simply because it is order, and the alternative to order is violence at worst and politics at best."[69]

As Sandifer notes, it is a rather strange kind of analysis that looks to authoritarianism as an antidote to violence, given the authoritarian penchant for violence. It is no less strange to see it as an alternative to politics, rather than a form of it (a perspective he shares with Thiel). Yet, Sandifer notes, Yarvin believes he can overcome this problem:

> How do you get a non-destructive authoritarian? "The answer: find the world's best CEO, and give him undivided control over budget, policy and personnel." But wait, he's even got a suggestion as to who: "I don't think there is any debate about it. The world's best CEO is Steve Jobs."[70]

Sandifer responds that this may be the worst idea possible, and not just because Jobs is dead.[71] At heart, Yarvin is no less committed to government-by-CEO than Thiel. Authoritarianism, however, functions not to ensure the general welfare or secure the common good, but quite explicitly to guarantee profit. The institutions of liberal society, particularly media and academia, which Yarvin refers to as the Cathedral, advocate for values, such as civil rights and feminism, that are destructive to the order (that is to say, the hierarchy) necessary for the production of profit.[72] Evoking yet another literary horror, Yarvin declaims: "Cthulhu may

67. Sandifer, *Neo-Reaction a Basilisk*,19.

68. Yarvin, *Open Letter to Open-Minded Progressives*, 3.

69. Yarvin, *Open Letter to Open-Minded Progressives*, 3, para. 30. Once again, we see a strange conception of the idea of politics as something inherently negative. Not a form of order, but its opposite.

70. Sandifer, *Neo-Reaction a Basilisk*, 19.

71. Sandifer, *Neo-Reaction a Basilisk*, 19.

72. Hui, "On the Unhappy Consciousness of Neoreactionaries."

swim slowly, but he only swims left"[73]—rewriting Martin Luther King Jr., Sandifer notes, as H. P. Lovecraft fanfic.[74]

Only by recasting monarchy as competent corporate governance can the Cathedral be overcome.[75] As with Thiel, democracy is fundamentally at odds with a key social imperative—freedom for Thiel, order for Yarvin. Only by placing governance "outside" of politics, and in the hands of ridiculously wealthy CEOs, can genuine social good be restored.[76] For Thiel, this involves detaching, Galt-style, from corrupted and coercive governance, either online, at sea, or in space. For Yarvin, it requires a (purportedly) bloodless coup, in which the power of the state is seized by the CEOs for the purposes of profit-making.[77]

At core, the fundamental error at the heart of these accounts of libertarianism is a broken conception of the political. Thiel, Yarvin, and their acolytes perceive politics as being fundamentally a question of coercion, rather than, to invoke Arendt once more, a "space of appearance," a realm

73. Yarvin, "Gentle Introduction to Unqualified Reservations," para. 94. Here again we can see the role that speculative fiction plays in the creation of the alt-right imaginary. References to Lovecraft, Howard, Tolkien, and others proliferate, as Jordan S. Carroll argues, though high fantasy and sword and sorcery genres tend to be backward-looking, as opposed to the futurity of science fiction. However, Carroll notes, the forward-looking character of science fiction does not prevent it from harkening to a nostalgic imagined past. "Because many on the alt-right believe that history moves in cycles and great men can revive ancient archetypes as if no time has passed, they see no contradiction between combining archaic and futuristic elements to make archeofuturism" (*Speculative Whiteness*, 23). Thus, Yarvin's repeated condemnation of the mass of human beings as "hobbits" worthy only of being dominated by the "dark elves" of technomonarchism (McManus, "Yarvin's Case Against Democracy").

74. Sandifer, *Neo-Reaction a Basilisk*, 21. This is obscene on several fronts, not least of which is Lovecraft's own avowed and explicit racism as well as Yarvin's own stated desire to reinstitute slavery.

75. McManus, "Yarvin's Case Against Democracy."

76. As Tait writes: "Because the most ordered system is a unitary command structure with a clear hierarchy, Moldbug's model for a new political order is the corporation. He proposes that the state is privatized to incentivize profit-maximizing governance by 'shareholders' (large owners) who vote for a CEO-monarch. More Steve Jobs than Henry VIII, the monarch has absolute authority but serves at the shareholders' pleasure. Moldbug calls this corporate-monarchy regime 'neocameralism.' By limiting politics to this narrow domain, Moldbug reasons it creates space for a libertarian paradise. Moldbug calls himself a 'Jacobite' and favors the restoration of the House of Stuart, but the details of his futurist monarchy are less important than the thirst toward total privatization and authoritarianism" ("Mencius Moldbug and Neoreaction," 197).

77. Lest one object that, even given Thiel's vast wealth, these figures and their ideas are marginal and have no potential to influence national policy, it is worth noting that both Thiel and Yarvin have already had an influence on J. D. Vance, the Vice President of the United States. See Flegenheimer, "How J. D. Vance Thinks About Power."

of discourse in which ideas are tested and contested, the primary tool of which is not violence, but moral suasion.[78] The *polis* is the public space within which human action is organized. The primary tool of political life is not force, but argument. It is mediated not with guns, but with words:

> The space of appearance comes into being wherever men are together in the manner of speech and action, and therefore predates and precedes all formal constitution of the public realm and the various forms of government, that is, the various forms in which the public realm can be organized. Its peculiarity is that, unlike the spaces which are the work of our hands, it does not survive the actuality of the movement which brought it into being, but disappears not only with the dispersal of men—as in the case of great catastrophes when the body politic of a people is destroyed—but with the disappearance or arrest of the activities themselves. Wherever people gather together, it is potentially there, but only potentially, not necessarily and not forever.[79]

The public realm, that is the realm in which the *polis* manifests itself, is constituted precisely by human communal expression and deliberation. It is the field in which human expression leaves that which is merely private and personal and is placed into confrontation with others in a condition of equality. Yet, the public, or political, is not yet the state. It precedes the state. Government is the creature of the public, and thus a second order expression of political action.

It is the realm of the *state*, not the political, that is reliant on violence for enforcement. As Max Weber notes, one of the key features that constitutes a state is a monopoly on the use of force.[80] But it is a mistake to reduce the political to the state. The state is the outcome of political deliberation. It is the place where political deliberation is expressed through institutional action, but political action is wider than merely its state expression. For all of their talk about rejecting the political, both Thiel and Yarvin are deeply involved in political discourse. Thiel's whole *modus operandi* has been an expression of political discourse, both in his

78. One can see in this respect the influence of Arendt's thought on the work of Jürgen Habermas, whose conception of public life is one in which, under ideal conditions, consensus prevails over coercion. See, for example, Habermas, *Theory of Communicative Action* and Habermas, *Moral Consciousness and Communicative Action*.

79. Arendt, *Human Condition*, 199.

80. Weber, "Politics as a Vocation."

advocacy of libertarian anti-politics and through his support of authoritarian political figures such as Donald Trump and J. D. Vance.[81]

Thiel's vision of a libertarian paradise in space or at sea is not an escape from the political, it is merely another expression of the political. And the result of a successful attempt at realizing his vision would not be an escape from the state, it would merely be a displacement of the authority of the state into the hands of private capital. This vision is not simply paradoxical—in the sense that the libertarian vision of an abandonment of state power merely reinscribes it in a different form—but contradictory, in the sense that, at least as Arendt has it, the private and the public represent two separate forums of human action. To render the role of the *polis* as a task of the *oikos* is to fundamentally misunderstand both realms.

There is also a fundamental misunderstanding of the concept of liberty at operation within the libertarian paradigm. Freedom, in this conception, is indelibly connected to the idea of private property. In a sense, only those who possess property are really free, and perhaps they are the only ones who deserve freedom. This is how it is possible for Thiel, Yarvin, and others to assert the idea that the wealthy are both the most competent to rule and have the greatest moral authority to do so—their wealth itself, the evidence of ownership, the quantity of property, arrogates to them the right of rulership. There is a kind of logic at work here that makes sense on the surface. If a just society is only possible when rulers are truly free from external compulsion, then the vast wealth of a Peter Thiel or a Jeff Bezos should in principle allow them to rule impartially.

This is, after a fashion, a reconceptualization of Plato's understanding of the "philosopher-king."[82] In *The Republic*, Plato argued that only those who were wholly disinterested in power could truly be trusted with it, and thus, the only ones fit to rule were those who had dedicated their lives to the contemplation of the Forms. Rulership was, for Plato, a responsibility and a burden of the wise, for whom the subordinate good of ruling was a necessary task, and yet a distraction from the highest good. The libertarian version of this same idea substitutes the good of wealth creation for

81. Vance, of course, is a late-comer to the authoritarian agenda, despite the fact that he at one time worked directly for Thiel. Nevertheless, his transformation from conservative analyst and critic of Trumpian authoritarianism to participant coincides with his decision to run for political office with the financial support of Thiel.

82. Plato, *Republic*, V, 473.d.

the good of contemplation. Furthermore, while Plato's philosopher-kings were disinterested precisely because the goods of wealth and acquisition held no attraction for them, in the libertarian mindset, it is precisely the interest that the very wealthy have in preserving and expanding their own freedom, and protecting it from the aberrant desires of those who wish to deprive them of their liberty (that is, property), that impels them to descend from on high (perhaps a space station orbiting the earth?) to take on the task of rule.

Liberty is thus not a human entitlement, but an acquisition. Freedom is not a right, but a purchase. And democracy is not a means by which a free people may govern itself, but a means by which the mob can steal from the few genuinely free human beings who are entitled by their vast wealth to real liberty. It is the most vulgar expression of Ayn Rand's ideology—Friedrich Nietzsche with a side of Adam Smith.

Needless to say, there are other, better ways to conceive of freedom. From the vast menu of superior alternatives, Amartya Sen's conception of freedom as the capacity to fulfill one's capabilities suggests itself as an obvious contender. For Sen, it is precisely the inability to achieve one's ends that is most indicative of the lack of freedom. For Sen, it is by expanding the field of choices through which individuals may engage in the process of self-actualization that society may become more free: "Development consists of the removal of various types of unfreedoms that leave people with little choice and little opportunity of exercising their reasoned agency. The removal of substantial unfreedoms, it is argued here, is constitutive of development."[83]

Poverty for Sen is "capability deprivation," the absence of freedom that accompanies the lack of basic resources for survival and development. A society, in this sense, becomes more free the more people, particularly those currently deprived of them, are given the resources for development. For Sen, the sheer scope of human misery described by the word poverty, the number of people without the basic resources of human development, is a moral affront. "Liberty" cannot then be understood simply as letting those with more than they can possibly use keep what they have, but in finding ways to ensure that the greatest possible number of people are able to actualize their capabilities, to exercise their freedom, and to participate in the space of appearance, the public sphere.

83. Sen, *Development as Freedom*, 7.

Thus the fundamental paradox of libertarianism—that an obsession with liberty serves as the ideological underpinning for authoritarianism—is resolved in Sen through an understanding of freedom as the opening up of the public sphere to participation, so that the capabilities of all, particularly those on the margins, can be developed and allowed to flourish.

What Thiel, Yarvin, and the flock of Randian disciples who follow in their wake hope to achieve is not something that exists purely on the level of thought. As noted, Thiel has contributed a large portion of his vast wealth into electing candidates for office who find his libertarian/authoritarian chimera to be appealing. Yet, all monsters grow beyond the capacity of their creators to control, and the authoritarian ideas unleashed by Thiel and company, and embodied by Trump and his acolytes, mutated in the wild. Mere authoritarianism doesn't represent the outer fringe of possibility for these dispositions. The kind of conspiracism represented by QAnon serves as a kind of apotheosis of the authoritarian mindset, one that may—or may not—be made to serve as a political expedient.

"TRUST THE PLAN": QANON AND THE CULT OF AUTHORITARIANISM

There is no shortage of evocative anecdotes one could select to illustrate the simultaneously bizarre and dangerous impact of QAnon in American political life over the past several years. Each example would reveal the broad sweep of QAnon, its capacity to absorb and mutate other conspiracy theories, incorporating them into the structure of its "superconspiracy."[84]

Grass Valley is located in Nevada County, California. Far from most urban centers, and with a population of around 13,000 people, it seems at first blush to be an unlikely target for the attention of QAnon. And yet, in early 2019, it became the focal point of QAnon's conspiratorial attention. That this happened is strange; *why* it happened is stranger still.[85]

It began with a tweet from former FBI Director James Comey.[86] In the tweet, which was tagged #FiveJobsIveHad, Comey lists former employment as:

84. Sommer, *Trust the Plan*, 106.

85. Rothschild, *Storm Is Upon Us*, 74.

86. Comey himself is a figure worthy of extended discussion in terms of the intersection of religion and contemporary American political life. Apart from his role in arguably aiding in the ascension of Donald Trump, only to be unceremoniously fired

1. Grocery store clerk.
2. Vocal soloist for church weddings.
3. Chemist.
4. Strike-replacement high school teacher.
5. FBI Director, Interrupted.

At first blush, this appears to be merely one of the many posts that appear every day on Twitter, in which a person shares some slice of their life or background with the world. But to QAnon, it was something more sinister. Through an imaginative interpretive process, a QAnon follower discerned that "Five Jobs I've Had" actually meant "Five Jihads." Furthermore, taking the first letter of each of the five listed jobs gave one the letters "GVCSF." A bit of googling later, and it was determined that these letters stood for Grass Valley Charter School Foundation, and that Comey was announcing a planned attack by the forces of the deep state on the foundation's upcoming Blue Marble Jubilee Auction.

Through the amplification system of QAnon's presence on social media, this information was broadcast to the larger conspiracy community, which began raising alarms. As Mike Rothschild notes, "It was the deep ugly concern of people who are determined to think you are in danger, and that its their job to protect you, when the only real danger is their protection."[87] The result was the cancellation of the event.[88] The response of the QAnon figure who amplified the conspiracy was to insist that he had done nothing wrong: "Comey's Twitter account is definitely being used to transmit coded messages to activate cells."[89] QAnon even took credit for an unrelated incident a few weeks later, which they insisted was proof that they had thwarted a terrorist attack engineered by the former director of the FBI.[90]

This story illustrates much about QAnon as a movement: Its obsession with the "deep state" and its conviction that major figures in American politics are involved in a (literally) diabolical conspiracy to impose

when Trump realized that he could not be easily manipulated, he was also apparently for several years active on Twitter, while running the FBI, under the moniker of @ReinholdNiebuhr. A revelation that caused simultaneous delight and consternation among many Niebuhr scholars.

87. Rothschild, *Storm Is Upon Us*, 76.

88. Rothschild, *Storm Is Upon Us*, 77.

89. Rothschild, *Storm Is Upon Us*, 77.

90. Rothschild, *Storm Is Upon Us*, 78.

tyranny; its use of online forums like Twitter and Facebook to magnify their theories; its capacity to cause danger and disruption in ordinary people's lives with little provocation; and its conviction that they are the heroes of a cosmic struggle against the forces of evil. The one core element of QAnon's identity that is not readily apparent from this story is its intense adulation of Donald Trump.

Unlike many conspiracy theories, the origins of which can be hard to identify, QAnon's origins are quite easy to trace. It emerged from the fever swamps of 4chan on October 28, 2017, with a post announcing the immanent arrest of Hillary Clinton. The purported author, "Q," went on to post a series of often cryptic and obscure messages (or "drops") over the ensuing three years, claiming to be an insider in the US government, working directly for Donald Trump as part of an operation to overthrow the liberal "deep state" and expose its cabal of adrenochrome-consuming child-murderers for the satanic cult that they were:

> Believers in the nascent conspiracy benefitted from being the first to know about the immanent upheaval. They would have the tools they needed to understand what was about to happen and to help participate in any necessary quelling that would take place. And that special status was emphasized in Drop #60, which noted that the only people who had the "full picture" of what was happening comprised "(less than 10 people) [and] only three are non military." Believers joined this hyper select and elevated group, thinking that they were seeing the first rays of a new rising sun.[91]

QAnon's approach to the reading, not only of Q's drops but of any text that happens to come to its attention, offers an example of what Eco refers to as the "hermetic model" of interpretation, a form of gnosticism in which the real Truth of the world is hidden within mysteriously encoded systems of symbols.[92]

91. Rothschild, *Storm Is Upon Us*, 23. It is worth noting that one of the features that makes QAnon a "superconspiracy" is its capacity to take on elements of conspiracies that, at least initially, have nothing to do with the content of Q's "drops." Thus, for example, the association of QAnon and the idea of cultural elites subsisting on chemicals taken from murdered children was inserted into the discourse of QAnon by its adherents, and is not directly referenced in any "official" Q communication. Yet, as with many equally outrageous claims, it has been absorbed into the heart of the QAnon conspiracy theory.

92. Eco, *Interpretation and Overinterpretation*, 34.

Drawing the connection between ancient hermeticism and much postmodern theory, Eco argues that the two approaches have a disquieting similarity. Both view the text as an "open-ended universe where the interpreter can discover infinite interconnections."[93] Both view language as inadequate to the interpretive task. Both reject the univocity of textual interpretation. And, in order "to salvage the text—that is, to transform it from an illusion of meaning to the awareness that meaning is infinite—the reader must suspect that every line of it conceals another secret meaning; words, instead of saying, hide the untold; the glory of the reader is to discover that texts can say everything, except what their author wanted them to mean."[94]

Eco acknowledges that his description caricatures much contemporary literary theory.[95] Furthermore, some texts genuinely *do* seek to open themselves to infinite interpretation. Yet, this hermetic approach allows the reader unqualified authority over what the text actually *does* mean, to the degree that it distorts most texts beyond recognition:

> *From a certain point of view everything bears relationships of analogy, contiguity, and similarity to everything else.* One may push this to its limits and state that there is a relationship between the adverb "while" and the noun "crocodile" because—at least—they both appeared in the sentence that I have just uttered. But the difference between the sane interpretation and the paranoiac interpretation lies in recognizing that this relationship is minimal, and not, on the contrary, deducing from minimal relationship the maximum possible. The paranoiac is not the person who notices that "while" and "crocodile" curiously appear in the same context: the paranoiac is the person who begins to wonder about the mysterious motives that induced me to bring these two particular words together. The paranoiac sees beneath my example a secret, to which I allude.[96]

"Suspicion," Eco notes, "in itself, is not pathological."[97] It becomes pathological, he argues, when the search for clues within a text or event falls victim to an "excess of wonder," which in turn leads to "overestimating

93. Eco, *Interpretation and Overinterpretation*, 39.
94. Eco, *Interpretation and Overinterpretation*, 39.
95. Eco, *Interpretation and Overinterpretation*, 40.
96. Eco, *Interpretation and Overinterpretation*, 48. Italics in original.
97. Eco, *Interpretation and Overinterpretation*, 48.

the importance of coincidences which are explainable in other ways.[98] Eco goes into detail on the history and application of this form of hermeticism, in both its ancient and modern forms, in order to distinguish between interpretations that are permissible on the basis of what he terms the *intentio operis* (the intention of the text itself), and those that engage in impermissible forms of "overinterpretation": If there are no rules to help ascertain which interpretations are the "best" ones, there is at least a rule for ascertaining which ones are "bad."[99]

This distinction between interpreting and overinterpreting, between relatively better readings of a text and "bad" readings, hinges on the distinction Eco makes between "open" and "closed" texts. The interpretation of the text is neither the exclusive domain of the author (as the exclusive arbiter of the text's meaning) nor of the reader (as hermetic interpreter). Rather, the text stands on its own, but also stands in relation to its author and the author's context. Eco distinguishes between "interpreting" a text, which requires one to take seriously the standpoint and setting of the author and the time and place in which the text was created, and "using" a text, in which the reader merely projects onto the text whatever happens to be convenient for the sake of their preferred interpretation.

Yet, he continues, the author too has to yield before the text itself: "Between the unattainable intention of the author and the arguable intention of the reader there is the transparent intention of the text.[100] An "open" text, according to Eco, is one that can sustain multiple interpretations.[101] Eco uses examples such as Joyce's *Finnegan's Wake* and some of his own novels to illustrate the way in which a text can be constructed to elicit a variety of interpretive options. On the other hand, "closed" texts are those that are constructed to produce a single idea, such as a stop sign or a Coca-Cola ad. Overinterpretation takes place when "closed" texts are treated as though they were "open" and thus generative of a potentially infinite variety of interpretive possibilities.

Q's 4chan drops were, to dignify them beyond their due, forms of "open" text. Their meanings were often intentionally, and increasingly, oblique so as to allow readers to project their own interpretive possibilities onto them. And project they did! However, James Comey's "Five Jobs I've Had" tweet is a quintessentially "closed" text, not written to provide

98. Eco, *Interpretation and Overinterpretation*, 50.

99. Eco, *Interpretation and Overinterpretation*, 52.

100. Eco, *Interpretation and Overinterpretation*, 78.

101. Eco, *Role of the Reader*, 41.

any more or different kind of information than that which it provided. It was in reading it as an open text, and playing semiotic games with it, that QAnon's interpretation became paranoiac, with the resulting fall out.

The same can be said, for example, of the idea that "pizza" is a euphemism for sex with minors, and thus an order of pepperoni pizza from a local restaurant is somehow evidence that the restaurant was a waypoint in a child sex ring: "These references were based on a supposed 'pedo code' that referred to young girls as 'pizza' and young boys as 'hot dogs.'"[102] This was the origin of the so-called "Pizzagate" conspiracy, which led to a shooting at the Comet Ping Pong Pizzeria in Washington, DC. Although Pizzagate was a precursor to QAnon, its core elements were incorporated into its superconspiracy along with many others.

One may be justified in wondering whether QAnon is worth the attention that it has garnered over the past several years, particularly as its prominence waned in the wake of Trump's electoral defeat in 2020.[103] Yet, according to Sommer, "QAnon is unmatched among modern American conspiracy theories in its ability to inspire violence."[104] Over one hundred of its adherents have committed crimes.[105] Furthermore, it is resistant to traditional counter-terrorism strategies.[106]

As a movement, QAnon is remarkable in several respects. As Sommer notes, it is a crypto-religious movement, and yet it lacks a charismatic leader.[107] The "Anon" in QAnon stands for "anonymous," and despite widespread speculation about the true identity (or identities) of the figure known as Q, they remain unknown. Nor, it seems, does their true identity actually matter. The role of charismatic leader has been taken on by a number of "priests," as Sommer notes: "thousands of QAnon entrepreneurs, who push their own individual versions of the theories that make up the fabric of QAnon . . . interpreting the Q clues for believers like clergy for a congregation."[108]

102. Rothschild, *Storm Is Upon Us*, 26.

103. To a large degree, the decline in QAnon's prominence is because its main theories and objectives have metastasized within Trump's conservative evangelical and Christian nationalist base. Many of its key ideas have been incorporated within mainstream Republican thought as the party has continued to lurch toward the authoritarian and extremist right.

104. Sommer, *Trust the Plan*, 135.

105. Jensen and Kane, "QAnon-Inspired Violence in the United States."

106. Jensen and Kane, "QAnon-Inspired Violence in the United States."

107. Sommer, *Trust the Plan*, 45.

108. Sommer, *Trust the Plan*, 45–46.

The role of charismatic leader is also, and more significantly, passed on to Donald Trump, who is cast in QAnon mythology, as among his Christian nationalist followers, as a messianic figure, standing up against the forces of evil, the central figure in a cosmic drama to wipe the vampiric adherents of the political left off the face of the earth. The eliminationist rhetoric running throughout QAnon's discourse is truly alarming—as appeals to extrajudicial imprisonment, mass executions, and the imposition of martial law are prominent elements: "How could any movement based around a 'secret war' between good and evil that ends with military tribunals and summary executions be considered anything other than violent?"[109]

This dimension of QAnon's rhetoric ties it firmly to the forms of white Christian nationalism discussed in chapter 1.[110] While QAnon is not *specifically* a form of Christian nationalism, in terms of its key tenets, with its at times overtly religious language and its appeal to mass violence as a means of destroying a form of satanic conspiracy, it appeals to, and is often embraced within, forms of white Christian nationalism.

CHRISTIAN NATIONALISM, IDENTITY, AND THE RHETORIC OF VIOLENCE

What QAnon takes to an absurdly conspiratorial extreme is the same trend that we have discussed—the increasing prevalence of white Christian nationalism as a major feature of the contemporary American right.[111] This is further grounded in the declining influence of white Christianity in American life. As Robert Jones notes: "Beginning in the 1970s—due to the twin forces of demographic change and religious disaffiliation—white mainline Protestants began to rapidly decline in both power and numbers. In this vacuum, white evangelical Protestants began to assert themselves as the face of white Christian America, only to find their own numbers dropping by the first decade of the twenty-first century."[112]

109. Rothschild, *Storm Is Upon Us*, 106.

110. This rise in religious nationalism generally can be observed globally beyond the American context, including Hungary, in Russia, Brazil, and the Philippines. India has its own variant grounded in Hinduism, and forms of Islamic nationalism can be found in several countries throughout the Middle East.

111. See Cooper-White, *Psychology of Christian Nationalism*.

112. Jones, *End of White Christian America*, 77.

In the same vein, Kristen Kobes Du Mez argues that American evangelicalism, with its increasing emphasis on a cult of aggressive masculinity, "must be seen as a cultural and political movement rather than as a community defined chiefly by its theology."[113] This is not, she states, to suggest that theology has no role to play. Rather, it is through the interplay of theology and culture that modern evangelicalism has taken on its current form: "Masculine authority, militarism, and the sexual and spiritual subordination of women have simply been part of the air evangelicals breath for decades."[114] This combination of elements is directly implicated in the increasing acceptance of authoritarian politics on the Christian right, along with the cult of personality that explains the widespread conservative (white) Christian allegiance to Donald Trump.

They are also implicated in the increase, not only in violent rhetoric, but in actual acts of violence on the American right. A Christianity defined, not by the teachings of Jesus, not by the willingness to suffer violence rather than inflict it, but instead by the belief that violence is right, proper, and a truly "American" way of Christianity offers no buffers to the increasingly tempting lure of terrorist violence on the right. When a particular conception of white Christian heritage is threatened, violence appears as both a morally appropriate solution, and perhaps even a necessary one.

Timothy McVeigh was never a particularly religious person, and has generally not been framed as a religious figure in American recollections of his bombing of the Murrah Federal Building in Oklahoma City in 1995. Yet his motivations resonate powerfully in the words and actions of contemporary Christian nationalists and others who participated in the January 6, 2021, riots at the US Capitol. As Jeffrey Toobin notes, McVeigh was motivated by "the obsession with gun rights; the perceived the belief in the value and power of violence."[115] As Du Mez notes: "A common sense of embattlement . . . links the rhetoric of the NRA to that of conservative white evangelicalism. For both, a bunker mentality strengthens identity and loyalty, and fuels militancy."[116] To be sure, not all the January

113. Du Mez, *Jesus and John Wayne*, 298.

114. Du Mez, *Jesus and John Wayne*, 298.

115. Toobin, *Homegrown*, 6.

116. Du Mez, *Jesus and John Wayne*, 296. One can see the connection between evangelicalism, conspiracism, and white supremacy even more clearly in the case of Randy Weaver, who was ultimately acquitted at trial after a standoff with federal officials at Ruby Ridge, Idaho. As Ganz describes the popular image of Weaver: "Here was a man who was just trying to keep his family safe from the New World Order, and when

6th rioters would have identified themselves with conservative evangelicalism, but the admixture of right-wing Christianity with the ideologies of groups such as the Proud Boys and the Oath Keepers makes it difficult to distinguish where the one leaves off and the other begins. The rhetoric shared with these groups by many of Donald Trump's evangelical supporters is striking.[117]

Jeff Sharlet documents this shared rhetoric in his book *The Undertow*. He describes contemporary America in a state of "slow civil war," as he shares his observations from his attendance at Trump rallies, megachurches, and random encounters in a cross-country trip. He sees the prosperity gospel as playing a significant role in the evangelical embrace of Trump. Both are transactional, trading faith for wealth, or the promise of wealth.[118] Although many evangelicals in 2016 were initially wary of Trump, eventually "the establishment Christian Right embraced the gospel of Trump, and it prospered: Trump's administration stocked top to bottom with its apostles, the movement mightier even 'post-Trump' than it was under George W. Bush or Reagan."[119] Sharlet also notes that Trump embraced a Manichean worldview, in which a "'spiritual war' with dark and hidden powers" was taking place.[120]

As with QAnon, Trump was given messianic status within the conservative evangelical community.[121] Examples include a billboard featuring Trump alongside the biblical verse "unto us a son is given and government shall be upon his shoulders."[122] As Sharlet notes, some of

he could not escape its clutches, they went and killed his family. The story of a vet vs. a tyrannical state intent on crushing white Christian Americans now looked plausible. Weaver's ties to the farthest fringe of politics would be played down. He was just an eccentric minding his own business" (Ganz, *When the Clock Broke*, 305).

117. For further discussion, see Kramer, *Politics of Resentment*; Denker, *Red State Christians*; Gorski et al., *Flag and the Cross*; Marti, *American Blindspot*.

118. Sharlet, *Undertow*, 112.

119. Sharlet, *Undertow*, 113.

120. Sharlet, *Undertow*, 113.

121. Or alternatively, as Dustin Byrd has argued, Trump has made a "Constantinian compact" with evangelical Christians: "In accepting the pagan Roman *quid pro quo* compact with the self-deifying Trump, American conservative Christians followed the example of the 4th century Christians: they compromised the inner-spirit of Christianity—its negativity—in exchange for access to power, a power which they believed would secure their continued existence and prosperity in capitalist America. However, unlike Emperor Constantine, who seemed to show at least some commitment to the religion of Christianity if only late in his life, Donald Trump has shown no movement towards a life dedicated to the values of the Gospels" (*Dark Charisma of Donald Trump*, 107–8).

122. Cooper, "Fort Oglethorpe Billboard Picturing Trump with Messianic Words

Trump's followers viewed him as a latter-day King Cyrus."[123] Of course, this was by no means universal. Many evangelicals spoke out against Trump as an amoral vulgarian.[124] Evangelical ethicist Russell Moore was a vocal critical of Trump, as were prominent pastors such as John Piper and Ed Stezer. Evangelical women such as Beth Moore were also vocal critics of Trump's evangelical supporters: "But on November 8 it became clear that the vast majority of evangelicals had come back around. Exit polls revealed that 81 percent of white evangelicals had handed Trump the presidency."[125]

The question of identity is at the heart of this otherwise baffling evangelical support of Trump.[126] As Du Mez documents in detail, over the course of a half century, (white) American evangelicalism underwent a transformation through which it came to identify far more with the mythology of American nationalism than with its own founding documents. It adopted the moral example of John Wayne, and projected that example onto the person of Jesus Christ, rather than adopting Jesus Christ in order to offer a vision to challenge the nationalism, racism, and glorification of violence embodied in the figure of John Wayne.

And as the mythology of American nationalism turns on the idea of righteous violence, the advocacy of violence was incorporated into the narrative of Christian nationalism. Sharlet reports from one church that seamlessly mixed the doctrines of QAnon, January 6th denialism, and American nationalist theology. There were no crosses on display, he explains. Rather, the pastor "compared the cross, the crucifix, the method by which Jesus is believed, by those who believe, to have died for our sins, to the tender dove: weak-tea figuration that fails to convey the great breadth of ass kicked by Christ once he was risen."[127]

> Now was the time for war, spiritual or otherwise. The resurrection, of Christ, yes, and also the red America, rising from the

Is Wrong-Headed." The verse is from Isa 9:6, although confusingly the billboard cites Rom 8:17. This is apparently a reference to the phrase "joint heirs," also featured on the billboard. The verse referenced reads: "And if children, then heirs: heirs of God and joint heirs with Christ, if we in fact suffer with him so that we may also be glorified with him."

123. Sharlet, *Undertow*, 113.

124. See, for example, Sider, *Spiritual Danger of Donald Trump*.

125. Du Mez, *Jesus and John Wayne*, 265.

126. Jardina, *White Identity Politics*. See also Sides et al., *Bitter End*.

127. Sharlet, *Undertow*, 174.

> grave, its symbol not the cross but, said Dave, "the empty tomb." Like the end of Mel Gibson's gory 2004 film *Passion of the Christ*, when Christ's death shroud collapses, the body disappeared, and then beside it the living savior is there, naked and ripped as mournful strings give way to the *da-d-a-da-dum-dum* of a military drum and buff Jesus marches to war.[128]

As Sharlet explains, in the ideology of American nationalism, the Old Testament gospel of the Father and the New Testament gospel of the Son is supplanted by the gospel of 1776: "apotheosis of revenge and redemption."[129]

How much of this can we really take seriously, though? Is there not an element of unseriousness that runs through much of this violent rhetoric? This question is helpful in providing a degree of plausible deniability to those who deploy this rhetoric. Through acts of ironic disavowal, they can make continual invocations of violence while at the same time insisting that it's all "really a joke." At times, the irony can become like a snake eating its own tail—like the OK sign, an anodyne gesture that was somehow transformed, through ironic disavowal, into a white supremacist symbol:

> It began as a joke; or rather, a "joke," in scare quotes, *ironic* White power, a "hoax" meant to trick liberals into believing that the raised fingers actually represent the letters *W. P.* The joke worked so well that it became real. Now, in certain circles, OK *does* mean White power—unless you say it doesn't.[130]

And of course, what the symbol means depends entirely on who is asking the question. It's a joke to outsiders, but deadly serious within the tribe—an open text, subject to multiple interpretations, but having a definite meaning to those who are inducted into the secret knowledge. Absurd memes like Pepe the Frog serve the same function, as do the Hawaiian shirts sported by the Boogaloo boys.[131] The purpose is the same, to provide ironic distance between the surface "joke" and the serious intent behind it.

128. Sharlet, *Undertow*, 185.

129. Sharlet, *Undertow*, 181.

130. Sharlet, *Undertow*, 109. Italics in original.

131. One can see the same dynamic in play in the response to Elon Musk's "my heart goes out to you" invocation of the Nazi salute, with supporters insisting that it was unintentional, or that it was a "Roman salute," followed by others, including a priest, echoing the gesture in a serious/not serious way.

But to say this is itself to fall for the joke, to become an object of mockery for taking it all "seriously," when after all, this violent rhetoric is only intended to "own the libs." And yet, to the heirs of Timothy McVeigh, it means much more. A 2009 Department of Homeland Security report declared that "rightwing extremists have capitalized on the election of the first African American president, and are focusing their efforts to recruit new members, mobilize existing supporters, and broaden their scope and appeal through propaganda."[132] The report was greeted with such hostility by conservatives that the Obama administration had it withdrawn.[133]

And yet, in the decade and more since it was released, right-wing extremist violence has only increased: "Indeed, the amount and degree of such violence offers a hidden history of the Obama years. The roll call of such acts runs into the dozens."[134] After Donald Trump assumed the presidency, these existing right-wing movements were emboldened, gathering in Charlottesville, Virginia, in 2017 for a rally dubbed "Unite the Right." There they marched through the streets with tiki torches chanting, "Jews will not replace us!" As Toobin notes, "The chant reflected the right-wing obsession with 'replacement theory'—the idea that the white majority in the United States would be replaced by people of color and immigrants. *The Turner Diaries* was an early expositor of this view, which was later made famous by Fox's Tucker Carlson."[135]

Ironic disavowal allows this rhetoric to go largely unchallenged under the guise of subversive humor. And yet the acts associated with those who use it are no joke. This culminated in the January 6th attack on the US Capitol, in which Trump supporters attempted to prevent the peaceful transition of power after Trump's loss in the 2020 election. As rioters stormed the Capitol building, declaring, "Hang Mike Pence!" and seeking out House Speaker Nancy Pelosi and others deemed to be traitors, they evoked *The Turner Diaries*'s "Day of the Rope" and QAnon's expectation of a violent "storm" in which its enemies would be subjected

132. Toobin, *Homegrown*, 357.

133. Toobin, *Homegrown*, 358.

134. Toobin, *Homegrown*, 359.

135. Toobin, *Homegrown*, 363. *The Turner Diaries*, written by neo-Nazi leader William Luther Pierce under the pseudonym Andrew McDonald, tells the story of a right-wing uprising sparked by a bombing similar to the one perpetrated by McVeigh, which climaxes in a spree of mass murder called "the day of the rope." As Toobin notes, the protagonist's mission in the novel was "to protect 'legacy Americans' from the depredations of Blacks, Jews, and the foreign born" (22). It was Timothy McVeigh's favorite book. Carlson, as of this writing, no longer works at Fox News.

to mass execution. A scaffold was even erected outside the Capitol building, with Vice President Pence hanged in effigy. Trump advisor Roger Stone declared even before the election, "Fuck the voting, let's get right to the violence."[136]

Yet, even after the violence of January 6th, the right, and particularly Trump, engaged in acts of ironic disavowal, declaring that nobody had actually encouraged violence that day. It was once again merely a "joke." The rioters were actually tourists, invited in by police or Congresspeople. No one was actually harmed or killed. To believe otherwise, once again, was to fall for the "joke." And the greatest punchline of all was that, in the end, Trump won election to a second term as president, notwithstanding the insurrection of which he was at the heart.

CONCLUSION

Identity is the connective tissue that binds together the various themes of this chapter. From Donald Trump's personal psychodrama and the dark charisma that binds him to his followers, to the more general appeal of authoritarian personalities; from the libertarian fantasy of an escape from politics into authoritarianism, and its mutation into QAnon conspiracism, to the allure of authoritarian violence on the Christian right; the desire to define and secure a sense of identity against its negation illuminates the authoritarian tendencies on the American political right, and particularly within the Christian right.

When the Christian foundation of American civil religion began to crumble in the mid-twentieth century, this represented not simply the rise of the secularization that was taking root in Europe at the same time, it represented a fundamental challenge to the affinity between American Christianity and the democratic forms and structures that provided the scaffolding for civic life. As ethnic and cultural differentiation brought more and different forms of symbolic expression to the public sphere, the idea of Christian ownership over American culture and politics could no longer be sustained. To be sure, there had been religious minorities in the United States since its founding, but it was precisely their status as *minority* that allowed Christians to accept and tolerate them under the rubric of religious freedom. Once Christianity itself became subject to the same

136. Toobin, *Homegrown*, 369.

conditions of public expression as other religions, overt Christian public power began to decline.

Of course, what is unsaid in the preceding paragraph is that this was really only true of *white* Christian power (and for much of American history, specifically white *Protestant* power). For non-white Christians, this was never the prevailing narrative. African American Christianity has always had to reckon with the reality of powerlessness and marginalization. Yet, as white Christian America lost cultural ground, the idea of American Christian nationalism began to take stronger and stronger root within the white evangelical community, providing as it did a narrative in which "traditional" conservative conceptions of masculinity, family, and nation became unquestioned premises of Christian identity. And once again, this can only be understood in the context of the changing racial dynamics of the post-World War II era. While patriarchal structures are no less prominent in African American and Latino forms of evangelicalism, the identification of ethnicity, Christianity, patriarchy, and nationalism takes on a particular form within white evangelicalism.

That being the case, the authoritarian threat facing the church raises a theological and moral challenge for the Christian community. Is democratic pluralism consistent with the elements of Christian faith? Is it possible to imagine a diverse, multiethnic, cosmopolitan society, which recognizes and respects secular forms of governance from within the contours of Christian theology, or must Christianity inevitably collapse into support for authoritarianism?

Underlying these dynamics is a dispute over the nature of identity itself—what it means to declare oneself to be American, or Christian, or male or female, or gay or straight, or any of the other myriad self-conceptions that people can adopt. The conservative response to this dispute is to seek to narrow the boundaries within which identity can be authenticated. However, the very nature of identity itself eludes that solution. To understand more fully the political and social moment in which we dwell then, we need a clearer understanding of what we mean by the idea of identity.

3

Contradictions of Identity

Rooted Cosmopolitanism and the Forging of the Self

Once I saw this guy on a bridge about to jump. I said, "Don't do it!" He said, "Nobody loves me." I said, "God loves you. Do you believe in God?"

He said, "Yes." I said, "Are you a Christian or a Jew?" He said, "A Christian." I said, "Me, too! Protestant or Catholic?" He said, "Protestant." I said, "Me, too! What franchise?" He said, "Baptist." I said, "Me, too! Northern Baptist or Southern Baptist?" He said, "Northern Baptist." I said, "Me, too! Northern Conservative Baptist or Northern Liberal Baptist?"

He said, "Northern Conservative Baptist." I said, "Me, too! Northern Conservative Baptist Great Lakes Region, or Northern Conservative Baptist Eastern Region?" He said, "Northern Conservative Baptist Great Lakes Region." I said, "Me, too!"

"Northern Conservative Baptist Great Lakes Region Council of 1879, or Northern Conservative Baptist Great Lakes Region Council of 1912?" He said, "Northern Conservative Baptist Great Lakes Region Council of 1912." I said, "Die, heretic!" And I pushed him over.

—Emo Philips, "The Best God Joke Ever—And It's Mine!"

ON BEING SOMEONE

In 2009, shortly after the birth of my third child, my parents came to Chicago for a visit. During our time together, my father revealed to us that, in confirmation of long-held family lore, he and his siblings were one-quarter Native American, making my brothers and me one-eighth Native American. My uncle, I was told, had been doing family genealogical research and had been able to establish family connections to two upstate New York tribes, and was only waiting for a few final details to be ironed out before our whole family would be formally recognized as tribal members.

I found this all very interesting, but also a bit perplexing. To be honest, I was more than a bit dubious about the entire thing. After all, I was well aware that such stories are exceedingly common among white Americans, who often seek identification with the Native American experience for a variety of complicated reasons. In most cases of course, these stories are vague enough and far enough back in the past to be largely unconfirmable and mostly legendary. What was unusual about the story my father told me was that, if true, my native ancestry was as recent as my great-grandmothers.

And yet I had to ask, what did this new information, if true, really mean for me and my family? After all, nothing in my upbringing had any connection to Native American culture. Growing up, the lore was simply that—lore. I had far deeper connections to my Irish grandparents and their heritage than to anything grounded in Native American experience. It seemed somehow inauthentic, and dishonest, to seek some kind of identification, let alone advantage, from a sudden revelation that I might have a Native American heritage.

I consulted one of my colleagues, a specialist in Native American religion, who cautioned me, wisely I think, about the complexities of white people attempting to claim Native American ancestry, and suggested that I not make a big deal about it, at least not until I had more information. So I more or less let the matter rest, pending more information from my father's side of the family.

But the situation gave me pause to reflect on the question of what it would mean for me to identify as Native American, indeed, what it meant for me to identify as anything at all. Like many Americans, I grew up with a kind of mongrel identity—German on my father's side, Irish on my mother's (though even there, the narrative is complicated). This idea, at least for white Americans, that what you "are" is somehow the sum of your ancestry, and that the celebration of that ancestry is somehow meaningful, is very powerful. But what did it mean, in my forties, to be given another thread of ancestry, particularly an ancestry that had been savagely oppressed and subjected to genocide throughout American history?

Around the same time, I began seeing a lot of commercials on television for genealogical testing services, such as 23-and-me and Ancestry.com. One set of these commercials hilariously suggested that the discovery of a previously unknown genetic heritage changed the way their recipients understood themselves culturally, trading kilts for lederhosen, or discovering a previously unknown passion for Native American pottery.[1] It was also during this time that Senator Elizabeth Warren came into criticism for having claimed Native American identity while on the faculty of Harvard Law School based on similar "lore" to that with which I had grown up. Nevertheless, I continued to ponder what it meant for me to be, all of a sudden, partially Native American.

The answer as it turned out was that it meant nothing. It wasn't true. None of it. I eventually took one of those genetic tests, if for no other reason than curiosity, and it turned out that there was not a scintilla of Native American genetic material in my genome. Whatever the family lore might have said, whatever my uncle's research had uncovered, whatever that might mean for some future tribal affiliation, the genetics were clear—I, and presumably my entire family, were not even remotely Native American, not in the smallest part.

But again, this just raised further questions about the nature of identity. If *being* Native American meant something about who I am, then *not* being Native American must have meant something as well, right? More broadly, it raised the question of what it even meant to *be* somebody in the first place, and what that sense of somebody-ness had to do with questions of genetics, culture, history, and heritage.

This is a subject that Kwame Anthony Appiah has addressed extensively. To what degree, he asks, do the "lies that bind" us as possessors of particular identities serve as a sound foundation for our self-perception, as well as in matters of social cohesion?[2] He shares his own experiences as the child of a Ghanaian father and a British mother, noting the many ways that his identity has been misascribed over the years: "Puzzled by

1. The latter commercial was particularly weird. The subject (I assume it was an actor playing a role), was shown to be 23 percent Native American, thus the love of pottery, apparently. But at the same time, she was shown to be 22 percent Iberian, and yet displayed no newfound love for tapas on the basis of this information. All of which suggested, to the degree that any of this was real in the first place, that these choices had much more to do with preference than with science.

2. Appiah, *Lies That Bind.*

the combination of my accent and my appearance, once our ride is under way, taxi drivers in the United States and the United Kingdom regularly ask me where I was born. 'In London,' I tell them, but that's not what they really want to know. What they mean to ask is where my family came from *originally*. Or, more bluntly, what are you?"[3] Yet, he notes, the answer to that question is inevitably complicated, not only for him, but for all of us: "Each person's sense of self is bound to be shaped by his or her own background, beginning with family but spreading out in many directions—to nationality, which binds us to places; to gender, which connects us with roughly half the species; and to such categories as class, sexuality, race, and religion, which all transcend our local affiliations."[4]

Yet, he maintains, each of these categories is exceptionally fraught. What it means to speak of religion, nationality, culture, or class is not nearly as clearly defined as we would like to make it. At first blush, to say that I am a Christian or that I am an American ought to provide some categorical basis for defining my identity. But, as Appiah argues, those categories are in themselves far more ambiguous than one might think. What constitutes a religion or a nation is as much a construction—a "lie" that binds—as it is a reflection of some objective set of criteria.

Even the very notion of identity, as it is used today, is of very recent vintage. Appiah identifies it with the work of George Herbert Mead prior to, and with Erik Erikson after, World War II.[5] For Mead, the self is formed through a confrontation between one's internal state of being and the external expectations of others—the "I"-self is transformed into a "me"-self when those expectations are internalized. To this, Erikson adds the role of group identity in the formation of the "ego-identity."[6] In the decades that followed, these accounts of identity were expanded and supplemented by other thinkers, as the subject of identity moved toward the center of American social and political discourse.

All of which is to say that these questions are distinctly modern in their form, and indeed distinctly *late* modern. As Francis Fukuyama notes, this question of one's identity could not have been framed (at least not in the way we do today), in the villages of pre-modern European societies:

3. Appiah, *Lies That Bind*, xi. Italics in original.
4. Appiah, *Lies That Bind*, xii–xiii.
5. Appiah, *Lies That Bind*, 3.
6. Appiah, *Lies That Bind*, 3.

> Consider the situation of a young peasant, Hans, who grows up in a small village in Saxony. Hans's life in the little village is fixed: He is living in the same house as his parents and grandparents; he is engaged to a girl whom his parents found acceptable; he was baptized by the local priest; and he plans to continue working the same plot of land as his father. It doesn't occur to Hans to ask "Who am I?" since that question has already been answered for him by the people around him.[7]

Yet, when Hans is dislocated from his local context by economic necessity, he comes into contact with people unlike those according to whom he had previously defined himself—people who think differently than he does, believe differently than he does, and want different things than he has been raised to want. At this point, the question of identity comes crashing down on Hans: "For the first time in his life, Hans can make choices about how to live his life, but he wonders who he really is and what he would like to be."[8] The question of identity, which would never have been a problem back in his village, now becomes central.[9] Fukuyama invokes Ferdinand Tönnies distinction between *Gemeinschaft* (community) and *Gesellschaft* (society) to explain how the expansion and simultaneous depersonalization of one's social relationships creates this crisis of identity within modernity, and the attendant rise of modern forms of political association such as nationalism.[10]

But this raises a further question. What *is* an identity? Appiah, drawing on Bourdieu, identifies identity first in terms of one's *habitus*, that is, "a set of dispositions to respond more or less spontaneously to the world in particular ways, without much thought."[11] Our *habitus* describes the way in which we are formed from a young age to interact unconsciously with the world around us—lessons about what it means to be polite, to eat properly, how to address elders, etc. These forms of action constitute much of what gives us our identity, and yet we don't generally think of them as an "identity"—they are just the way things are. This

7. Fukuyama, *Identity*, 63.

8. Fukuyama, *Identity*, 64.

9. Fukuyama, *Identity*, 64.

10. Fukuyama, *Identity*, 64–65. In particular it is the move from local rural forms of association to urban forms that create this rift, as the local context of the countryside allowed for the more personal forms of association to flourish, while in the cities, the far larger and more diverse population prevents the same kinds of relationship that emerged in the village context.

11. Appiah, *Lies That Bind*, 21.

habitus is not simply a psychological disposition, but is also embodied through our actions, our temperament, our manner of speech, and our manner of dress.[12]

Appiah uses gender norms as a way of explaining how this *habitus* is formed and policed:

> Girls in Japan see other girls covering their mouths when they laugh. They do likewise. If they don't, they are corrected. But because of this, some gay men in Japan also cover their mouths when they laugh, and this reflects the fact that they identify to some degree with women. Because the ways in which men and women dress and walk in different social groups are different, you end up walking and dressing in ways that reflect your identity, not just your gender but your class and your ethnicity.[13]

Of course, these ways of expressing identity can be altered. Through altering these forms of bodily expression—clothing, manner of speech, ways of comporting oneself, what Bourdieu calls one's "bodily hexis"—one can alter the perception of one's identity, often unconsciously.[14] At the same time, the reality that these elements of our identities derive either from environment or from choice means that they are not *essentially* aspects of our human nature. Nothing about my behavior can be said to be *essentially* male or masculine, or essentially grounded in my ethnic or class identity. And yet, those aspects of my *habitus* do reflect real aspects of my identity that disclose the cultural and social setting in which I was raised or which I have adopted.

Though again, even given this account, the question remains, why should identities matter? Appiah notes several elements that identities share which makes them important to our self-conception. First, he says, identities ascribe labels to us. These labels are, in a sense, sorting mechanisms, through which we can categorize people we encounter and understand them in terms of their relationship to a collectivity. Of course, as he illustrates, understanding the boundaries between these categories can be difficult, particularly to those outside of their discourses, as in, for example, distinguishing between members of particular West African ethnic or linguistic groups.[15]

12. Appiah, *Lies That Bind*, 21–22.
13. Appiah, *Lies That Bind*, 23.
14. Appiah, *Lies That Bind*, 25.
15. Appiah, *Lies That Bind*, 8.

At the same time he notes, these identities matter to people, because they offer them an account of their place in the world. "Every identity," he writes, "makes it possible . . . for you to speak as one 'I' among some 'us': to belong to some 'we.'"[16] Identities, he states, give us "reasons for doing things."[17] He continues:

> People who give reasons like these—"Because I'm a this, I should do that"—are not just accepting the fact that the label applies to them; they are giving what a philosopher would call "normative significance" to their membership in that group. They're saying that the identity matters for practical life: For their emotions and their deeds. And one of the commonest ways in which it matters is that they feel some sort of solidarity with other members of the group. Their common identity gives them reason, they think, to care about and help one another. It creates what you could call norms of identification: Rules about how you should behave, given your identity.

This, in one sense, is why it mattered whether or not my family was in an identifiable way Native American. It validated and endorsed the normative significance of our affiliation with and solidarity with Native American tribes. This could be seen, for example, in the memes that relatives would post to social media expressing support for Native causes. Of course, there were very good reasons to support those causes regardless of our identification with Native American culture, but as Appiah notes, the common identity that we (supposedly) shared offered us reasons that did not require additional justification. Because we were this, we did that (even if we weren't).[18]

There is a third reason identities matter as well, which is that, in addition to giving you reasons for doing things, "it can give others reasons for doing things to you."[19] This can have both positive and negative connotations. On the one hand, a shared identity can be grounds for other group members to offer a person help. On the other hand, identities can validate particular forms of power. To be identified, for example, with

16. Appiah, *Lies That Bind*, 9.

17. Appiah, *Lies That Bind*, 9.

18. I hasten to add that there was no doubt within my family at least as much romantic desire to be affiliated with Native American culture as there is in other predominantly white American families, and that this romantic desire did not have any particular ethical or political content. However, it remains the case that, at least on occasion, it did serve as a justification for expressions of solidarity with Native causes.

19. Appiah, *Lies That Bind*, 10.

particular castes in an Indian context can inform how others are authorized in treating a person. "Dominant identities can mean that people will treat you as a source of authority; subordinate identities can mean you and your interests will be trampled upon or ignored."[20]

This quality of identity—the way that we are treated—also accounts for the conflicts that often arise among different conceptions of identity. When one is privileged or disadvantaged because of qualities of one's identity, the division that this creates risks social discord. The relative positions created by differences of identity are contested in social life, as members of different groups vie to either maintain their privilege or to overcome the privileges of others. And one's relative advantage or disadvantage is usually not a position one chooses; it is ascribed. One may reject or fail to conform to some stereotypical aspects of that ascribed identity, but it continues to function beyond one's capacity to control. And thus the conflicts that arise coalesce around the moral question of how members of various identities may expect to be justly treated within society. A roughly egalitarian society will strive to minimize disparate treatment on the basis of diverse identities; but particularly in societies, such as the United States, that continue to deal with centuries of racial and ethnic oppression, the realities of colonialism, and the ongoing effects of barbaric practices of slavery and the genocide of Native Americans, equality may appear to be a distant hope.

In the case of my own family saga around our alleged heritage, I took the genetic test to be the end of the story. Whatever tales continue to circulate within my wider family circle, I don't have any reason to give them credence. But the question still remains as to what difference it could make to me, personally. There are at least two conclusions that I draw. First, I would not want to adopt any identity to which I was not entitled, especially when that identity came with particular moral claims on the rest of society of which I might feel tempted to take advantage. And second, my moral commitment to stand with Native Americans on particular issues should not and does not depend on my own heritage, but upon my understanding of the inherent rights of all human beings to live with equal dignity in a just society. And it is this second principle that leads to the next section, where I wish to dig more deeply into what this commitment to dignity might mean.

20. Appiah, *Lies That Bind*, 11.

DIGNITY AND RECOGNITION

The relationship between identity and the demand for human dignity is arguably one of the central political problems of modernity. Francis Fukuyama makes the argument that we can see these themes developing as early as the philosophy of Rousseau, and even earlier via the theology of Martin Luther, stating that "Luther was one of the first Western thinkers to articulate and valorize the inner self over the external social being."[21] Our inner self is the realm of faith, the ground of our spiritual existence, which cannot be determined or finally influenced by our exterior existence. It is that interior state—faith—that is salvific for Luther, rather than any external acts we might perform.

At the same time, Fukuyama argues, what we think of as identity in the modern sense is not yet present in Luther, and developed throughout modernity. What is central for identity as it has been defined in the contemporary sense is not simply an acknowledgment of an inner self distinct from our external circumstances, but a demand for the *recognition* of the inner self's validity. This desire for recognition is what Fukuyama connects with the concept of *thymos*, or what Plato identifies as the "spirited" part of the soul. *Thymos*, Fukuyama argues, "is the part of the soul that craves recognition of dignity."[22] That is to say, it is the dimension of ourselves that seeks the acknowledgment and acclaim of others. This is not to say that it is mere egocentricity. Rather *thymos* is grounded in the understanding that we, simply by virtue of being selves, persons with a distinct inner being, are deserving some kind of recognition.

Further, he continues, the nature of recognition matters. *Isothymia* is the desire for equal recognition, while *megalothymia* is the desire for the proper and appropriate recognition of one's superiority.[23] *Isothymia* is the recognition that Jack White and I are both human beings and American citizens entitled to equal respect on those bases. *Megalothymia* is the recognition that, as a guitar player, White is far superior to me, no matter how much I might wish it to be otherwise. Here again, this is not a question of egocentrism, but rather of judgment—the ability to distinguish between the relative merits of persons on relevant grounds. Were Jack White to come to my house to play guitar, it would be foolish of me to pretend that I was his equal in that regard. At the same time, it would be

21. Fukuyama, *Identity*, 26.

22. Fukuyama, *Identity*, xiii.

23. Fukuyama, *Identity*, xiii.

equally foolish for White to assume that his musical skill entitled him to greater rights than me as a citizen.

This desire for recognition lies at the heart of G. W. F. Hegel's *Phenomenology of Spirit*, and is encapsulated in his account of the master-slave dialectic. Hegel describes this dialectic as the contradiction between the one who is recognized and the one who recognizes the other.[24] In its most basic form, consciousness, according to Hegel, is wholly self-regarding. It is "Being-for-Itself."[25] But when it comes into conflict with another consciousness, they each confront the reality of their otherness, and their own self-sufficiency is called into question:

> Each is indeed certain of its own self, but not of the other, and therefore its own self-certainly still has no truth. For it would have truth only if its own being-for-self had confronted it as an independent object, or what is the same thing, if the object had presented itself as this pure self-certainty. But according to the Notion of recognition this is possible only when each is for the other what the other is for it, only when each in its own self through its own action, and again through the action of the other, achieves this pure abstraction of being-for-self.[26]

In other words, each consciousness seeks to subject the other consciousness to itself as an object, and thus a struggle ensues in which each consciousness must risk its own being. The victor in this struggle subjects the other consciousness to itself, but finds it cannot exist without it, and indeed both find the other essential for their own existence. Thus, through their struggle they come to the mutual recognition of one another. This abstract account of recognition provides the basis for Hegel's understanding of the meaning of history (and in particular the history of conflict) itself. As Fukuyama notes: "Hegel argued that the struggle for recognition was the ultimate driver of human history, a force that was key to understanding the emergence of the modern world."[27]

Hegel's description of the master-slave dialectic illustrates the way in which the struggle for recognition drives human social and political action. When we are reduced to a thing among things, or to a lesser being

24. Hegel, *Hegel's Phenomenology of Spirit*, 113. See also Kojeve, *Introduction to the Reading of Hegel*. Kojeve makes the theme of recognition central to his interpretation of Hegel.

25. Hegel, *Hegel's Phenomenology of Spirit*, 113.

26. Hegel, *Hegel's Phenomenology of Spirit*, 113.

27. Fukuyama, *Identity*, 10.

among beings, then we rebel and struggle to be understood as equal to those who would thus reduce us (*isothymia*). However, Fukuyama notes that the same dynamic can work the other way. We also rebel when we perceive ourself as being dragged down to the level of those who are less deserving (at least in our own estimation) of merit than we are (*megalothymia*).

For Fukuyama, this provides the lens through which to understand contemporary conflicts over identity—on the one hand are those who desire and deserve to have their human equality and dignity recognized by others, and on the other hand are those who desire to have their superior merit recognized by others. Modern democratic politics is grounded in *isothymia*, the basic dignity through which all people can participate in public life. However, even in the context of a democratic polity, there are those who are more, and those who are less, deserving of recognition.

"The desire for the state to recognize one's basic dignity has been at the core of democratic movements since the French Revolution. A state guaranteeing equal political rights was the only rational way to resolve the contradictions that Hegel saw in the relationship between master and slave, where only the master was recognized."[28] At the same time, however: "Recognition of everyone's equal worth means a failure to recognize the worth of people who are actually superior in some sense."[29]

The phrase "in some sense" is carrying a lot of the weight of that sentence, however. Because it is precisely the sense in which superiority is understood and measured, and the contexts in which it is relevantly applied, that matter in terms of the democratic character of a society. As Fukuyama notes: "The rise of modern democracy is the story of the displacement of *megalothymia* by *isothymia*: societies that only recognized an elite few were replaced by ones that recognized everyone as inherently equal."[30] For Fukuyama this is a net good. But it also becomes the basis for much of the contemporary conflict over the nature of identity—if my equality comes at the expense of your privilege, then your *megalothymia* is challenged, and the Hegelian struggle for recognition is renewed.

It is also the case that *isothymia* can bleed into *megalothymia*, the desire for equal recognition, argues Fukuyama, can become the basis for claims of superior merit:

28. Fukuyama, *Identity*, 49.
29. Fukuyama, *Identity*, 23.
30. Fukuyama, *Identity*, 22.

> Contemporary identity politics is driven by the quest for equal recognition by groups that have been marginalized by their societies. But that desire for equal recognition can easily slide over into a demand for recognition of the group's superiority. This is a large part of the story of nationalism and national identity, as well as certain forms of religious politics today.[31]

Fukuyama's analysis of the role of *thymos* in the understanding of contemporary conversations about the relationship between dignity, recognition, and identity provides a useful analytical lens. While he has some critical words to say about "identity politics" broadly construed, his perspective is grounded in the presumption that the desire for recognition is a wholly legitimate human aspiration. At the same time, he rightly notes the danger that the desire for recognition poses to the structures of democratic society, most clearly in the global resurgence of ethno-nationalism, sparked at least in part by the backlash to new patterns of migration.

As Hegel notes, the contradiction between consciousnesses in the struggle for recognition is accompanied by very real violence grounded in the refusal to admit the equal humanity and dignity of those who possess a different identity. He writes of the "trial by death" that accompanied the struggle for recognition.[32] "Just as each stakes his own life," he writes, "so each must seek the other's death."[33] The ensuing struggle, in which each consciousness attempts to eliminate the other, ultimately resolves itself through the domination of one over the other—in which the master ultimately asserts himself against the slave. Yet the irony that Hegel sees in this struggle is that, through that struggle and domination, the master is ultimately forced to acknowledge the self-consciousness of the slave—the dominant other recognizes his own dependence on the dominated, and the dominated his own equality with the one who dominates.[34]

In concrete terms, the resurgent nationalism seeks by violence to kill, drive out, or subordinate those whom it deems to be inferior—the "alien other" that exists like an infection within the body politic. For Hegel, this is ultimately an illusion grounded in a failure to honor the mutual dignity within all human consciousness. Yet the confluence of conceptions of identity and the willingness to use violence for the purpose of asserting and defending that identity is deeply enmeshed within

31. Fukuyama, *Identity*, 22.
32. Hegel, *Hegel's Phenomenology of Spirit*, 114.
33. Hegel, *Hegel's Phenomenology of Spirit*, 114.
34. Hegel, *Hegel's Phenomenology of Spirit*, 119–20.

nationalist ideology—sometimes for better, but mostly for worse. It is to a deeper analysis of this that we now turn.

VIOLENCE AND IDENTITY

The diversity of identities does not inevitably result in violence. In situations where *isothymia* prevails and equal dignity and recognition are taken as the baseline presumption of public participation, a pluralism of identities cannot only exist, but can contribute to the thriving of a vibrant culture. When the pluralism of identities celebrates and reinforces one another in their particularity and also provides a welcoming setting for the discovery of new ideas, it can be crucial to the creation of a thriving society.

However, as Amartya Sen notes, "identity can also kill—and kill with abandon."[35] When solidarity between the members of one identity group stands in tension with the interests of the members of another identity group, violence becomes a means by which each group seeks to advance its interests.[36] The assumption that the competition for social goods is a zero sum game leads to conflict over perceived limited resources. But more than that is simply the perception of others as *Other*—as in some sense alien from the basic elements of humanity that we share in common—that allows for the belief that violence can be justified. In violent conflicts, the enemy is often labeled with dehumanizing terms in order to prevent the recognition of the fundamental sameness that underlies their perceived otherness. When our enemy appears to us in their full humanity, it becomes difficult, sometimes impossible, for us to act violently toward them.

Michael Walzer reports an episode from Robert Graves's autobiography, in which he refrains from shooting an enemy soldier in war because the man was bathing: "I saw a German, about seven hundred yards away, through my telescopic sights. He was taking a bath in the German third line. I disliked the idea of shooting a naked man, so I handed the rifle to the sergeant with me."[37] George Orwell tells a similar story from the Spanish Civil War, in which he refused to shoot a half-dressed man precisely because "a man who is holding up his trousers isn't a 'Fascist,' he

35. Sen, *Identity and Violence*, 1.

36. Sen, *Identity and Violence*, 2.

37. Quoted in Walzer, *Just and Unjust Wars*, 140.

is visibly a fellow-creature, similar to yourself."[38] Measures must be taken, by those who wish to enact violence on some alien Other, to crystalize them in their otherness. But when those attempts at crystallization fail, or when the illusion of otherness is penetrated by the revelation of their humanity, we often find, as Graves and Orwell found, that we cannot pull the trigger.

Of course, it is a truism that we do not possess one singular identity. Rather we are made up of multiple, sometimes competing, identities that determine the totality of what makes us who we uniquely are. The identity conflict is as often an internal struggle to define who we are, and to whom we belong, as it is an outward struggle between groups. This is why the question of my own alleged Native American heritage mattered, both to me and to members of my family. It was not solely, or perhaps even primarily, a question of group membership, but of internal self-identification. For me at least, the question was not "do I belong to this or that group" (although that was an obvious and important element of the discussion), but *what am I* if I am to incorporate this new understanding of my identity into my self-understanding—particularly as someone who had managed to enter middle age without having ever understood himself in those terms. And, equally important, what responsibilities and obligations does this new self-conception impose upon me, if I am to adopt this understanding of my identity?

Yet, regardless of the multiplicity of identities that constitute our selves, others often insist on ascribing a singular identity to us, for the purpose of either elevating their own sense of *megalothymia* or diminishing our sense of *isothymia*. Racism, anti-Semitism, sexism, homophobia, and a long litany of other bigotries function on this basis: by reducing their designated opponents to mere things, demeaning them through words and actions, they impose a singular identity through which the other can be described and discounted. "In opposing external imposition, a person can both try to resist the ascription of particular characteristics and point to other identities a person has."[39] Sen offers the example of Shakespeare's Shylock in *The Merchant of Venice*, who pleads for the recognition of his fundamental humanity in the face of anti-Semitism. In the same way, Bharadvaja in *The Mahabharata* criticizes the caste system by noting the common human attributes shared by members of all castes.[40]

38. Quoted in Walzer, *Just and Unjust Wars*, 140.

39. Sen, *Identity and Violence*, 7.

40. Sen, *Identity and Violence*, 7–8.

Sen argues that the solution to these dilemmas is not to be found in suppressing the diversity of identities that people inhabit, but perhaps paradoxically, in encouraging the multiplicity of identities:

> Identity can be a source of richness and warmth as well as violence and terror, and it would make little sense to treat identity as a general evil. Rather, we have to draw on the understanding that the force of a bellicose identity can be challenged by the power of *competing* identities. These can, of course, include the broad commonality of our shared humanity, but also many other identities that everyone simultaneously has. This leads to other ways of classifying people, which can restrain exploitation of a specifically aggressive use of one particular categorization.[41]

A person who defines themselves according to only one identity (e.g., as "only" a Hutu or a German) can be convinced to engage in violence against individuals and groups identified as enemy others (Tutsis or Jews respectively). However, recognizing that they are, while being those things, also at the same time African or European, or belonging to other identities—worker, lawyer, teacher, father or mother, husband or wife—can diminish the power that claims of exclusive identity hold over us.[42] Furthermore, as Sen notes: "Along with the recognition of the plurality of our identities and their diverse implications, there is a critically important need to see the role of *choice* in determining the cogency and relevance of particular identities that are inescapably diverse."[43] In other words, our identities are not just imposed upon us, but are to at least some degree chosen.

However, to suggest that we choose our identities is not to suggest that any and every identity is open to us to choose. The fact that I *might* have been partly Native American did not give me the power to simply *adopt* that identity, even less so after it was established that I was *not*. The well-publicized case of Rachel Dolezal offers another instructive example of how identity choice can be constrained.

Dolezal was an instructor at Eastern Washington University in 2015, teaching a number of courses in the field of Africana education, and identifying as African American. She was also the president of the Spokane, Washington, NAACP. That year, it was revealed that, despite

41. Sen, *Identity and Violence*, 4. Italics in original.

42. Sen, *Identity and Violence*, 4.

43. Sen, *Identity and Violence*, 4. Italics in original.

her claims to the contrary, Dolezal was not African American, but of European descent. She received a barrage of criticism over what was widely perceived as a form of deception, and was removed from her teaching and community leadership positions as a result.

At the same time, some observers defended her on the grounds that, even though she was not black, she "identified" as black. One commentator noted that, for many white Americans, "who are disconnected from European heritage or legacy, it often feels like whiteness as a concept is empty."[44] Some of her colleagues in the Spokane area offered her support on the basis of her work on behalf of the African American community, while other observers denounced her on the grounds that she was performing a kind of "blackface."[45]

At stake in the controversy was the question of what it meant for a white woman to inhabit an African American identity. Was it an expression of solidarity with the African American community? Was it a form of cultural appropriation? Did she take positions as an African American that could have been occupied by someone who was actually African American? And what, indeed, does that term mean? I remember vividly a colloquy I once attended, in which a white South African spoke of being naturalized as a US citizen, thus himself becoming "African American," to the deep skepticism of the black participants at the conference.

Compounding the controversy, two years later the feminist journal *Hypatia* published an article by Rebecca Tuvel that compared the response to Dolezal to that of Caitlyn Jenner's coming out as transgender.[46] In the article, Tuvel put forward the thesis that "generally, we treat people wrongly when we block them from assuming the personal identity they wish to assume."[47] For example, she suggests that it would be wrong to prevent a person who strongly identifies with Judaism to undertake the necessary steps to convert. She argues that there are two elements to what she terms "a successful identity transformation."[48] The first is how the person in question self-identifies (e.g., in her example, does the person identify as Jewish, and in the same vein, does Jenner identify as a woman or Dolezal identify as black). The second is "whether a given society is

44. Holpuch, "Rachel Dolezal Identifying as African American."
45. Capehart, "Damage Rachel Dolezal Has Done."
46. Tuvel, "In Defense of Transracialism."
47. Tuvel, "In Defense of Transracialism," 264.
48. Tuvel, "In Defense of Transracialism," 264.

willing to recognize an individual's felt sense of identity by granting her membership in the desired group."[49]

In the American context, religious conversion tends to be relatively non-controversial. Individuals join and depart from religious communities with relatively little social friction, although individual and local circumstances play a large role even there. For several years, transgender identity was beginning to achieve an increasing amount of acceptance on the basis of Tuvel's second principle, although recent backlash in the United States, particularly accentuated in the 2024 presidential election, has undermined some of that acceptance.[50]

The move that Tuvel makes, which resulted in intense criticism of her article, was her claim that "reasons similar to those we accept with regard to individuals who transition to another sex extend to those who wish to transition to another race."[51] Although Tuvel attempts to account for and address objections to her position, in some corners she was perceived to be undermining the case for a (legitimate) desire to transition one's gender by advocating on behalf of an (illegitimate) desire to transition one's race.[52]

In fairness to Tuvel, a close reading of the article makes it clear that she is intentionally grappling with the philosophical implications of these questions of identity in order to understand what kinds of distinctions, if any, exist between these two understandings of identity-transition. While her approach was arguably excessively abstract, it was not in any way out of line as a philosophical argument. However, this is less of an exoneration than it might at first appear, since it is the very abstractness of her argument that creates problems.

The issue is not whether, in the abstract, one should be permitted to adopt one's own identity. The issue is whether, *in these particular circumstances*, such an identity should be adopted or affirmed. Dolezal's

49. Tuvel, "In Defense of Transracialism," 264.

50. One marker of that backlash is the amount of legislation targeting members of the trans community. In 2024, there were 701 bills proposed across 44 states, 51 of which passed. See Trans Legislation Tracker, "2024 Anti-Trans Bill Tracker."

51. Tuvel, "In Defense of Transracialism," 272.

52. A number of additional arguments were also advanced in response to the article, including claims that Tuvel did not cite, and did not show sufficient familiarity with, the existing literature on transgender identity, and that in the process of laying out her argument, she dead-named Jenner. The website *Daily Nous* covered the controversy and the specific claims made by Tuvel and her critics. See Weinberg, "Philosopher's Article on Transracialism."

self-identification as black existed in the context of a deeply fraught history of American racism, a history from which the nation still struggles, often feebly, to emerge. In those circumstances, to identify publicly as black is to claim membership in the community that has suffered generationally from the trauma of that racism. Dolezal may indeed have desired to claim such membership, but it is not so easily granted when one has not dwelt within that identity for one's entire life. It was this realization that lay behind my own reticence about claiming any sort of Native American identity—what did I really know about being Native American?[53] What did Dolezal really know about being black?

There is an important distinction to be made between this kind of identity transformation and religious conversion. As Tuvel notes, one can opt to convert to Judaism, but one does not just *decide* to convert. One goes through a *process* of conversion, which involves learning about the history and tradition of the Jewish people in the context of a relationship with a rabbi and a congregation. The same can be said of other religions—for example, Christianity and Buddhism, each of which have strong traditions of winning converts, also generally have rigorous processes by which conversion takes place.

Conversion is always a conversion *with* and *alongside* as well as *to*. In a similar though definitely distinct way, gender transition usually takes place under medical supervision and care. It is not *public* precisely, but it has a public context, through which one's identity transition is recognized and acknowledged. Yet, Dolezal's identification as black was a personal, and intentionally deceptive, decision, that required her to keep the reality of her past hidden, rather than to be fully integrated into a new form of community.

Again, Tuvel recognizes aspects of this objection in her second principle—that identity transformation is dependent on the acceptance of the community as much as it is on one's own personal preferences. And yet this aspect of her analysis, which should have prompted a much deeper excavation of the particulars of Dolezal's case, is subsumed within a general discussion of the category of "white privilege."

The assumption of an identity is thus inescapably intertwined with the context in which that identity is exercised. The identities we adopt are

53. By contrast, consider the case of Elizabeth Hoover, a professor of Native American studies who was raised to believe she was Native American and who regularly took part in Native practices from a young age, and yet whose Native heritage has been called into serious question by critics. Kang, "Identity Crisis."

chosen with reference to the social situation in which we adopt them. As Sen notes, "choices are always made within the limits of what is seen as feasible."[54] And part of what is factored into the question of feasibility is what others are willing to accept, and what they are not. And Sen goes on to note that the struggle for choice in identity is at least as much about convincing others of the legitimacy of our identity as it is in coming to adopt that identity ourselves.

Sen argues that the concept of destiny lies at the heart of the relationship between identity and the prospect of violence. Insofar as identity is perceived as being in some sense unitary and predetermined, as opposed to pluralistic and contended, it contains the seeds of violence. The belief that one's identity is grounded in a pre-established, and unchosen, personal or cultural matrix demands, further, that such conceptions of identity be enforced through some mechanism of coercion. This could be with the goal of policing individual identity choices, or of maintaining some illusory sense of social or cultural "purity," through which outsiders and aliens are forcibly excluded. As Sen notes:

> The illusion of singular identity, which serves the violent purpose of those orchestrating such confrontations, is skillfully cultivated and fomented by the commanders of persecution and carnage. It is not remarkable that generating the illusion of unique identity, exploitable for the purpose of confrontation, would appeal to those who are in the business of fomenting violence, and there is no mystery in the fact that such reductionism is sought.[55]

The connection between violence and the desire for purity is also reflected in René Girard's analysis of the connection between violence and mimesis. For Girard, however, it is uniformity of identity that provides a central problem, as we seek to mirror the desires of others—wanting what they want—and struggling to possess that which is already possessed by the other. The contagion of violence is grounded in this "mimetic desire."[56] In this sense, too much sameness as much as too much difference is a threat. Twins, for example, represent a potential threat to social order precisely because of their similarity: "Twins invariably share

54. Sen, *Identity and Violence*, 5.

55. Sen, *Identity and Violence*, 175.

56. Girard, *Violence and the Sacred*, 143.

a cultural identity, and they often have a striking physical resemblance to each other. Wherever differences are lacking, violence threatens."[57]

Sen's account of the rootedness of violence within the desire for purity can be squared with Girard, who argues that "twins are impure in the same way that a warrior steeped in carnage is impure, or an incestuous couple, or a menstruating woman."[58] Twins are an interesting case precisely because they bear a similarity to one another while also diverging from the norm *through their very similarity*. As Girard notes, to the extent that violence is grounded in mimetic rivalry, the figure of the twins represent a particular threat, as the many literary depictions of twins struggling for a common object illustrate. The figure of the twin exemplifies the paradoxes rooted in sibling rivalry. Girard writes:

> We instinctively tend to regard the fraternal relationship as an affectionate one; yet the mythological, historical, and literary examples that spring to mind tell a different story: Cain and Abel, Jacob and Esau, Eteocles and Polyneices, Romulus and Remus, Richard the Lion-Hearted and John Lackland. The proliferation of enemy brothers in Greek myth and dramatic adaptations of myth implies the continual presence of a sacrificial crisis, repeatedly alluded to in the same symbolic terms. The fraternal theme is no less "contagious" *qua* theme for being buried deep in the text than is the malevolent violence that accompanies it. In fact, the theme itself is a form of violence.[59]

On the one hand, the figure of the twins seems to represent identity in its purest form—two people who share almost all their characteristics in common. But in this sense, they are too close, they share *too much* in common. They are distinct from the community of identity precisely through their similarity, and thus risk violating the boundaries of purity that the community of identity seeks to maintain, as the symbolic struggle to which Girard alludes suggests. As Girard notes: "Difference that exists outside the system is terrifying because it reveals the truth of the system, its relativity, its fragility, and its mortality."[60]

Yet, as Sen notes, the sense of identity is grounded in an understanding of collective destiny that can brook no deviation. Those who violate the communal sense of purity are thus subject to violence, and in

57. Girard, *Violence and the Sacred*, 57.

58. Girard, *Violence and the Sacred*, 58.

59. Girard, *Violence and the Sacred*, 61.

60. Girard, *Scapegoat*, 21.

this regard, Girard's understanding of the role of the scapegoat becomes relevant to understanding the connection between communal identity and violence. As Girard argues, the communal struggle caused through mimetic desire leads ultimately to violence. The role of the scapegoat in this regard is to become the bearer of communal guilt, the one recognized, named, and persecuted within the community as responsible for the violence.[61] The scapegoat is thus both perpetrator and victim. Being singled out for blame, it is driven from the community or killed. Girard writes:

> Ultimately, the persecutors always convince themselves that a small number of people, or even a single individual, despite his relative weakness, is extremely harmful to the whole of society. The stereotypical accusation justifies and facilitates this belief by ostensibly acting the role of mediator. It bridges the gap between the insignificance of the individual and the enormity of the social body. If the wrongdoers, even the diabolical ones, are to succeed in destroying the community's distinctions, they must either attack the community directly, by striking at its heart or head, or they must begin the destruction of difference within their own space by committing contagious crimes such as parracide and incest.[62]

The scapegoat is quintessentially an outsider—one who possesses an identity distinct from the community. This outsider identity allows the community to pile the worst possible crimes onto them. Then, through violence directed at the scapegoat, Girard claims, the community restores a kind of equilibrium that temporarily quells mimetic violence, at least for a short time. Eventually though, a new scapegoat must be sought and thus the sacrificial cycle begins again.[63]

61. Girard, *Scapegoat*, 14.

62. Girard, *Scapegoat*, 15.

63. Girard's thought, it must be noted, is complex and multifaceted, having evolved over decades. Pinning his thought down to one overly simplified explanation is bound to leave out a great deal of important detail. Furthermore, his work has been extensively commented upon, and thus there is a large body of secondary literature that explores both the anthropological and the theological dimensions of his thinking. Of particular significance for the purposes of this study, see Bailie, *Violence Unveiled*. Also Jones, *Did God Kill Jesus*. Both of these volumes explore the theological dimensions of Girard's theory, with particular attention to the connection between his understanding of the scapegoat mechanism and the Christian account of redemption, about which more in a subsequent chapter.

By distinguishing between the "pure" insiders bound together by a sense of common identity and the contaminating influence of the alien Other—racial, ethnic, sexual, or what have you—a ready source of scapegoats is always at hand. As Sen notes: "The advocacy of a unique identity for a violent purpose takes the form of separating out one identity group—directly linked to the violent purpose at hand—for special focus, and it proceeds from there to eclipse the relevance of other associations and affiliations through selective emphasis and incitement."[64]

Sen's analysis is grounded in an essentially secular liberal account of justice, drawing heavily on the work of John Rawls. As such, his prescription for the problem of violence is the creation of a more just and equitable form of liberal society (although he expresses skepticism about that society reaching to a global extent). Elsewhere, Sen discusses the economic and moral mechanisms by which such equity is to be achieved.[65] Here, he focuses on the development of multiculturalism as a potential cure for the problems of identity and violence.

The form of multiculturalism for which Sen advocates is one which "focuses on the freedom of reasoning and decision-making, and celebrates cultural diversity to the extent that it is as freely chosen as possible by the persons involved."[66] The challenge, however, is the connection between identity as that which is imposed versus identity as chosen. If not all identity choices are available or acceptable in all contexts, the question of the extent to which freely chosen identity is possible remains largely context-dependent, even within liberal societies.

At the same time, Sen argues, "a nation can hardly be seen as a collection of sequestered segments, with citizens being assigned fixed places in predetermined segments."[67] A genuine freedom to choose with

64. Sen, *Identity and Violence*, 175. It should be noted that Sen does not use Girard's understanding of mimetic violence as an aspect of his own understanding, yet there is significant overlap between Sen's approach and Girard's with respect to how purity and contamination function as concepts. Girard goes deeper than Sen's diagnosis in terms of his analysis of the deep cultural and religious wells from which these concepts draw.

65. Sen, *Development as Freedom*.

66. Sen, *Identity and Violence*, 150.

67. Sen, *Identity and Violence*, 165.

whom to affiliate, and from whom to disaffiliate, is a crucial dimension of identity in a multicultural context. Yet, in the end Sen does not do more than gesture toward the hope that such a society may be possible, under conditions through which forms of violence-provoking "solitarism" are replaced by an embrace of social pluralism as a form of global identity:

> There is a compelling need in the contemporary world to ask questions not only about the economics and politics of globalization, but also about the values, ethics, and sense of belonging that shape our conception of the global world. In a nonsolitarist understanding of human identity, involvement with such issues need not demand that our national allegiances and local loyalties be altogether *replaced* by a global sense of belonging, to be reflected in the working of a colossal "world state." In fact, global identity can begin to receive its due without eliminating our other loyalties.[68]

It is hard to disagree with the contention that asking such questions is an important sign of progress toward a view of pluralism that resists the pull of violence grounded in solitarist conceptions of identity. But as a conclusion, "ask questions" seems a bit weak. What is needed is a more robust defense of multiculturalism and social pluralism as positive moral programs for the sake of overcoming violence.

Wolfgang Huber offers such a robust defense in his book *Violence*. Huber focuses not on freedom as the moral core grounding multiculturalism, but rather on human dignity, a recognition that multiculturalism "can only unfold where the existence and the rights of other cultures are respected."[69] This requires, he argues, a recognition of the basic humanity of those who are unlike us: "Respect for human dignity in the person of strangers, tolerance for their way of life, and nonviolence when participating in a conflict between different claims to truth, are decisive conditions not only for the pluralistic society as a whole but for the multicultural society as well."[70] This is not a denial of the central role of freedom that Sen emphasizes, but by grounding the insistence on nonviolent cooperation across social and cultural differences in a normative moral claim about human dignity, Huber forcefully insists that it is our humanity, not any particular condition of our humanity, that provides the basis for a resistance to the scapegoating of others on the basis of identity.

68. Sen, *Identity and Violence*, 185. Italics in original.

69. Huber, *Violence*, 63.

70. Huber, *Violence*, 63.

The perennial challenge to the claims of a universal appeal to human dignity is what seems to be the equally compelling claims of social particularity. To stake a moral claim on the basis of one's humanity cuts against the recognition that I am not *merely* human, but rather *this* human being in *this* context, and can be meaningfully described according to a particular set of characteristics. Many of the appeals that Sen identifies throughout his analysis—to be Indian or American, male or female, Christian or Hindu—are grounded in this recognition of the moral force of particularity. Human dignity in the abstract sense appears too general a category to encompass what it means to have an identity of any kind. And of course that is true. Huber's case for human dignity is not intended to divest us of our particularity. But the ability to maintain our particularity in a pluralist and multicultural society relies on those claims of human dignity. That universal recognition entails the kind of common respect that allows us to yet remain together in our particularity in spite of our differences.

IDENTITY POLITICS: FOR AND AGAINST

Before continuing, it may be useful to make a brief foray into the discourse surrounding "identity politics," not because the term itself, or the debates surrounding it, are particularly illuminating, but precisely because they are not. To talk about identity in the context of its social and political dynamics inevitably leads to charges that one is playing "identity politics," as though that is a definitionally bad thing. And yet, it is unquestionably the case that issues of identity in a pluralistic context have political implications, not only on the level of public policy but perhaps more significantly on the level of cultural self-understanding.

Critics of the concept of identity politics, often though not exclusively from the political and cultural right, ground their critique in the assumption that our particular identities are, or should be, subsumed into some larger common political identity. Canards such as the claim that Black History Month preferences Africa American identity over a common American identity, or that Pride celebrations highlight gay experience at the expense of common experience, are frequent. A charitable interpretation of these complaints is that they object to the singling out of a group or groups for celebration and thus highlight the fragmentation that accompanies social and cultural pluralism. A less charitable, and I think more accurate, interpretation is that these complaints are grounded in the suspicion that the celebration of pluralism is a threat to the hegemony of dominant racial, sexual, and class hierarchies.

The phrase "identity politics," much like the term "woke," has been co-opted by the political right and removed from its original context in such a way that its use frequently obscures more than it reveals. As Adrian Daub notes, people talk about these ideas "so that they don't have to talk about other things, in order to legitimize certain topics, positions, and authorities and delegitimize others."[71] Used as a term of opprobrium, it has become a way of evading the discussion of genuine questions of social and political justice rather than engaging forthrightly with the critical stance that the term originally conveyed.

As Olúfẹ́mi Táíwò has argued, the concept of identity politics as it was originally conceived was a radical assertion of the right of groups to define their own identities and interests in the context of conditions of oppression and marginalization.[72] It was only subsequently appropriated as a means of pacifying marginalized groups while maintaining a status quo that served to perpetuate their marginalization. One can see this dynamic in play in the institutional responses to the police murder of George Floyd in 2020. Governments, universities, and corporations, sensitive to the very legitimate claims of racism surrounding not only the killing but their own practices, chose to respond by expanding Diversity, Equity, and Inclusion (DEI) programs, which, while they may have beneficial effects on the margins of the discussion, did not engage in an immanent critique of the very institutions and structures that promote them.

Rather than address the deep-seated interplay of racism, policing, and capitalism, many institutions instead contented themselves with assigning readings from Robin D'Angelo and Ibram X. Kendi.[73] While such projects may have had some small-scale beneficial effects, they were more effective at defanging more trenchant criticisms provoked by the murder. They also created an easy target for right-wing backlash, which caricatured these programs as progressive propaganda campaigns rather than, as Táíwò suggests, programs of social pacification.

What these efforts did do was, on the one hand, convey the impression that solutions to institutional racism could be achieved on the level

71. Daub, *Cancel Culture Panic*, viii–ix.

72. Táíwò, *Elite Capture*.

73. D'Angelo, *White Fragility*; Kendi, *How to Be an Antiracist*.

of bureaucracy with a sufficient degree of oversight and a great deal of wishful thinking, and on the other hand, to provoke a backlash that made it difficult to discuss the genuine issues raised by the Floyd murder without being effectively shouted down for being "woke" or "playing identity politics." Multiple states passed laws cracking down on the machinery of DEI at state universities, while more and more progressive discourse was simply dismissed for trafficking in "wokeness." The terms themselves became meaningless imprecations that allowed for their dismissal as mere expressions of "identity politics."[74]

But that disingenuousness obscures the substance of what identity politics actually signifies. Critics of the term engage in argument by anecdote to suggest that any of the issues raised under the identity politics rubric lack legitimacy, but the conversation is far more complex than either the institutional supporters of diversity initiatives or critics of identity politics care to acknowledge.[75] As Yascha Mounk argues, the discourse around identity politics "is the product of a rich set of intellectual influences, including postmodernism, post colonialism, and critical race theory" which "can be pressed into the service of diverse political causes from a radical rejection of capitalism to a tacit alliance with corporate America."[76]

Mounk offers up the phrase "identity synthesis" to describe the broad set of concepts that go into making up the various ways in which identity is addressed in the public sphere, a "body of ideas that draws on a broad variety of intellectual traditions and is centrally concerned

74. A similar tactic was used to attack the field of Critical Race Theory, which has become, in the right-wing imaginary, a blanket term for academic discourse that recognizes the history and continuing existence of racism in the United States. This, it apparently needs to be said, is not at all what Critical Race Theory entails. However, the strategy was clearly and unabashedly articulated by Manhattan Institute Fellow Christopher Rufo on Twitter, writing: "The goal is to have the public read something crazy in the newspaper and immediately think 'critical race theory.' We have decodified the term and will recodify it to annex the entire range of cultural constructions that are unpopular with Americans." He continued in a subsequent tweet: "We have successfully frozen their brand—'critical race theory'—into the public conversation and are steadily driving up negative perceptions. We will eventually turn it toxic, as we put all of the various cultural insanities under that brand category." For his trouble, Rufo was made a Trustee at New College in Florida.

75. As Adrian Daub remarks wryly: "Something that just happens to irritate you—talk of gender identity, debates about dreadlocks, trigger warnings, DEI (diversity, equity, and inclusion) programs—conveniently also turns out to be a threat to Western culture" (*Cancel Culture Panic*, 8).

76. Mounk, *Identity Trap*, 9.

with the role that identity categories like race, gender, and sexual orientation play in the world."[77] Mounk is critical of many of the ways in which that identity synthesis is expressed on the level of policy while also recognizing that there is a serious set of theoretical concepts and empirical observations that ground its critique. He notes the reality that these issues of race, class, gender, and culture grow out of real conditions of marginalization and oppression, while also arguing that an excessive concern for the particular ways in which those forms of oppression have been enforced against particular groups prevents an acknowledgment of the universal obligations of justice and fairness that ground the legitimate desire to overcome social disparities.

Yet, the term "identity politics" is typically weaponized only against those on the left. To the extent that its critics recognize right-wing forms of identity politics at all, it is only in passing, *en route* to a condemnation of the perceived excesses of diversity programs designed and intended to open up a wider space in public discourse for those who have been pushed to the margins. One thinks of John Roberts, Chief Justice of the Supreme Court, whose insights on the question of racial equality barely rose to the level of a high school freshman, arguing, "the way to stop discrimination on the basis of race is to stop discriminating on the basis of race."[78] As though such blatant question-begging provided any solution to the underlying problems diversity policies are intended to address.

Yet, even taking into account the potential for excesses in movements intended to open up those areas of society closed by discrimination, forms of right-wing identity politics, which perhaps we can distinguish by calling "identitarian," are far more dangerous to the aspirations of equality and democracy than their liberal analogs, and indeed, identitarian politics are much older and more pernicious than the forms of identity politics that have come under such recent scrutiny. It was not excessive concern for diversity and inclusion that led to the transatlantic slave trade, the Jim Crow era in the South, or redlining in urban neighborhoods.

This is not to suggest that there are no grounds to criticize the current approaches to DEI in the institutional context. In addition to serving largely to support and justify the institutional status quo, one can see how efforts like D'Angelo's to psychologize racism serve to make it seem as

77. Mounk, *Identity Trap*, 9.

78. *Parents Involved in Community Schools v. Seattle School Dist. No. 1*. 551 U.S. 701 (2007), 748.

though the issues are primarily therapeutic, rather than structural. Attempts to reduce the discourse on racial discrimination to simple formulas, as in Kendi's insistence that the only two relevant categories in the discourse on race are "racist" and "anti-racist," do not serve to illuminate either the structural problems or their potential solutions. Both of these approaches have been co-opted by the forms of "elite capture" that Táíwò identifies.[79] Yet, as he argues, "In reality, we may not be able to entirely eliminate elite capture from the world."[80] It is a feature of the structures that engage in the kind of cooptation he critiques to preserve themselves by incorporating their critics into that structure.

But, even faced with the (arguable) excesses of identity politics, the risk is minor compared to the forms of identitarian politics that have emerged on the contemporary right—forms of white nationalism and ethnic chauvinism that desire, not only to roll back the gains made on matters of racial and gender equality over the last fifty years, but to reassert white male dominance and hegemony under the banner of authoritarian movements that desire to undermine democracy itself. Once again it is worthwhile to invoke the words of Joe Sobran: "Now that democracy has overthrown communism, we can turn to the problem of how to overthrow democracy."[81]

In the contemporary context, resurgent forms of ethno-nationalism threaten to push universal claims of human dignity, inclusion, and universality to the margins in the name of narrowly conceived forms of particularity. It is important to take those particular claims seriously as a dimension of identity, yet at the same time, it must be possible to make distinctions between understandings of national identity that work within the broader claims of human dignity, and those that do not.

NATIONALISM AND COSMOPOLITANISM

Nationalism is a fraught category in the discussion of identity. Earlier, I analyzed nationalism largely in the context of contemporary forms of ethno-nationalism, and the role of Christian nationalism, specifically

79. It should be noted, however, that this does not imply that Táíwò and Kendi are opposed to one another's projects. Kendi offered a positive review of Táíwò's book, writing that it "acutely reminds us that building power globally means we think and build outside of our internal confines" (back cover).

80. Táíwò, *Elite Capture*, 11.

81. Ganz, *When the Clock Broke*, 79.

in the United States. The "neo-nationalist" projects, if we can call them such, offer considerable grounds for skepticism about the prospects for any form of inclusive multiculturalism. Yet in the wider sense it is a more complex concept than its contemporary expressions might lead one to believe.

The general concept of nationalism can be understood in two possible ways. The first understands nationalism as grounded in citizenship. This "civic" form of nationalism conceives of national identity as connected to a shared set of principles and norms and can be connected to the more "aspirational" conception of the American mythos discussed in chapter 1. The other form of nationalism, corresponding to the more pathological "ethno-nationalist" model described earlier, grounds conceptions of nation in particular cultural, ethnic, or racial identities. It is only possible to belong to the nation, in this understanding, if you possess the requisite characteristics, regardless of one's acceptance of a set of civic ideals and principles.

Contemporary arguments about immigration, in the United States as well as Europe, center on this distinction: does participation in civic life and the adoption of national identity rest on one's values, or one's blood; one's acceptance of a certain civic compact, or one's association with a specific cultural or ethnic heritage? At the height of the Syrian civil war, as refugees attempted to flee to safety in Europe, much of the backlash was rooted in the idea that the refugees were a quintessentially alien Other. As Arab and mostly Muslim, they were seen as lacking essential characteristics to participate in European society by those who attempted to exclude them. Part of this was rooted in Islamophobia, but it was at least equally based on the assumption that, as Arabs, Syrians were not capable of becoming "truly European."

A similar dynamic is at play in American immigration debates. In spite of the oft-repeated claim that the United States is a "nation of immigrants," arguments surrounding immigration, usually focusing on migrants from Central and South America, frequently evoke the specter of the alien Other. This is quintessentially embodied in the rhetoric of Donald Trump, for example in his declarations that immigrants (many from what he has referred to in the past as "shithole countries") are "poisoning the blood" of the country.[82] Such language evokes Girard's

82. Gabriel, "Trump Escalates Anti-Immigrant Rhetoric."

scapegoat dynamic in identifying blameworthy outsiders as responsible for contaminating ("poisoning the blood" of) the national corpus.

Earlier I evoked the idea of America as a "melting pot," which was a common metaphor for the United States throughout the twentieth century. The phrase originates with writer Israel Zangwill. As Samuel Goldman puts it: "Zangwill saw America as more than one people entitled to a 'separate and equal station' among 'the powers of the earth.' Instead he understood it as a process of transformation leading to a new human type, designated to redeem the world."[83] Framed in this way, the United States is not merely a place where many identities are melded into a singular American self-understanding, but is rather a heroic-romantic ideal of human aspiration. Its importance "lies less in its sociological accuracy than as a shorthand for a distinctive account of American purpose."[84] It is "God's crucible," yet, as Goldman suggests, it is a "broken crucible."[85] The existence of those excluded from this ideal—Native Americans and the enslaved, particularly—demonstrates that not everyone was invited to participate in the transformation. Furthermore, the presence of "unmeltable ethnics" entering the country via immigration calls into question the entire premise of that myth.[86]

Nationalism writ large, however, need not be a project either of dedifferentiation (the melting of everything into one civic agglomeration) nor of marginalization (isolating the "unmeltables" and subjecting them to the dynamics of scapegoating). Nationalism in the wider sense has positive as well as negative dimensions, and it is only by acknowledging its positive dimensions that we can develop a cogent critique of the way it currently functions, not only in the United States, but in other countries with burgeoning ethno-nationalist movements. As Francis Fukuyama argues, *pace* Europe:

> The region is not threatened by immigrants so much as by the political reaction that immigrants and cultural diversity create. The anti-immigrant, anti-EU demons that have been summoned

83. Goldman, *After Nationalism*, 40.

84. Goldman, *After Nationalism*, 42.

85. Goldman, *After Nationalism*, 40.

86. Novak, *Unmeltable Ethnics*. Novak, of course, was later to affiliate with the rising "theocon" movement associated with *First Things* in the 1990s. At this stage, his thesis was simply to question the "melting pot" assumptions of Zangwill and others. Though in the second edition, written after his theocon turn, he does sharply critique the place of multiculturalism in the discourse of American pluralism, perhaps having found a way to become meltable after all.

> are often deeply illiberal and could undermine the open political order on which the region's prosperity has been based. Dealing with this backlash will depend not on a rejection of identity itself, but on the deliberate shaping of national identities in ways that promote a sense of democratic and open community.[87]

Viktor Orbán, the leader of Hungary, which Fukuyama specifically names as creating "deliberate barriers to the assimilation of immigrants" has openly embraced the moniker of "illiberal democracy" to describe his vision of the country, a vision that has been adopted by the National Conservative movement in the United States.[88]

Fukuyama argues that the alternative to ethno-nationalism is not the abandonment of national identity altogether, but the reassertion of those forms of national identity grounded in universal human dignity and civil equality (*isothymia*) rather than ethnicity. Furthermore, conceptions of national identity are crucial to resistance, at times, to the expansion of regimes dedicated to the elimination of competing identities or the deprivation of human dignity and democratic aspirations.[89]

In the contemporary context, it's hard to argue, for example, that Ukrainian nationalism, in opposition to Russian aggression, is not a positive thing. In the nineteenth century, nationalisms of various kinds worked hand in glove with movements for liberalization and democracy throughout Europe. Those forms of nationalism recognized that there was something of significance in viewing one's identity in cultural and geographic terms in opposition to the arbitrary claims of emperors and kings, while the American "melting pot" mythos sought to ground national identity not simply in cultural or geographical terms but on the basis of adherence to a particular narrative and accompanying set of norms.

As noted in chapter 1, that American mythos always existed alongside one that was grounded, more or less explicitly, in ethno-nationalist (or at least crypto-ethno-nationalist) terms, often subordinating the more inclusive norms to an emphasis on white and Christian forms of

87. Fukuyama, *Identity*, 153.

88. See, for example, Chamberlain et al., "National Conservatism," which sees itself as opposed to "universalist ideologies now seeking to impose a homogenizing, locality-destroying imperium over the entire globe" (para. 3).

89. Yoram Hazony intensifies Fukuyama's arguments and makes the (highly dubious) case that the desire to transcend ethnic and national categories in the name of cosmopolitan values is actually an invitation to greater hatred and hostility among and between different tribal affiliations, rather than a means of seeking to overcome the conditions that cause that hatred. See Hazony, *Virtue of Nationalism*.

identity, excluding almost by definition blacks and Native Americans from the equation, and ultimately including white ethnics—e.g., Irish and Italians—only begrudgingly.[90] Over the past decade, that ethno-nationalist vision has been in ascendance, not only in the United States, but globally. The more inclusivist values that were initially associated with certain forms of nationalism diverged early into forms of socialism and anti-colonialism, as national aspirations became increasingly connected with the emergence of racial "science" in the nineteenth century.

Ultimately, the need to identify a relevant "us" in terms of national or ethnic identity was accompanied by the need to identify a relevant "them" to serve as an object of hate and the victim of Girardian violence. The story of the connection between nationalism and fascism in the twentieth century illustrates how that dynamic evolved. That the same dynamic continues to play a role not only in Hungary, but also in Brazil, India, the Philippines, and other countries besides the United States reveals the close connection between nationalism and the scapegoating mechanism.

That is not to say, however, that nationalism cannot play a positive role when there are legitimate national questions at stake. Again, the example of Ukraine in the contemporary context illustrates the point—Ukrainian national identity stands in opposition to forms of Russian nationalism that extend back to the czarist period, and construe the entirety of the former Russian Empire as belonging "properly" to Russia, regardless of local national aspirations. In a similar way, Kurdish and Palestinian nationalisms stand in tension with the artificially constructed national boundaries established throughout the Middle East after the dissolution of the Ottoman Empire.

Indeed, the history of colonialism itself complicates the very notion of what it means to *be* a nation. European colonialism disrupted and often destroyed local conceptions of identity wherever it imposed its presence. Whether through the wholesale destruction of African societies through the transatlantic slave trade and the exploitation of natural resources throughout the continent, through the genocide of Native American populations throughout the Americas, or through the subversion of traditional structures of governance in Asia, European colonial projects did immeasurable damage to conceptions of local identity that

90. See, for example, Ignatiev, *How the Irish Became White*, as well as Roediger, *Working Toward Whiteness*.

might have formed the basis for the organic development of national self-understanding.

At the same time, European colonial presence around the world caused the development of anti-colonial forms of nationalism through which national identity coalesced specifically in opposition to colonial exploitation. Throughout the twentieth century, anti-colonial movements organized around the world to expel governing European authorities. The Indian independence movement, for example, grounded its self-understanding in the recognition that Indian national identity was crucial to successfully expelling the British colonial government. However, competing conceptions of national identity, combined with religious fears, resulted in the creation of two separate countries in the aftermath of independence.

And again, the artificial designation of national borders throughout the Middle East in the aftermath of two world wars resulted in the creation of "nations" which were grounded in neither a shared sense of ethnic nor civic identity, resulting in many of the fractures within national governments throughout the region over the past half century. It is difficult to see how these polities can be considered nations in any meaningful sense of the word, grounded as they are neither in a shared sense of ethnicity nor in a shared sense of civic unity.

Fukuyama defends the principle that national identity need not be exclusive, but can be grounded in liberal values and democratic practices. "Such an inclusive sense of national identity," he argues, "remains critical for the maintenance of a successful modern political order."[91] Such polities offer physical security and stability for economic development and provide a "wide radius of trust" within society that provides the grounds for better governance as well as the establishment of social safety nets.[92] Furthermore, he argues, liberal democracy itself is only possible in the context of a well-defined understanding of national identity:

> A liberal democracy is an implicit contract between citizens and their government, and among the citizens themselves, under which they give up certain rights in order that the government protects other rights that are more basic and important. National identity is built around the legitimacy of this contract;

91. Fukuyama, *Identity*, 128.
92. Fukuyama, *Identity*, 128–30.

> if citizens do not believe they are part of the same polity, the system will not function.[93]

And yet, while one might infer from Fukuyama's argument that national identity may be a *sufficient* condition for the creation of a liberal democratic order, it is not clear that it's a *necessary* condition. There is nothing that connects the criteria he lays out exclusively to *national* identity per se. It is certainly possible to envision a broader, transnational or postnational understanding of identity that can sustain a global liberal democratic order. While Fukuyama may be correct that no such system can function in the absence of a sense of shared citizenship, the idea of citizenship can (and at times has) extended beyond national identity.[94] In a federal context, one's identity as a citizen can straddle multiple understandings of citizenship—for example, one can be an American *and* a Texan, or European *and* Polish, Danish, or Spanish.

The acknowledgment that national identity and liberal democracy arose alongside one another does not require the assumption that they are inseparable from one another. Indeed, the rise of "illiberal democracies" such Orbán's Hungary suggests at a minimum that national identity can thrive quite well in the absence of a set of liberal democratic principles. It is at least worth entertaining the possibility that the disjunction may work as well in the other direction, given the proper circumstances.

Whatever positive benefits nationalism provides in certain particular circumstances, it inescapably draws a line of demarcation between whatever definition of "us" corresponds to the national character, and every potential "them." The lesson that the resurgent forms of exclusionary nationalism offers is that such boundary lines, even in the best of circumstances, create the possibility of dehumanizing the alien others who fall outside those borders. Kwame Anthony Appiah offers an alternative approach in his analysis of cosmopolitanism as a means of understanding human community in an emerging global context.

Appiah begins by noting the way in which culture and society have escaped the boundaries of national identity. Like Fukuyama, Appiah recognizes that the (post-)modern context inevitably pushes us beyond the local communities that constituted human identity for much of history.

93. Fukuyama, *Identity*, 130–31.

94. One can, for example, look at the concept of citizenship in ancient Rome, in which the nature of citizenship extended beyond the territorial boundaries of Rome to include members of different *ethne*, who acquired Roman citizenship through a variety of means. See Sherwin-White, *Roman Citizenship*.

As he notes, during most of human existence on earth, "we were born into small societies of a few score people, bands of hunters and gatherers, and would see, on a typical day, only people we had known for most of our lives."[95] Now, however, as the subtitle of his book states, we live in "a world of strangers." And yet, our actions, and the actions of our representatives, affect people and places we will never see:

> Only in the past couple of centuries, as every human community has gradually been drawn into a single web of trade and a global network of information, have we come to a point where each of us can realistically imagine contacting any other of our six billion conspecifics and sending that person something worth having: A radio, an antibiotic, a good idea. Unfortunately, we could also send, through negligence as easily as malice, things that will cause harm: A virus, an airborne pollutant, a bad idea.[96]

As these increasingly porous borders among peoples carry artifacts, for both good and ill, among different nations and cultures, existing institutions and structures proved inadequate to deal with their effects. National boundaries break down in the face of the economic, technological, and social dynamics of a global set of relationships. Yet, Appiah argues, "globalization" as a term does not quite capture the challenge this represents, nor does "multiculturalism." What "cosmopolitanism" offers as a term that these others do not is an ancient philosophical and moral pedigree, signaling, Appiah argues, "a rejection of the conventional view that every civilized person belonged to a community among communities."[97] Instead, the cosmopolitan seeks community, not with the *polis*, the local political community, but the *kosmos*—not merely humanity writ large, the world, but the universe itself.[98]

This cosmopolitan vantage point, Appiah argues, unifies Cynic and Stoic philosophers on the one hand with the earliest Christians on the other. As he notes "It is profoundly ironic that, though Marcus Aurelius sought to suppress the new Christian sect, his extraordinarily personal *Meditations* . . . attracted Christian readers for nearly two millennia."[99] In the words of Christoph Weiland, "Cosmopolitans . . . regard all the

95. Appiah, *Cosmopolitanism*, xi.
96. Appiah, *Cosmopolitanism*, xii.
97. Appiah, *Cosmopolitanism*, xiv.
98. Appiah, *Cosmopolitanism*, xiv.
99. Appiah, *Cosmopolitanism*, xiv.

peoples of the earth as so many branches of a single family, and the universe as a state, of which they, with innumerable other rational beings, are citizens, promoting together under the general laws of nature the perfection of the whole, while each in his own fashion is busy about his own well-being."[100]

Which is not to suggest that cosmopolitanism is a flawless alternative to either of these other ways of describing the encroaching global reality in which we dwell or the resurgent forms of nationalism that have grown in response. Appiah notes the way in which it can convey an impression of effete superiority, of "a Comme des Garçons-clad sophisticate with a platinum frequent-flyer card, regarding, with kindly condescension, a ruddy-faced farmer in workman's overalls."[101] Beyond this, however, is the criticism that cosmopolitanism encourages the love of humankind at the expense of expressing love toward any actual human beings.[102] Appiah critically notes the perspective of those who have "urged that the boundaries of nations are morally irrelevant—accidents of history with no rightful claim on our conscience."[103]

Nevertheless, given the alternatives, Appiah argues that as a term cosmopolitanism offers a better account of universal human responsibility on the ground that "the one thought that cosmopolitans share is that no local loyalty can ever justify forgetting that each human being has responsibilities to every other."[104] He argues for a "partial cosmopolitanism," which recognizes the role that our local loyalties and identities play in defining who we are, while at the same time possessing a horizon that extends, as the name implies, to the entire cosmos—recognizing that we do not only have obligations to clan and kin, but do in fact have moral obligations to strangers (and, to extend the cosmopolitan vision even farther, perhaps even to our enemies).

Appiah argues that the sort of de-contextualized "ruthless" cosmopolitanism embodied by the clichés of platinum card elites and self-absorbed misanthropes lacks necessary connections to *history*, *place*, and

100. Appiah, *Cosmopolitanism*, xv.

101. Appiah, *Cosmopolitanism*, xiii.

102. Appiah, *Cosmopolitanism*, xvi.

103. Appiah, *Cosmopolitanism*, xvi. At the same time, one can certainly criticize nationalism as fundamentally incoherent on the same grounds of George Bernard Shaw, who stated, "Patriotism is, fundamentally, your conviction that this country is superior to all others because you were born in it" (Shaw, "Music in London").

104. Appiah, *Cosmopolitanism*, xvi.

people that give substance to the milieu in which human beings pursue their individual projects of self-development. He refers to this alternative conception as "rooted cosmopolitanism":

> A form of cosmopolitanism worth pursuing need not reflexively celebrate human difference; but it cannot be indifferent to the challenge of engaging with it. So, on the one hand, we should distinguish this project from the diversitarianism of the game warden, who ticks off the species in the park, counting each further one a contribution to his assets. On the other hand, we should distinguish it from simple universalism. You wouldn't be a cosmopolitan—or anyway, you wouldn't share in what was distinctively valuable in cosmopolitanism—if you were a humanitarian who (to invert Marx's slogan) sought to change the world but not to understand it. A tenable cosmopolitanism, in the first instance, must take seriously the value of human life, and the value of particular human lives, the lives people have made for themselves, within the communities that help lend significance to those lives. This prescription captures the challenge. A cosmopolitanism with prospects must reconcile a kind of universalism with the legitimacy of at least some forms of partiality.[105]

Thus, a rooted form of cosmopolitanism recognizes the value of both humanity and particular humans, and connects our attachment to particular humans to the larger goal of creating a society suitable for all human beings.

The challenge as Appiah describes it is in determining the boundaries between what we owe those with whom we have particular relationships and what we owe to humanity as a whole. It is one thing to say that I have moral duties to persons *qua* persons, it is another thing to say that those duties necessarily trump my obligations to family and friends. Moral obligation can often seem hopelessly abstract in the context of the responsibilities we feel toward those with whom we have identity-forming relationships.

Nationalism relies on an account that assumes that our identity as citizens is uniquely identity-forming, although Appiah notes that it is in many ways no less abstract than being a "citizen of the world." It requires no less of a mental leap to identify with the nation than it does to prefer humanity as a whole, and in both cases, the idea that we would prefer

105. Appiah, *Ethics of Identity*, 222–23.

them to the more immediate relations of kin can seem somewhat monstrous, as for example in the case of the Roman consul Titus Manlius Torquatus.

According to Livy, when he was consul, Torquatus's son Silanus was accused of corruption. Torquatus stood in judgment over his son's trial and found him guilty, banishing him, after which Silanus died by suicide. Torquatus refused to attend the funeral.[106] On the one hand, this account suggests that Torquatus acted in an exemplary manner as consul, refusing to allow kinship obligations to interfere with his duty to impartially apply the law. On the other hand, it appears monstrous (at least to modern eyes) that a father should behave so callously toward his son, not only condemning him, knowing that suicide was Silanus's only honorable option, but then also refusing to mourn his death.

This is not to suggest that Torquatus had an obligation to suborn or approve his son's corruption. But his personal intervention in the trial, leading to his son's death, suggests that Torquatus went well beyond the bounds of his duty as consul *precisely in order to make a lethal example of his son*. It is also noteworthy that Torquatus's other son, also named Titus, displayed his father's death mask prominently in his house, as an object lesson to his own son.[107] Of course, the past is a foreign country, and it may be fruitless to pass judgment on Torquatus on the basis of modern moral standards, but the story is illustrative of the uneasy boundaries between the particular and the universal. Is it really the case, or should it be, that the wider, more abstract obligations we have toward the nation as a whole, or toward the cosmos as a whole, negate the particularities of our intimate relations? Appiah makes the case that they neither do, nor should.

The particular bonds that we share as individuals with larger or smaller groups, however defined, are identity-forming aspects of who we are. Whether our identity is grounded in family, tribe, or nation, our *belongingness* to these groups defines us in a way that our abstract humanity does not. To speak as an American, or as someone from a particular heritage, or as the son of my parents and the sibling of my brothers and the father of my children, means something that cannot be merely subsumed

106. Titus Livius, *The History of Rome*, LIV. It is notable that Valerius Maximus tells a different version of events, stating that Torquatus had his son executed directly, rather than inducing him to suicide, and that the crime was not corruption but disobeying orders. (Valerius Maximus, *Facta et Dicta Memorabilia*, 5.8.3.)

107. Valerius Maximus, *Facta et Dicta Memorabilia*, 5.8.3.

into the general qualities of personhood. This, in the end, is what it means to be rooted. And one can see how it can be that these identities can motivate us in a way that cosmopolitan claims of universalism cannot: "Supranational economic organizations [such as the European Union] don't seem to involve the shared memories, the thick narratives, that nations (or families, or religions) do. They don't furnish *identities*. Their sway is purely formal; a matter of contract and treaty. If nobody will *give* his life for these organizations, it might have something to do with the fact that nobody *makes* his life out of them."[108]

Our "thick" relationships with identity-forming groups possess a sway on us that cosmopolitanism cannot match. This, for Appiah, is what it means for us to be "rooted." And it is for this reason that, at least in the present context, nationalisms of various kinds continue to hold an appropriate place in our collective self-conceptions. Again, should one say to a Ukrainian, in the midst of a war of national self-preservation, that nations are an abstract illusion?

What then does it mean to embrace a cosmopolitan vision? For Appiah, it comes down, not to an abandonment of the particularities of kin, tribe, and nation, but rather to a broader perspective on the relations of our particularities to those of others. It is not that the specifics of our rooted self-understandings do not matter, but rather that we are morally compelled to recognize that the rooted self-understandings of others also matter, and that there is not a moral argument to be made that ours is inherently superior simply by virtue of being ours. As Appiah notes, cosmopolitanism is a task more than it is an ideology, a project of viewing the specifics of our own being from the wider reflective equilibrium of the multitude of identity-forming contexts that others also possess. As he states:

> The cosmopolitanism I want to defend is not the name for a dialogue among static closed cultures, each of which is internally homogenous and different from all others; not a celebration of the beauty of a collection of closed boxes. What I want to make plausible is, instead, a form of universalism that is sensitive to the ways in which historical context may shape the significance of a practice. At the same time, I want to elaborate on the notion that we don't often need a robust theoretical agreement in order to secure shared practices.[109]

108. Appiah, *Ethics of Identity*, 243. Italics in original.

109. Appiah, *Ethics of Identity*, 256.

The "thin" agreements that bind together a cosmopolitan commitment to institutions that extend beyond the identity-forming contexts of tribe and nation need not, and probably cannot, negate the "thick" bonds of our specific cultural self-understandings. And yet, in acknowledging the fundamentally arbitrary nature of those self-understandings, we can recognize and defend those broader, more abstract cosmopolitan relations that push our sense of obligation beyond the particular communities in which we are rooted.

THEOLOGY AND ROOTED COSMOPOLITANISM

In the final analysis, the contradictions of identity we have been examining throughout this chapter cannot be resolved by appeals to the moral or cultural interplay between universal and particular, or thick and thin conceptions of our collective obligations. What might be revealed by restricting the analysis to these levels is how intractable the problem may ultimately be. The issues of community and society, or solidarity within or beyond our national self-conceptions in the end turn back upon themselves. They are never permanently resolved, but merely deferred to the next moment of social crisis, only to reemerge in the form of new appeals to the particularity of our ethnic or national affiliations.

A rooted cosmopolitanism of the kind that Appiah endorses may indeed be the pragmatically best option available for resolving the contradictions on the level of politics, though again, the tendency to retrench into more narrowly defined conceptions of identity in moments of social, economic, or political emergency suggest that it may not be possible to create a lasting solution on the political plane.

It is here that theology becomes an indispensable tool for addressing these questions of identity. I am aware that even at this junction we may be on the horns of an insoluble dilemma, since theology itself is notoriously embedded within thick conceptions of identity. If theology is always grounded within a particular religious tradition, and always an expression of particular faith commitments (even if those commitments address questions of universality), how can it provide an escape from the problems of particularity?

In the chapters to come, I want to face those questions in detail, but for now I will simply admit that this may indeed be another contradiction. However, I do not think that the solution to these contradictions is found in seeking some universal standpoint from which to address these questions. If nothing else, I believe that Appiah has successfully argued that seeking such a standpoint is neither possible nor desirable. If there is no "view from nowhere" from which to resolve these contradictions, then we must begin from where we stand, which in my case is within the Christian theological tradition.

What I hope the remainder of this book will do is provide a way in which those who share that standpoint may engage critically and creatively with the questions raised by these contradictions of identity, not in order to escape their own particularity, but in order to find within that particularity a way of working cooperatively with those grounded in other standpoints to find a common way forward, one that is "rooted" in Appiah's sense, but which finds value in a pluralistic and democratic polity through which many viewpoints may collaborate for the sake of a larger, and more diverse, common good.

4

Christianity and Identity

Personhood, Community, and Responsibility

When I discover who I am, I'll be free.

—Ralph Ellison, *Invisible Man*[1]

IDENTITY, RESPONSIBILITY, AND IMAGO DEI

In the previous chapter, we noted the tension that exists between the particular and the universal in questions of identity. We have also observed the tension between fate (for lack of a better word) and choice. Is identity something that is imposed upon us from without, or something we are free to adopt or discard? Is my individual identity subsumed or overridden by my belonging to a family, an ethnicity, a nation? Can I abandon one identity for another? Are the most important aspects of who I am those things that I share with others, or those things that are unique to me?

In 1944, Dietrich Bonhoeffer wrote about this struggle of self-identity from his cell in Tegel prison. He expressed the struggle to discern who he truly was from the way that he was perceived by others. "Who Am I?" He writes:

1. Ellison, *Invisible Man*, 239.

They often tell me
I would step from my cell's confinement
calmly, cheerfully, firmly,
like a squire from his country-house.
Who am I? They often tell me
I would talk to my warders
freely and friendly and clearly,
as though it were mine to command.
Who am I? They also tell me
I would bear the days of misfortune
equably, smilingly, proudly,
like one accustomed to win.[2]

As he reflects on the way that others see him, the way that they define who he is, Bonhoeffer is aware of the gap between the way that he portrays himself—calm, friendly, proud, even in the midst of his imprisonment, someone who appears to be in charge even though he is under guard—and the way in which he perceives himself:

Am I then really all that which other men tell of?
Or am I only what I know of myself,
restless and longing and sick, like a bird in a cage,
struggling for breath, as though hands were compressing my throat,
yearning for colours, for flowers, for the voices of birds,
thirsting for words of kindness, for neighbourliness,
trembling with anger at despotism and petty humiliation,
tossing in expectation of great events,
powerlessly trembling for friends at an infinite distance,
weary and empty at praying, at thinking, at making,
faint, and ready to say farewell to it all?[3]

Bonhoeffer recognizes the contradiction between his inner self-perception and how others see him: "restless and longing and sick, like a bird in a cage." Rather than calm, he is angry; instead of proud, he is powerless. He asks which of these people he really is, or whether he is both, alternating hypocritically between the one and the other, "a contemptible woebegone weakling." Yet, in the end, he recognizes the fundamental truth of his identity is found not in how he is perceived by others, or even how he sees himself: "Whoever I am, thou knowest, O God, I am thine."[4]

2. Bonhoeffer, *Letters and Papers from Prison*, 347–48.
3. Bonhoeffer, *Letters and Papers from Prison*, 347–48.
4. Bonhoeffer, *Letters and Papers from Prison*, 347–48.

In this poem Bonhoeffer encapsulates the contradictions of identity, the way in which the very idea pulls us in different directions. And yet, for Bonhoeffer, they are less contradictions than paradoxes—he is both what others perceive him to be and how he experiences himself internally. However, those paradoxes are not eternally unresolved, but find their resolution within the being of God. It is God who defines our identity because our very nature is grounded in who God is. This is what it means to be *imago Dei*, in the image of God.

Elsewhere Bonhoeffer connects the idea of the *imago Dei* with the ethical responsibility we have for one another. The image of God within us is, as he writes, a "gift," which is given to us by God.[5] We have our origin in the divine being; it is when, he argues, we seek to define ourselves according to our own possibilities that we fall away from that origin into the realm of the ethical. As strange as it may sound, Bonhoeffer argues that it is precisely, as Genesis has it, our "knowledge of good and evil," that is the surest sign of estrangement from God:

> In knowing about good and evil, human beings understand themselves not within the reality of being defined by the origin, but from their own possibilities, namely, to be either good or evil. They now know themselves beside and outside of God, which means they now know nothing but themselves, and God not at all. For they can only know God by knowing God alone. The knowledge of good and evil is thus disunion with God. Human beings can know about good and evil only in opposition to God.[6]

Yet, we live in a world where that estrangement is unavoidable. It is an element of the "disintegration of the world" of which we are a part, a world created by God.[7]

This does not imply, however, that ethical judgment and discernment are inescapable elements of our estrangement. Rather "just as there is a false human activity that is itself a judging, so now there is also, surprisingly enough, a judging that is a genuine human activity, that is, a 'judging' that springs from the accomplished unity with the origin, with Jesus Christ."[8] Bonhoeffer continues:

5. Bonhoeffer, *Ethics*, 300–301.
6. Bonhoeffer, *Ethics*, 300.
7. Bonhoeffer, *Ethics*, 299.
8. Bonhoeffer, *Ethics*, 316.

> Just as the judgement of Jesus Christ consisted in his coming not to judge but to save—"and *this* is the judgment, that the light has come into the world" (John 3:19; cf verse 17, 18)—so will those reconciled with God and with human beings in Christ judge all things by not judging, and know all things by not knowing good and evil. Their judgment will consist in a Christian way of helping others put things right, lifting them up, guiding them onto the right path, admonishing and comforting them. . . . It will be a judgment of reconciliation and not of disunion, a judgment by not judging, judgment as an activity of reconciliation.[9]

Once again, Bonhoeffer expresses the paradoxical condition of Christian life—to be within the realm of the ethical, but not bound by the forms of judgment that are expressed within ethics; judging and discerning, not from the condition of estrangement, but from the condition of salvation.

What this means in the context of Bonhoeffer's larger project is that Christian moral action is defined by the idea of *responsibility*. Bonhoeffer's understanding of responsibility is grounded in his experiences in the anti-Nazi resistance in Germany. As part of the underground movement to overthrow (and eventually to assassinate) Hitler, Bonhoeffer was forced to grapple with the question of what it meant to engage in ethically necessary actions that violated what he took to be his moral obligations as a Christian. Once again, he dwells within the paradox: "those who act responsibly become guilty without sin; and only those whose conscience is free can bear responsibility."[10] To take on guilt out of a responsibility for one's neighbor is to freely choose to act in the knowledge that our identity is rooted, not in our acts, but in God's grace: "They do so not out of a sacrilegious and reckless belief in their own power, but in the knowledge of being forced into this freedom and their own dependence on grace in its exercise. Those who act out of free responsibility are justified before others by dire necessity; before themselves they are acquitted by their conscience, but before God they hope only for grace."[11]

The connection between our identity within the Being of God and our responsibility, even in the midst of guilt, is crucial for understanding the moral claims made upon us by the identity claims we carry (whether chosen or imposed). To claim or be claimed by an identity entails the responsibilities that come along with that identity in the context of the

9. Bonhoeffer, *Ethics*, 316.

10. Bonhoeffer, *Ethics*, 282.

11. Bonhoeffer, *Ethics*, 282–83.

social and material relations of the society to which we belong. We are thrown, as it were, into those relations, precisely because we are created in the image of God as social and communal creatures. Even within the context of self-chosen identity claims, we are not free from the context in which those claims are made. But as a result we are also thrown into the ambiguity of those relations. To be responsible means to carry the burden of our own decisions, including the forms of identity that we chose for ourselves.

Yet, Bonhoeffer understood that responsibility only takes on moral gravity in the context of our relationship with God. We cannot know with certainty whether the identity we have chosen, or one that is thrust upon us and we have accepted, is the "right" one. In Bonhoeffer's case, he was clear that, even in choosing to side with the victims, those who are crushed "beneath the wheel" of oppression,[12] he was not granted the certainty of knowing whether or not his acts were morally correct, let alone pure in the sight of God. He was placed into a position of acting on behalf of those under threat of violence, and therefore had to choose without certainty. In this respect, he reflects the condition described by Jean Paul Sartre, in which there is no absolute standpoint, not even that of God, which can assure us with complete certainty of our own rectitude.[13] Faith in God is not faith in God's approval of our actions, but in God's grace in the face of our failures. What Bonhoeffer understood was that, regardless of the ambiguities of our identities or our actions, we belong ultimately to God.

If this is the case, then the questions of universality and particularity as they relate to identity are ultimately grounded in our understanding of the God-human relationship. To speak of a "human nature" in any sense is to make a universal claim—to be human is to be created in the image of God, in which case there is no distinction to be drawn along the lines of nation, ethnicity, gender, or any other category of particularity. We are,

12. Bonhoeffer, "Church and the Jewish Question," 374.

13. Sartre, *Existentialism and Human Emotions*, 51. "Existentialism isn't so atheistic that it wears itself out showing that God doesn't exist. Rather, it declares that even if God did exist, that would change nothing. There you've got our point of view. Not that we believe that God exists, but we think that the problem of His existence is not the issue. In this sense existentialism is optimistic, a doctrine of action, and it is plain dishonesty for Christians to make no distinction between their own despair and ours and then to call us despairing." Elsewhere in the text Sartre tells of a Jesuit he met during the war, who chose the order after a series of misfortunes, viewing these as signs that God was leading him to the priesthood. "He saw the hand of God in all this, and so he entered the order. Who can help seeing that he alone decided what the sign meant?" (28–29).

individually and collectively, bound together within the unity of God's being (a unity which, as we will discuss, is itself irreducibly pluralistic). In this sense, the claim that any particular conception of identity has on us is unavoidably relative—nation or ethnicity can never be *absolute* standards of judgment with regard to ourselves or others.

That said, the burden of responsibility that we accept takes place *within* particular contexts and relationships, which again are often chosen for us. For Bonhoeffer, that meant grappling with the reality of his identity as a German under Nazism. As he was well aware when he made the choice to return to Germany and participate in the resistance against Hitler rather than remain safely in New York, he could divest himself neither of his self-understanding as, nor ignore the burden of, being German. For him, that meant taking an active role in the anti-Nazi resistance within Germany. As he wrote: "I shall have no right to participate in the reconstruction of Christian life in Germany after the war if I do not share the trials of this time with my people."[14]

This was not the only legitimate option open to him. Other German expatriates, such as Paul Tillich, took a different path. Tillich chose to resist the Nazis by broadcasting anti-Nazi speeches into Germany.[15] But he was no less aware of his German identity, or of his responsibility to participate in the anti-Nazi resistance than Bonhoeffer was.[16]

On the other hand James Cone, writing from the perspective of black theology, expressed skepticism toward universal claims grounded in the idea of the image of God: "black theology is suspicious of those who appeal to a universal, ideal humanity. Oppressors are ardent lovers of humanity. They can love all persons in general, even black persons, because intellectually they can put blacks in the category called Humanity."[17] For Cone, as for Appiah, the risk of universal claims is precisely that they swallow up the particular, along with the recognition of oppression that takes place within those particularities: "God did not become a universal human being but an oppressed Jew, thereby disclosing to us that both

14. Bethge, *Dietrich Bonhoeffer*, 665.

15. Tillich, *Against the Third Reich*.

16. Tillich, *Against the Third Reich*, 6.

17. Cone, *Black Theology of Liberation*, 85. In language that again echoes the argument made by Appiah, Cone quotes Dostoevsky: "I love humanity, but I wonder at myself. The more I love humanity in general, the less I love man in particular."

human nature and divine nature are inseparable from oppression and liberation."[18]

For Cone, "Jesus is not a human being for all persons; he is a human being for oppressed persons, whose identity is made known in and through their liberation."[19] At the same time, liberation is itself dialectical—liberation from being oppressed must also mean liberation from being oppressor. It entails a reconfiguration of the very nature of human relationality within society.[20] What Hegel's master-slave dialectic correctly understood was that the final stage is the mutual recognition between oppressor and oppressed that frees both of them from entrapment within that relationship.

Ultimately though, this requires a transition from the discussion of the *imago Dei* as an abstract concept to an understanding of how it is necessarily grounded within human particularity. As Cone notes, Christian identity is based, not simply within an idea of the universal human, but within the life and history of a particular human, and the connection between his history and our own.

IMAGO DEI TO *IMAGO CHRISTI*

What the idea of the image of God contributes to Christian theology is the understanding that theology has a universal horizon, encompassing humanity as a whole. However, it is with the idea of the *imago Christi* that Christian theology proper begins. Moving from the abstract and general to the specific, historical, and particular, it grounds the theological understanding of identity within the experience and context of Jesus

18. Cone, *Black Theology of Liberation*, 85.

19. Cone, *Black Theology of Liberation*, 85–86.

20. This is a point that Jürgen Moltmann makes in *The Spirit of Life*. "God himself is the victim of the violent. God himself suffers the wrong they do. And God will judge according to what he has experienced in the poor and in all vulnerable creatures. God, that is to say, creates justice for the people who have been deprived of it, and for those without any rights, he does so through his *solidarity* with them" (129–30, italics in original). At the same time: "On the cross of Christ this love is there for the others, for the sinners—the recalcitrant—enemies. . . . So how does this atonement reach the people who commit injustice and violence? It reaches them out of the compassion of the Father, through the vicariously suffered God-forsakenness of the Son, and in the exonerating power of the Holy Spirit. It is a single movement of love, welling up out of the Father's pain, manifested in the Son's sufferings, and experienced in the Spirit of life. In this way God becomes *the God of the godless*. His righteousness and justice justifies the unrighteous and the unjust" (137, italics in original).

of Nazareth. This means, on the one hand, that God's relationship with humanity is not one that only exists in the heavens and above the fray, but one that takes place in the flesh and blood history of the person Jesus, who existed in a specific time and place, with its own specific social and political context to which Jesus, as a human being, was subject and of which he was the victim. It also means, on the other hand, that our own flesh and blood, our own time and place, and our own specific social and political contexts are bound up in what God undertook in the life and history of Jesus. His history does not bound his relevance, but rather allows us to understand that God's involvement in history extends, through Jesus, to our own context.

As God identifies with Jesus and Jesus identifies with humankind, so our identities are taken up into the identity of God. But the reverse action also takes place, as our identities are taken up into the identity of God, God identifies with us in our own particularity through the particularity of Jesus Christ—the particularity of our struggles, our suffering, our joy, our fellowship, and the totality of the lives we live in our own particular time and place. Jürgen Moltmann places this dynamic within the Trinitarian life of God:

> The Trinity . . . means the history of God, which in human terms is the history of love and liberation. The Trinity, understood as an event for history, therefore presses towards eschatological consummation, so that the "Trinity may be all in all," or put more simply, so that "love may be all in all," so that life may triumph over death and righteousness over the hells of the negative and of all fore . . . God is, God is in us, God suffers in us, where love suffers, we participate in the trinitarian process of God's history. Just was we participate actively and passively in the suffering of God, so too we will participate in the joy of God wherever we love and pray and hope.[21]

Jesus, as the incarnate *Logos*, stands both as God before humanity and humanity before God.[22] Through his humanity he both represents and stands in solidarity with the whole of human experience, and in his divinity he redeems and transforms all human experience within the divine identity. In this sense, the *imago Christi* is the *imago Dei* and vice versa, and as all human beings are created in the divine image, they are

21. Moltmann, *Crucified God*, 255.

22. Barth, *Church Dogmatics IV.1*, 122.

redeemed through Christ's identification with the human condition, even, as Moltmann insists, to the point of abandonment by God:

> When God becomes man in Jesus of Nazareth, he not only enters into the finitude of man, but in his death on the cross also enters into the situation of man's godforsakenness. In Jesus he does not die the natural death of a finite being, but the violent death of the criminal on the cross, the death of complete abandonment by God. The suffering in the passion of Jesus is abandonment, rejection by God, his Father. God does not become a religion, so that man participates in him by corresponding religious thoughts and feelings. God does not become a law, so that man participates in him through obedience to a law. God does not become an ideal, so that man achieves community with him through constant striving. He humbles himself and takes upon himself the eternal death of the godless and the godforsaken, so that all the godless and godforsaken can experience communion with him.[23]

Within Christian life, the motion goes in the other direction, approaching God through being "conformed to the image of his Son" (Rom 8:29). Through God's self-emptying in Christ (Phil 2:7), humanity is made capable of overcoming the condition of God-abandonment and embracing the image of Christ as a reflection of the "divine imperative" governing our moral lives.[24] Thus the calling of Christ is a calling to a new form of life, a new identity, one that is grounded in the covenantal relationship between God and God's people. As J. Kameron Carter writes: "To exist in Christ is to be drawn into such an understanding of identity, into the ecstatic and eschatological identity of Israel's covenantal promises."[25]

To live life *coram deo*—in the presence of God—is to experience a transformation of one's self, a shift within the "inner disposition of the heart," to use Calvin's phrase.[26] In this sense, one becomes more fully the image of God to the degree to which one's heart is reshaped in the image

23. Moltmann, *Crucified God*, 276.

24. Brunner, *Divine Imperative*.

25. Carter, *Race*, 251. As Carter notes, "An understanding of Christ as the Image of God and of all human persons as existing in the Image, who is Christ, cannot bypass or supersede YHWH's promises to Abraham and thus to Israel, for it is from the history of this people's covenantal interactions with God and thus from God's history that God takes up the history of the world. Moreover, they are the people whose identity, in being a covenantal and thus a nonracial identity, is always eschatologically in front of them. It always exceeds them" (250–51).

26. Calvin, *Institutes of the Christian Religion*, 3.3.16.

of Christ, so that, as Paul states "the same mind may be in you that was in Christ Jesus" (Phil 2:5). It is this dialectic of identification—God with Christ, Christ with Humanity, Humanity with Christ, and ultimately with God—that provides the moral foundation for the Christian insistence on the centrality of human dignity. As all are created in the divine image, are redeemed in Christ, and thus recipients of the gift of divine grace, all human beings are both entitled to that basic human dignity as children of God and obligated to honor it as subjects of divine grace.

IDENTITY AND HUMAN DIGNITY

A consistent theme in the discussions of identity we've examined throughout this project has been the desire for the recognition of one's essential human dignity. This struggle is at the heart of Hegel's dialectical method, and represents, in his analysis, the core dynamic of human existence—the desire for, and denial of, one's essential humanity to be honored in the context of our relations with other human beings. This also entails the recognition of relationality as the fundamental characteristic of human being. When we speak of the *imago Dei*, we speak, among other things, of the human relationality that echoes the triune relationality of the divine persons. In Christ, that relationality is extended to humanity through God's embrace of Christ's humanity, and so the struggle for human dignity is itself taken into the divine being. When God identifies with human being in Christ, thus does human dignity become a divine mandate.

Human dignity and identity are thus inescapably intertwined. To be given one's dignity is not done in the abstract, but in one's particularity, within the specific contours of what makes each of us a unique individual self. It is not sufficient to insist that mere respect for human dignity is possible without including the recognition of that personal uniqueness, as the stripping of those particular characteristics of our selves is precisely a denial of our dignity as individuals. As Christ's assumption of human nature was nevertheless the assumption of the particular characteristics of the human person Jesus of Nazareth, so our human dignity in the broader sense cannot be properly honored in the absence of our own particularly.[27]

27. This enters into the early church dispute between Alexandrian and Antiochian understandings of Christology. The Alexandrian *Logos-Anthropos* Christology insisted on the union of Christ with humanity writ large, while the *Logos-prosopon* Christology

Carter argues that it was precisely in severing Christ from his particularity, specifically his Jewishness, that Western Christianity set the stage for the construction of "race" as a vehicle for the establishment of white supremacy:

> Modernity's racial imagination has its genesis in the theological problem of Christianity's quest to sever itself from its Jewish roots. This severance was carried out in two distinct but integrated steps. First, Jews were cast as a race group in contrast to Western Christians, who with the important assistance of the discourses of Christian theology and philosophy, were also subtly and simultaneously cast as a race group. . . . Second, having racialized Jews as a people of the Orient and thus Judaism as a "religion" of the East, Jews were then deemed inferior to Christians of the Occident or West. Hence, the racial imagination (the first step) proved as well to be a racist imagination of white supremacy (the second step). Within the gulf enacted between Christianity and the Jews, the *racial* which proves to be a *racist* imagination was forged.[28]

He argues that, in abstracting Jesus from his context, Christianity embedded whiteness within the Western theological imagination as the normative standard by which human being, and thus human dignity, were measured. To move beyond this racist theological imaginary requires a reaffirmation of the particularity of the human person Jesus in the context of his divinity. This entails a reemphasis on his identity as a Jew: "At the genealogical taproot of modern racial reasoning is the process by which Christ was abstracted from Jesus, and thus from his Jewish body, thereby severing Christianity from its Jewish roots."[29] Within the early church, there were countervailing figures who resisted, in diverse ways, the emergence of this abstracted, and thus ultimately white supremacist, account of Jesus's identity—specifically, Carter argues, Irenaeus of Lyon, Gregory of Nyssa, and Maximus the Confessor. Through recovering the theological themes they articulate, it may become possible to reaffirm the

of Antioch emphasized the unity of the Logos with the particular human being Jesus. The Chalcedonian formulation of Christ as "true God and true human" sought to resolve this tension while at the same time maintaining the contributions of each formulation. Christ is truly human *both* in the sense of taking on a general human nature *and* in the sense of being incarnated in the particular life, history, and context of Jesus of Nazareth.

28. Carter, *Race*, 4. Italics in original.

29. Carter, *Race*, 6.

particularity of Christ, and thus overcome the racialization of the Christian theological imaginary.

Carter's emphasis on particularity is crucial to the recovery of an account of human dignity grounded in contextuality. At the same time, it continues to stand in dialectical tension with the universality of Christ's human nature as a resource for the consideration of the foundational role of human dignity in Christian moral thought. In the recognition of Christ's human specificity, Christianity affirms the significance of the specific and determinate identity of each individual, and the dignity of our specific and determinate identities. The recognition of Christ's embodiment of human nature in the more general and abstract sense, however, affirms that *all* conceptions of identity are included within the particular human incarnation of the divine Logos.

What does this emphasis on human dignity actually contribute to the understanding of identity though? In the first place, it offers a broad foundation on which to build an ecumenical discourse on issues of identity. Human dignity is certainly a core concept within Catholic Social Teaching, even as there remain deep disputes about the legitimate boundaries of identity within the Catholic tradition.[30] At the same time, it offers a grounding for the discussion of human rights within the Christian tradition, as articulated and defended by theologians such as Jürgen Moltmann.

Human rights, for Moltmann, are not an abstraction grounded in philosophical principles, but are grounded explicitly within the drama of creation and incarnation as articulated within the Christian story. Human rights are an expression of God's care for the beings created in the divine image and reconciled with God through the life, death, and resurrection of Jesus Christ. Thus the case for human rights is explicitly theological. "We see the theological contribution of the Christian church in the grounding of the fundamental human rights upon God's right to human beings."[31]

30. See, for example, Paul VI, *Dignitatis Humanae*, which offers an interesting contrast to the Christian nationalist and integralist understandings of religious freedom and self-determination discussed in previous chapters.

31. Moltmann, *On Human Dignity*, 15. At the same time, Moltmann is quick to add that "The Christian faith has over and above the different rights and duties of humanity to esteem the one individual dignity of the human being in his or her life with God—without, in so doing, excluding other religious or humanistic conceptions of human rights."

Collectively and individually, human beings have a right to live lives of dignity. What the specific details of such a life of dignity might be is a subject of discussion, but Moltmann understands those rights, however they might be articulated, to "be looked at against the background of the suffering and of the present struggles of individuals, nations, and states."[32] The particular expression of those rights has already been laid out in documents such as the United Nations Declaration of Human Rights and other treaties and legal and political documents.[33] What theology can contribute to the discourse on human rights is precisely in its understanding of how God's claim upon all human life requires that the rights and dignity of all human beings be respected. Those rights, he argues, are fundamental that are directly grounded in the divine claim, and are, on that basis "inalienable and indivisible."[34]

This principle excludes Christian participation in authoritarian or tyrannical forms of government. "Human beings do not exist for the sake of rule; rule, rather, exists for the sake of human beings."[35] Contrary to a Peter Thiel or Curtis Yarvin, democracy is a direct requirement of our divine origin:

> The rulers and the ruled must be recognizable in like manner and in common as being human. This is possible only when there is an equality under the law for all citizens. A constitution (the covenant) must guarantee the fundamental human rights as basic rights of those citizens. It must bind together those who are ruling and those who are ruled. Only on the basis of equality under the law can expression be given to the common human identity of rulers and ruled alike. The human rights and duties implied in the image-of-God concept are honored in history through the constant, open, and incessant process of democratizing the shaping of the people's political will. The control of the exercise of rule through the expiration of powers, the limitation of the mandate to rule to a stipulated period of time, and the extensive self-rule and participation of the people are the historically developed means for honoring the image of God present in human beings.[36]

32. Moltmann, *On Human Dignity*, 20.
33. Moltmann, *On Human Dignity*, 19.
34. Moltmann, *On Human Dignity*, 23.
35. Moltmann, *On Human Dignity*, 23.
36. Moltmann, *On Human Dignity*, 24.

The right to democratic participation in society also entails an obligation to take responsibility for one's participation and an obligation to the community within which one lives. "There is," Moltmann argues, "*no* priority of individual rights over social rights." Though, he immediately adds, "just as conversely there is no priority of social rights over individual rights."[37] The two stand in direct and necessary relation to one another as "the processes of socialization and the individualization of people mutually condition one another."[38] He goes on to add that the identity of human beings as created in the image of God also entails the community of humanity with the whole of creation, including the environment and non-human animals, as well as a community with future generations.

At the same time that the *imago dei* grounds human rights and responsibilities, and connects us to the whole of the divine creation, the incarnation connects us with the messianic mission of Jesus and the way of life associated with that mission. Christian life entails a particularly Christian ethic, and thus a particular understanding of Christian public responsibility:

> If there is no specifically Christian ethic, then the acknowledgement of Christ is itself called into question; for then Jesus' message cannot have been ethically meant, in the sense of making a public ethical claim. It was then either purely religious, and hence non-political; or wholly apocalyptic, and hence without relevance for changes in the world itself; or confined to personal life, and hence without any relation to the public conditions in which personal life is lived. But then can Jesus still be called the messiah in a sense that is in any way relevant? In Israel's history of promise, to which all the gospels are related, the messiah is a public person. His proclamation of the messianic Torah in the messianic era is addressed to the whole people of God and, with this people, to all the peoples of the earth. If Jesus came forward without any messianic claim of this kind, why did the Romans crucify him?[39]

Christian identity is thus both particular and public. It is an identity that is to be enacted in the context of the social setting in which Christians find themselves, and to be understood as grounded fundamentally in the relationship of Christ to the community he founded and the participation

37. Moltmann, *On Human Dignity*, 25. Italics in original.

38. Moltmann, *On Human Dignity*, 26.

39. Moltmann, *Way of Jesus Christ*, 117–18.

of Christians in that community. It cannot be collapsed into a mere general social ethic, but can be understood only in relation to Christ. There is, in this case, no place for Christians to ignore or subvert the Christian commitment to democracy or the recognition of human rights and responsibilities, including the social rights to the fundamental goods of human existence—food, shelter, care, etc.[40]

To claim one's identity as a Christian is thus to accept the moral claim of that identity and the responsibilities encompassed by that moral claim, which includes both a respect for democratic norms and the dignity of all persons. It also entails a recognition that the Christian community has a particular responsibility for those pushed to the margins within a society that does not accept those responsibilities. Christian identity does not confer any special public or political rights, but does require special responsibilities to those who are among the poor, the dispossessed, and the outcast. It requires a journey from the center to the margins, and a solidarity with those who have had their identities stripped from them, an entering into their experience.

IDENTITY AND NONIDENTITY

Christian moral life means entering into an identification with Christ, which in turn means, as noted above, having the same mind in us as was in Jesus. Paul continues in that passage, stating that Christ:

though he existed in the form of God,
did not regard equality with God
as something to be grasped,
but emptied himself,
taking the form of a slave,
assuming human likeness.
And being found in appearance as a human,
he humbled himself
and became obedient to the point of death—
even death on a cross. (Phil 2:6–8)

This idea of "self-emptying," or *kenosis*, describes the process by which Christ abandons his divinity in order to enter into the experience of those

40. The nature of these social goods is well articulated within the Catholic tradition through the United States Catholic Bishops letter *Economic Justice For All*, which offers an extended argument in favor of providing these basic social goods as fundamental obligations of a society toward its participants. (United States Catholic Conference).

who are separated and alienated from God. In the incarnation, Christ takes on identity with humanity so that humanity may identify with him, but in so doing, he at the same time enters into a condition of nonidentity, stripping himself of divinity in order, not simply to express the divine solidarity with humanity, but to stand beside those most alienated from God, one another, and themselves.

The biblical narrative offers an account, on the one hand, of Christ's particular identity within the historical and cultural context of a poor, colonized, subjugated carpenter in first-century Judea. The specificity of that identity grounds the human person Jesus within the condition of oppression and marginalization of those alongside whom and as one of whom he lived. On the other hand, it also describes the movement of the divine Logos from the condition of pure identity (in Hegelian terms) to complete non-identity.

Moltmann powerfully describes this process as an event within the history of God. The cross, as the locus of complete God-abandonment, is the place where Christ experiences the abyss of human despair, and brings that despair into the divine life, giving it its full weight while at the same time overcoming it:

> Only if all disaster, forsakenness by God, absolute death, the infinite curse of damnation and sinking into nothingness is in God himself, is community with this God eternal salvation, infinite joy, indestructible election and divine life. The "bifurcation" in God must contain the whole uproar of history within itself. Men must be able to recognize rejection, the curse and final nothingness in it. The cross stands between the Father and the Son in all the harshness of its forsakenness. If one describes the life of God within the Trinity as the "history of God" (Hegel), this history of God contains within itself the whole abyss of godforsakeness, absolute death, and the non-God.[41]

Christian life, then, is a following of Jesus from the condition of power and identity into the situation of powerlessness and non-identity, to undergo a *kenosis* of our own as we abandon status, privilege, and authority and, like Christ, join those whose own experience is that of disadvantage, death, and godforsakeness. Christian ethics is, in a very real way, an ethics of kenosis.

And yet, the shape of the self-emptying that the Christian life demands remains a question. For those who are already pushed to the

41. Moltmann, *Crucified God*, 246.

social margins, the demand for a kenotic way of life seems redundant, if not callous, while for those located closer to the center of those dynamics, the question of how one can empty oneself in a Christlike way presents its own challenges. This is something James Cone recognized throughout his writing. Whatever else Christian ethics might entail, it requires a proactive engagement with the struggle for human liberation from oppression, which requires an identification with those pushed to the margins. For Cone, the declaration that "God is black" is a recognition of God's liberating power within the community of the oppressed.[42] That power stands in opposition to the understanding of God that identifies divinity with social control and power as wielded within a racist society. To accept the prevailing understanding of God, to accept the dynamics of those racist power structures, is to refuse the kenotic demand within Christian ethics. Elsewhere, Cone writes:

> The basic problem with theological ethics cannot be solved through a debate on the deliberative, prescriptive, and relational motifs of ethical norms. Neither can it be solved through a discussion of the relative merits of the institutional, operational, and intentional motifs in the implementation of ethical decisions, although these issues are important for Christian ethics. Rather, we must unmask this error by analyzing its theological origin. The matter may be put this way: *Theologians of the Christian Church have not interpreted Christian ethics as an act for the liberation of the oppressed because their views of divine revelation were defined by philosophy and other cultural values rather than by the biblical theme of God as the Liberator of the oppressed. . . .* An ethic derived from this God, then must be defined according to the historical struggle of freedom. It cannot be identified with the status quo.[43]

For the oppressed, the rejection of the status quo involves an assertion of their identity as human beings of worth and dignity in a world that insists on their inferior status. For the oppressors, it involves a recognition of that worth and a refusal to accept the presumption that it is they who are at the center of the historical drama, rather than the process of God's unfolding salvation. In either case, however, this rejection of the status quo is a form of self-emptying, as both oppressors and oppressed refuse to accept the account of the world that has been given to them.

42. Cone, *Black Theology of Liberation*, 63.

43. Cone, *God of the Oppressed*, 199–200. Italics in original.

The dynamic of oppressor/oppressed, as Hegel noted, is inescapably reciprocal, as the identity of each is bound up in the reciprocal recognition of the other. As Cone notes: "While it is true that *all* are oppressed (and especially those who rule over others), *only* those whose existence (and thus consciousness) is defined by the liberation of people from social, political, and economic bondage can understand the dialectic of oppression and freedom in the practice of liberation."[44]

Kenosis entails, then, not a self-emptying in the sense of an absolute letting go of power, but rather of letting go of those configurations of power that deny the humanity and dignity of particular human beings in particular conditions of oppression.

In this sense, one's identity, whether imposed or chosen, informs one's relation to systems of power and privilege, and thus one's responsibility within the dynamics of oppressive systems. The kenosis of the oppressor, letting go of the systems and ideologies of oppression, is different from the kenosis of the oppressed, letting go—or more forcefully stated, *resisting*—the condition of being oppressed.

The Christian journey then is one that migrates from center to periphery, from identity to non-identity. This, however, is not an abandonment of identity, but a reconfiguration, as who we are is fashioned in the image of the Christ who emptied himself for the sake of others. It is crucial to recognize that this journey is not the same for everyone, nor is it a stripping away of the particularities of our history or circumstances. Rather, it is a reconstitution of our essential selves in the light of divine grace and within the context of Christ's messianic calling. It is not a journey into anonymity, nor do we become faceless drones absorbed into some larger body. Who we are, created and loved by God, remains in all of our individuality, and what it *means* for us to be who we are is fundamentally changed as we embark on the journey of self-emptying.

44. Cone, *God of the Oppressed*, 148. Italics in original. As Cone notes, concretely this entails the self-emptying by whites of their presumed authority to dictate the grounds on which theology and ethics should be done in a black context. He writes: "White oppressors must be excluded from this black ethical dialogue, because they cannot be trusted. To those whites who continually proclaim their goodwill, despite the long history of racism, the most blacks can say: 'There may be a place for you, but you will have to do what we say, without suggesting that you know what is best for our liberation.' Few if any whites can accept this" (216).

SELFHOOD, IDENTITY, AND THE OTHER

All of which raises the question of what the self is that needs to be emptied in this kenotic journey, and what it means to speak of the "self" in distinction to one's "identity." In one sense, the terms are synonymous. My identity *is* my self, and vice versa. There is an obvious sense in which the terms are interchangeable, but there is another sense in which their meanings are subtly yet meaningfully distinct, in which identity is, as it were, the outer shell of one's selfhood, which goes deeper than the labels and ascriptions which are applied to us, whether by ourselves or others.

At its most fundamental level, the self is that which is made possible within us through our capacity for self-reflection and examination. It arises within us through our capacity for consciousness and our ability to develop and cultivate an inner life that is distinct from our public presentation. The self "maintains a rather constant internal dialogue in which it approves or disapproves its actions, or even itself. . . . The self pities and glorifies itself as well as accuses and excuses itself. . . . The self in one of its aspects is making the self, in another of its aspects, its object of thought."[45] This self-reflexivity of consciousness creates the inner life through which we engage with our own sense of being and orient ourselves toward our lives and the societies to which we belong. It is this self which adopts or rejects the particular features of identity with which it is confronted.

Reinhold Niebuhr, drawing on psychoanalysis and depth psychology, argues that the self in this sense is inescapably dialogical. We dialogue within ourselves, among ourselves, and, ultimately with the transcendent source of value which we identify with God. Who we are in our dialogue with others is often hidden, and in some sense inescapably so. We never fully reveal the whole of ourselves to one another. But at the same time, we do not fully reveal ourselves to ourselves. We may be a mystery to others, but we are no less mysterious to ourselves. The inner dialogue in which we are constantly engaged is a continual process of self-revelation, as we act and think in ways contrary to our own expectations and challenge our own concepts of who we are or should be.

Niebuhr analyzes this process of continual disclosure of the self to itself in terms of the conflict between the conscience and the will within the human person. Conscience and will are, as Niebuhr conceives of

45. Niebuhr, *Self and the Dramas of History*, 6.

them, "two levels of the transcendence of the self over itself."[46] More particularly, the will confronts us with the question of attaining our own desires and impulses, and subordinates our reason to its own purposes. It is in this sense that Hume's dictum that reason "is and ought to be the slave of the passions," is true.[47] We experience ourselves as a collection of drives and impulses that not only do not emerge from our reason, but in fact often operate *contrary* to it.

In this sense what Niebuhr is describing is Schopenhauer's concept of the Will, a "blind, irresistible impulse," without knowledge, but to which our rational selves are subordinated:

> Life, the visible world, the phenomenon, is only the mirror of the will. Therefore life accompanies the will as inseparably as its own shadow accompanies the body; and if will exists, so will life, the world, exist. Life is, therefore, assured to the will to life; as long as we are filled with the will to life, we need have no fear for our existence, even in the presence of death.[48]

For Schopenhauer, the domination of the will was the inescapable fact of human existence which could not be escaped, but only evaded and sublimated, and even then only partially. For Freud, this becomes the pathological root of neurosis, as the Ego becomes trapped between the drives of the Id and internalized authority of the Superego. Niebuhr, on the other hand, sees the conscience as an essential corrective to the domination of the will. It is "any aspect of the self's judging its actions and attitudes in which a sense of obligation in contrast to inclination is expressed."[49] Put differently, conscience is that within us that, reflecting

46. Niebuhr, *Self and the Dramas of History*, 12.

47. Hume, *Treatise of Human Nature*, 415.

48. Schopenhauer, *World as Will and Idea*, 177. For Niebuhr, of course, Schopenhauer was primarily mediated through Freud, in which the Will is reconceptualized in terms of the Id. However, the key conceptual framework is grounded in Schopenhauer's thought.

49. Niebuhr, *Self and the Dramas of History*, 13. Niebuhr tries to draw a distinction between the understanding of conscience he is elaborating and the Freudian Superego by pointing to those whose conscience puts them in conflict with their communities: "The modern martyrs who have given their life to defy communities which sought to make total claims upon the individual have vividly refuted all theories, whither psychological, sociological or anthropological, which sought to reduce the sense of moral obligation to a purely sociological phenomenon. More particularly they refuted the Freudian theory of the 'super-ego' which was no more than the pressure of the community on the 'ego.'" It should be noted that, even if Niebuhr is correct in his analysis of the relationship between the fate of the "modern martyrs" of whom he speaks and

on its drives and desires, recognizes an obligation that transcends or supersedes the demands of the will. It is, in short, the recognition of a transcendent moral principle which we are bound to obey. Thus the connection of the self to its source of transcendent value allows for an escape from the pessimistic accounts of Schopenhauer and Freud.

For Niebuhr, the nature of the self is not defined solely by the reflexivity of self-consciousness. On the contrary, the community in which the self encounters both itself and others is an essential dimension of what it means for us to be morally aware human beings. Yet, as noted, we encounter other human beings as "a mystery which cannot be fully penetrated."[50] At the same time, and again echoing Hegel, we perceive other human beings instrumentally, as objects for our use rather than creatures with their own divinely granted integrity. Within its interpersonal relationships, the self perceives others as "a completion for its incompleteness."[51] We look to others to fulfill that within us that we cannot fulfill for ourselves.[52]

Yet, our relations with others, according to Niebuhr, do not need to be understood purely instrumentally. Rather: "The self can not be truly fulfilled if it is not drawn out of itself into the life of the other."[53] Yet:

> Even a mutual partnership . . . requires something more than calculated mutuality to initiate it and to preserve it. . . . This fact gives social relevance to what would otherwise seem to be a socially irrelevant form of love, defined in the New Testament as *agape*. This dimension of the dialogue between selves clearly transcends all canons of prudence; and reveals how the dialogue is enriched and sustained by viewpoints which are not directly derived from the ordinary level of mutuality.[54]

We encounter other selves as a limitation on our own freedom. Yes, as Charles Taylor notes, "I am a self only in relation to certain interlocutors: in one way in relation to those conversation partners who were essential to my achieving self-definition; in another in relation to those who are

---

the social theories to which he refers, it's far from clear that those theories have been so "vividly refuted" as he seems to believe.

50. Niebuhr, *Self and the Dramas of History*, 30.

51. Niebuhr, *Self and the Dramas of History*, 31.

52. This is at the heart of Aristophanes's speech in Plato's *Symposium*—the idea that the true nature of love is expressed through union with one's "other half." See Plato, *Symposium* (191.a).

53. Niebuhr, *Self and the Dramas of History*, 31.

54. Niebuhr, *Self and the Dramas of History*, 31–32.

now crucial to my continuing grasp of languages of self-understanding—and, of course, these classes may overlap. A self exists only with . . . 'webs of interlocution.'"[55] These webs of interlocution provide the setting through which our self-definition takes place.

For Niebuhr, our participation in these webs need not result in the Hegelian struggle for recognition. While the encounter with another self poses an inescapable mystery "which even the most imaginative love cannot penetrate," we are not bound to seek to subjugate the other to our own power. In some settings, as in a marital context, "each such partnership is a unique and distinctive drama of mutual adjustment which exhibits some unrepeatable elements. It becomes a moral and artistic achievement rather than a scientific one."[56] As selves, we find ourselves perpetually "open" to the reality of other selves, even at a great distance (a reality that social media has, in some ways, both revealed and exploited).

The family is, in a concrete way, the first encounter of the self with the reality of wider community, but it is hardly the last. Familial relationships that successfully form us to be open to the reality of other selves train us to participate in the wider public world to which we belong as citizens and contributors to society. On the other hand, it is entirely possible for those same relationships to curdle and malform our sense of social solidarity. If we learn to turn inward and away from others, or are taught that others exist as threats to be managed or objects to be exploited, or that others truly are an obstacle to our own self-realization, an unjust curtailment of our self-actualization, then we will not learn the skills of public participation that are necessary for the development of a democratic society.

Communities themselves can fail to exercise those skills of public participation, when they collectively turn against the values of democratic participation, or choose to isolate themselves from the risk of contamination by others, and form the identities of their members in such a way that they see the larger social context to which they belong as a hazard to be evaded rather than the setting within which to expand their openness to the reality of other people, ideas, and experiences.

55. Taylor, *Sources of the Self*, 36.

56. Niebuhr, *Self and the Dramas of History*, 33. It is unclear whether Niebuhr is arguing this as applying solely to marital relationships. However, the broader context of his work does entail the idea that, at least on the level of individual relationships, such creative love is possible beyond the setting of marriage.

There is certainly a place for "contrast communities" within any social order. When the church is fulfilling its social vocation, it is always simultaneously a contrast community as well as a training ground for public participation. The distinction is between a community that performs both of these tasks, and one that seeks only separation out of fear of contamination. The so-called "Benedict option" advocated by Rod Dreher may well fall victim to this tendency, along with the "resident aliens" approach of Stanley Hauerwas.[57] This being said, to the extent that the Christian community can become a training ground for morally responsible and engaged public participation, it necessarily contrasts itself with the larger social setting to which it belongs, not in order to separate itself from that setting, but in order to engage it on the ground of that sense of responsibility.

As Niebuhr notes, when communities come into conflict with one another, "the individual tends to become identified with his community so that its pride and prestige become his own. . . . This fact makes the pride of national and racial communities particularly attractive to individuals who suffer from various forms of individual frustration."[58] This is precisely the dynamic that has played out in the movements of reaction that have taken place around the world—in India, Hungary, Brazil, the Philippines, and in the United States. Frustrations associated with the economic and societal transformations that have taken place over the past half-century and more, associated with climate change, technological change, and globalization have contributed to the global rise of right-wing identitarian movements. At the same time, the erosion of traditional cultural and familial patterns associated with more conservative political ideologies have been deployed against progressive reform movements in ways that bolster the forces of reaction. As people see their "pride and prestige" decline in the face of changing mores, or experience resentment over demands that they share pride and prestige with

57. While speaking of these two in the same sentence, I want to make clear that they are not on the same level of sophistication or insight. While both advocate for the idea that the Christian community is and must be separate from the wider social setting in order to remain faithful, Hauerwas's arguments are grounded in a deep theological analysis of the relationship between, and contradictions between, the church and the wider society. Dreher, on the other hand, seems to be grinding a very particular political axe, one that Hauerwas might very well find abhorrent to his own understanding of Christian moral responsibility. See Dreher, *Benedict Option*. See also Hauerwas, *Peaceable Kingdom*.

58. Niebuhr, *Self and the Dramas of History*, 38.

previously marginalized groups, they tend to move toward reactionary politics.

Ultimately though, our self-conception is relativized through our encounter with the ultimate Other, which is to say, God. Our sense of identity is grounded as much in how we understand ourselves to be related to the realm of Ultimate Concern (as Tillich called it) as it is through our internal process of self-reflectivity and confrontation with other finite selves. Even those who deny the existence of God in the classically theistic sense nevertheless are forced to confront the abyss of meaninglessness in a godless world, and its implications for their own finite existence.

Within the Christian narrative, the confrontation with God is one in which our very sense of self is eroded and diminished in the face of God's infinity, as Job experienced when God spoke to him from the whirlwind. As God demands that Job account for himself and his words, God reveals the divine character as one of overwhelming power and majesty, before which human beings vanish into insignificance:

> Then the LORD answered Job out of the whirlwind:
> "Who is this that darkens counsel by words without knowledge?
> Gird up your loins like a man;
> I will question you, and you shall declare to me.
> Where were you when I laid the foundation of the earth?
> Tell me, if you have understanding.
> Who determined its measurements—surely you know!
> Or who stretched the line upon it?
> On what were its bases sunk,
> or who laid its cornerstone
> when the morning stars sang together
> and all the heavenly beings shouted for joy?" (Job 38:1–7)

God continues in this vein for 73 verses. Job, recognizing the overpowering presence of the divine, responds:

> See, I am of small account; what shall I answer you?
> I lay my hand on my mouth.
> I have spoken once, and I will not answer,
> twice but will proceed no further. (Job 40:4–5)

And these are indeed Job's final words. The justice of his case is forgotten in the face of God's presence. And it would seem, on its face that, in silencing Job, God has reasserted an unquestionable divine omnipotence. And yet . . . God does speak to Job; God offers an answer, or at least a response, to Job's case. And while that answer seems to be a demand for silence, God's willingness to confront Job recognizes Job's inherent dignity as a creature before God, and is itself a kind of recognition of the justice of Job's cause. Had Job been complaining unjustly, God might simply have ignored him. But given the obvious rightness of Job's position, God is forced to reply.[59]

Niebuhr argues that the dialogue between humanity and divinity, as understood in the Christian interpretation, "results in the conviction of the self," in the face of the reality of sin:

> [The self] is convicted . . . of its pretension or "sin"; of claiming too much for its finiteness, and for the virtue and wisdom which it achieves in its finiteness. The idea of such an encounter therefore permits the Biblical faiths both to affirm the life of the self in history and to challenge its achievements in any particular instance. . . . The fact that the self is judged for every inclination which affront's God's "majesty" by pride or lust for power is the religious dimension of sin. The prophets are however equally conscious of the social dimension which is the inclination of the self to take advantage of its fellow men. This "injustice" is never speculatively defined, as in Greek philosophy, but rigorously defined by reactions to injustice in particular situations."[60]

Thus on the one hand the dignity of human being as such is affirmed in God's willingness to engage humanity in dialogue. On the other hand, human ego and self-assertion, in seeking to supplant God and place ourselves at the center of the "dramas of history," as Niebuhr would have it, places us in the wrong in our relationship with the divine.

However, there is another dimension to this that needs to be explored in order to grasp the relationship between our sense of self and our relationship to the divine, which is grounded in the divine interrelationship of the Trinity.

59. Carl Jung offers a fascinating analysis of the book of Job from a psychoanalytic perspective in *Answer to Job*. In sum, Jung argues that Job effectively shames God, who has no recourse except to cow Job through the force of his presence, but Job is still ultimately denied justice. It is, as Jung argues, through Christ's incarnation that the justice Job demands is finally granted, not only to him, but to humanity as a whole. It is a transformation, he argues, in the divine–human relationship that is made necessary through God's abuse of humanity in the person of Job.

60. Niebuhr, *Self and the Dramas of History*, 65.

TRINITY, IDENTITY, AND RELATIONALITY

A crucial dimension of identity is that it cannot exist in isolation. We are and become selves, as Niebuhr notes, only in the context of and in relation to other selves. To be a self is to be interconnected. This insight grounds not only Christian theological anthropology, but is also at the heart of its understanding of divinity as well. God must also be understood as being ontologically relational within the very substance of the divine being. It is this that renders the doctrine of the Trinity indispensable to a fully developed Christian conception, not only of God, but of the nature of self and society.[61]

In stating this, I do not mean to imply that the doctrine of the Trinity only serves a utilitarian or ethical function. Rather, I am arguing that the Christian conception of the self, and therefore the Christian conception of moral responsibility, is inescapably embedded within the conception of God as triune. The early disputes within the church as to the nature of the Godhead were so hotly contested precisely because they carried implications for the whole of Christian being in the world.[62] What it means to worship a God who only "appears" triune, or whose triunity is somehow not embedded within an ontological unity, is very different from what it means to worship a God whose unity and trinity cannot be separated from one another. The perichoretic relationality of the persons of the Trinity offers an account of precisely what it means to be made in the divine image and likeness. It is, as Catherine LaCugna argues, "ultimately a practical doctrine with radical consequences for Christian life."[63]

And yet, the doctrine of the Trinity seems abstract from the perspective of Christian moral life in the contemporary world. Many churches, at least within the Protestant tradition, struggle to make sense of the doctrine in even its broadest terms, let alone articulate its significance for Christian life and practice. "The Western church," wrote Robert Jensen, "now little uses or understands Christianity's heritage of trinitarian reflection and language."[64] If this is the case, however, the blame lies

61. I make no claims in this section to offer anything resembling a comprehensive discussion of the doctrine of the Trinity. My hope is only to underscore the applicability of the doctrine to the question of Christianity and identity, particularly as it relates to the Christian community as the context in which identity is shaped and Christian values are formed.

62. Rusch, *Trinitarian Controversy*.

63. LaCugna, *God For Us*, 1.

64. Jensen, *Triune Identity*, ix.

squarely with a Christian theology that has failed to make the significance of trinitarian thought clear to the Christian community, and this is at least in part due to the failure to teach both the doctrine itself and its practical implications. And yet, a particularly Christian understanding of human life and society is impossible without it.

Over the past several decades, a renewed emphasis on what has become known as "social trinitarianism" has given new life, not only to the theological discussion of the trinity, but also to reflection on its moral implications. If God in God's inmost being is inherently relational, and if human beings, made in the *imago Dei* are as well, then our lives as moral beings and our obligations to one another are grounded in that understanding of triune identity.

Jürgen Moltmann grounds his own retrieval of trinitarian thought within the experience of divine suffering in the incarnation. In this respect, as he delineated first in *The Crucified God* and then further elaborates in *The Trinity and the Kingdom*, the experience of the cross is the baseline for trinitarian thought. As the Son suffers on the cross, the Father suffers alongside him, but they suffer in distinct ways. In Christ, the Son experiences the physical pain and torture of crucifixion, but far more significantly experiences the existential suffering of God-abandonment—the loss not only of life but of all connection to his own divinity. This is, in a real way, what the "descent into hell" signifies for Moltmann: That in his God-abandonment, Jesus experiences the full range of human experience, not only death, but the absence of God.

At the same time, the Father suffers the death of the Son. God does not stand aloof from the pain of the crucifixion, though Moltmann emphasizes, does not suffer the pain of *being* crucified. Rather, "the Father who abandons him and delivers him up suffers the death of the Son in the infinite grief of love."[65] But the God-abandonment of which Moltmann writes is not a withdrawal of divine love, but an expression of it, a surrendering of the intimate relationship between Father and Son for the sake of the redemption of creation:

> God does not just love as he is angry, chooses, or rejects. He *is* love, that is, he exists in love. He constitutes his existence in the event of his love. He exists as love in the event of the cross. Thus in the concepts of earlier systematic theology it is possible to talk of a *homoousion*, in respect of an identity of substance, the community of will of the Father and Son on the cross. . . . In the

65. Moltmann, *Crucified God*, 243.

> cross, Father and Son are most deeply separated in forsakenness and at the same time are most inwardly one in their surrender. What proceeds from this event between Father and Son is the Spirit which justifies the godless, fills the forsaken with love and even brings the dead alive, since even the fact that they are dead cannot exclude them from this event of the cross; the death in God also includes them.[66]

This approach entails an understanding of the persons of the Trinity as existing not simply as "modes of being" within the single divine substance of God, as Barth argued, but as inherently relational in their persons.[67] Through the incarnation, humanity is brought into the trinitarian relationality through Christ's own humanity: "In the incarnation of the Son *the Trinity* throws itself open, as it were. The Father of the Son becomes the Father of the new, free, and united human race. Through the brotherhood of the Son God's children enter into the trinitarian relations of the Son, the Father, and the Spirit. As people in the world, they simultaneously exist 'in God' and 'God in them.'"[68] As such, human community becomes grounded in the community of the triune God.

Catherine LaCugna takes as her starting point for developing a renewed focus on the trinitarian relations Karl Rahner's insight that God's being is grounded in God's triune self-communication.[69] "His theology as a whole is a profound meditation on the essential unity of 'theology' and economy, premised on the idea that God is by nature self-communicating. The incomprehensible God *is* God by sharing, bestowing, diffusing, expressing Godself."[70] From this she continues: "trinitarian theology is par excellence a theology of relationship; God to us, we to God, we to

66. Moltmann, *Crucified God*, 244.

67. Barth, *Church Dogmatics* II.1 §29, 326–27: "It is of decisive importance to recognize the three modes of being, not only economically as modalism does, but according to the seriousness of the divine presence and power in the economy of His works, as modes of being of the one eternal God Himself, so it is equally important to understand that God in Himself is not divested of His glory and perfections, that He does not assume them merely in connexion with His self-revelation to the world, but that they constitute His own eternal glory."

68. Moltmann, *Church in the Power of the Spirit*, 121–22. Italics in original.

69. Rahner, *Trinity*. It is worth noting that the idea of God's being as grounded essentially in self-communication can be found in the American context as early as the theology of Jonathan Edwards. See Edwards, *Observations Concerning the Scripture Oeconomy of the Trinity and Covenant of Redemption*. See also Lee, *Philosophical Theology of Jonathan Edwards*.

70. LaCugna, *God For Us*, 210. Italics in original.

each other. The doctrine of the Trinity affirms that the 'essence' of God is relational, other-ward, that God exists as diverse persons united in a communion of freedom, love, and knowledge."[71] The relational conception of the Trinity, she argues, offers a way of describing this communicative and relational dimension of the divine being which has definite implications for Christian life. Drawing on the Orthodox theology of John Zizulous and Stanley Harakas, she argues:

> There is an intrinsic connection between ethics and soteriology, because the praxis of the good is *theōsis*. *Theōsis*, or becoming God is the proper *telos* of the Christian person. . . . The human being as a moral agent has the ability to be ethically self-determining (*autexousion*). . . . *Theōsis* would be the harmony between personhood and nature as each becomes transfigured by the Holy Spirit in union with Christ to bring about union with God through communion with others. This harmony (or lack thereof) becomes evident in the extent to which there is a correlation between inner motive and external behavior. Good intentions do not make an evil act good. *Agapē* is the ethical requirement of *theōsis*: Just as God loves creation through the divine energies, we image God if we ourselves love creation with agape love.[72]

As LaCugna notes, there is an inescapable connection between our theological conception of God as relational, our anthropological understanding of human beings as created for community, and our moral conception of human life as oriented toward action grounded in agapic love. God's triune identity in the final analysis grounds our human conception of identity, and that conception of identity ultimately grounds our practice.

This is a point made by David Cunningham. Echoing Wittgenstein's dictum that "*Practice* gives words their sense," Cunningham argues that a trinitarian theology implies a set of trinitarian virtues, which in turn entail their own trinitarian practices.[73] "Theologians should be concerned," he continues, "not merely with the words that are uttered with respect to this doctrine, nor merely with what we think while we are uttering them, but with the difference they make at various points in our lives."[74]

71. LaCugna, *God For Us*, 243.

72. LaCugna, *God For Us*, 283–84.

73. Cunningham, *These Three Are One*, 3. Italics in original.

74. Cunningham, *These Three Are One*, 3.

Cunningham discusses these trinitarian virtues as "polyphony," the metaphorical harmony of voices through which the community expresses oneness in the midst of difference;[75] "participation," through which individuals are invited into the gathered fellowship "called out" to become the church (*ekklesía*);[76] and "particularity," through which our identities as persons are understood in the context of our relations and actions within the Christian community.[77]

This discussion is grounded in the understanding of the diversity-within-unity of the three persons of the trinity, what Daniel Migliore calls the "exquisite divine dance" of perichoretic triune relations within the godhead.[78] Just as each of the *hypostases* within the godhead is distinct while being unified within the one *ousion* of God, each person within the Christian community maintains their identity while nevertheless being part of the one community of the church.[79]

These trinitarian virtues themselves produce particular trinitarian practices, which Cunningham describes as "peacemaking," "pluralizing," and "persuading." He writes:

> These practices underscore one of the principal claims of this book: that, for God and for us, "these three are one" in a way that requires us to rethink our understanding of oneness and difference. On the one hand, I have argued against the notion that oneness is achieved only by means of homogeneity; or . . . that the kinds of difference embodied in polyphonic music or table-fellowship are also constitutive of unity. And on the other hand, I have resisted the notion that multiplicity is necessarily a scattering to the winds, leading to naïve forms of relativism and isolationism; the trinitarian virtue of particularity does not

75. Cunningham, *These Three Are One*, 127.

76. Cunningham, *These Three Are One*, 165.

77. Cunningham, *These Three Are One*, 196.

78. Migliore, *Faith Seeking Understanding*, 70.

79. As with all things involving the Trinity, one must be careful to avoid collapsing human concepts and categories into descriptions of the divine. God remains unfathomable mystery even in the midst of revelation. As Cunningham states "Christians believe that God has been revealed to us, and that this has been accomplished by God's own act. Nevertheless, we also believe that we have not fully comprehended, nor can we hope to express, the fullness of God" (*These Three Are One*, 5). In a similar vein, any derivation of anthropological implications from the doctrine of the Trinity can never be said to be univocal but only analogical. See also Placher, *Triune God*.

> exclude the possibility of harmonious consensus and mutual participation.[80]

The Christian community is thus defined by a commitment to nonviolence in the sense of a refusal to seek to impose homogeneity through coercion. It resists "the desire to eliminate one's enemies, to efface or consume the otherness of the other, to exercise power in such a way that the difference implied by an opposing force is subordinated and ultimately extinguished."[81] Rather, Christians are called upon to be peacemakers, to respect and celebrate the diverse identities that co-exist within a pluralistic and multivalent social setting.

Speaking of which, by "pluralizing," Cunningham means that Christians "must not only 'make room' for multiple modes of discourse and multiple forms of practice; it is in fact *defined* by such multiplicity."[82] Christian moral life is delineated by a recognition that there are many ways in which the ideas and practices that govern Christian life can be expressed while still remaining faithful to the Gospel. The church in this sense, he argues, is both "catholic" and "evangelical"—proclaiming the good news authentically throughout the world. I would add the term "ecumenical" to this description, recognizing that the church takes on many different forms while remaining the one body of Christ, and in that way reaffirming the simultaneously polyphonic and particular character of Christian life together.

Christian identity—or more broadly, human identity as understood in the context of the Christian faith—is thus inherently communal. A person is not, as described in much modern political and economic theory, an atomized individual, but constituted by and through relationships. As Appiah argued in chapter 3, our *habitus* is not simply chosen, but is a response to the social context in which we come to understand ourselves as particular persons. To have an identity is to have an identity in connection to a particular set of social relations.

What a trinitarian account of human personhood adds to the philosophical and sociological descriptions of personal identity is the recognition that these social relations are themselves grounded in and validated through our status as *imago Dei*. The image of God within us is our relational character, and therefore there can be no sense of identity that is

80. Cunningham, *These Three Are One*, 234.

81. Cunningham, *These Three Are One*, 235.

82. Cunningham, *These Three Are One*, 235. Italics in original.

not in some sense grounded in divinity. Indeed, as LaCugna argues, if our *telos* as human beings is to become divine, then the more our identity reflects with integrity that relational character, the more we strive toward a genuine *theōsis*.

The church then becomes the institutional setting within which we come to understand precisely *how* we are to be relational, to understand what it actually means for that relationality to have integrity. The church is, as Miroslav Volf argues, "the image of the Trinity."[83] But what does this mean in terms of how Christian life together is understood?

For Volf it is about the embrace of "unity in multiplicity." "Since God is the one God, reality does not . . . degenerate into individual scenes like a bad play; yet since the one God is a communion of the divine persons, the world drama does not degenerate into a boring monologue. Trinitarian thinking suggests that in a successful world drama, unity and multiplicity must enjoy a complementary relationship."[84] The issue is not, he insists, that there is only one ecclesial model that corresponds to this trinitarian understanding. On the one hand are those who embrace a greater sense of multiplicity (he notes feminist, political, and liberation theologians specifically) and on the other, those who emphasize universality (Orthodox and Catholic theologians, in his analysis).[85] The church, as the body of Christ, "already forms a communion with the triune God."[86] However, he goes on to write:

> Ecclesial correspondence to the Trinity can become an object of hope and thus also a task for human beings. The correspondence between the trinitarian and ecclesial relationships is not simply formal. Rather, it is "ontological" because it is soteriologically grounded. Jesus' high-priestly prayer, that his disciples might become one "as you, Father, are in me and I am in you, may they also be in us" (John 17:21), presupposes communion with the triune god, mediated through faith and baptism, and aims at its eschatological consummation. . . . The relations between the many in the church must reflect the mutual *love* of the divine persons.[87]

83. Volf, *After Our Likeness*, iii.
84. Volf, *After Our Likeness*, 191.
85. Volf, *After Our Likeness*, 193–4.
86. Volf, *After Our Likeness*, 195.
87. Volf, *After Our Likeness*, 195. Italics in original.

Echoing LaCugna, Volf too recognizes that the core value to be cultivated within the Christian communion is that of agapic love. What this looks like in practice resonates with Jürgen Moltmann's understanding of the church as a community of open friendship.

Whereas traditionally friendship (in the sense of *philia*) has been understood in the Aristotelean sense as a relationship of those who are equal and alike, Moltmann argues that in Christ, the nature of friendship is opened up to include not only those who are alike, but those who are different, strangers, alien to our lives and experiences:

> The closed circle of friendship among peers is broken in principle by Christ, not only in relation to the despised humanity of "bad society" but in relation to God. Had he abided by the peer principle, he would of necessity have had to stay in heaven. But his incarnation and his friendship with sinners and tax collectors breaks through the exclusive circles. For this reason Christian friendship also cannot be lived within a closed circle of the faithful and pious, of peers in other words, but only in open affection and public respect of others. Through Jesus, friendship has become an open term of proffer. It is forthcoming solidarity.[88]

The openness of the triune God to creation, the overflowing of divine grace from within the Trinity and into the world, provides the moral basis for a Christian community that itself overflows in love through recognition of the mutual humanity, the relational *imago Dei* even within those who are perceived to be Other. The Christian church is never authorized to exclude or shun those who do not conform to some established model of proper belonging to the community, but remains (or should remain) radically open to the stranger. To follow a Savior who dines with prostitutes and tax collectors is to be willing to sit, and even more to embrace, those who are targeted for exclusion by the established powers of the wider society.

This is indeed the identity-forming core of what it means to call oneself a Christian. If the doctrine of the Trinity is to have any moral valence at all, it is to be found in that radical self-emptying undergone by the Son, through which he enters into the uttermost depths of the human experience, even into damnation, out of solidarity with the human condition, thus simultaneously bringing the divine down to the level of the lowest human degradation and raising humanity to the height of

88. Moltmann, *Open Church*, 61.

divinization. The Christian community, then, has no basis upon which to evade responsibility for standing side by side with all of those deemed unacceptable by society.

The church is the training ground in which Christian identity is formed and cultivated. It is what William Johnson Everett refers to as a "theaterola"—a small stage on which we rehearse our larger responsibilities as moral agents and citizens.[89] It becomes the place where we cultivate the trinitarian virtues of which Cunningham writes, and practice the basic actions of radical welcome to the stranger and radical acceptance of the other.

The identity-forming character of the Christian community does not negate the other circumstances and locations through which our identities are formed. What it does do is contextualize those identities in terms of the core values expressed through the trinitarian relationality that the church represents. The church tells us what it means to be made in the image of God, what it means to live and act in the image of Christ, and what that entails in terms of our relations to others, inside and outside of the church. It becomes, in principle if often not in fact, the core formational dimension of Christian identity, through which other dimensions of our identity are understood and evaluated. The radical acceptance that is central to the church's attitude toward the world becomes the moral standard by which we gauge our own actions and the actions of others, particularly those others who call themselves Christian.

We are created, not merely as *zoon politikon* in the Aristotelean sense, nor merely as social beings, but as, in the form of the triune God, persons-in-communion, which is most fully expressed when we open ourselves up in vulnerability to the agapic love proclaimed by Jesus Christ.

WHO ARE WE?

When Dietrich Bonhoeffer asked in his prison cell, "Who am I?" He expressed a universal human question, to which his own poem does not provide a definitive answer. "Whoever I am," he writes, "Thou knowest, O God, I am thine." As we have seen throughout this book thus far, we may indeed be many things simultaneously, and always within the complexity of our self-examination remain mysterious even to ourselves. Yet, what

89. Everett, *God's Federal Republic*, 157.

Bonhoeffer affirms at the end of his poem is that, even if we don't know in the fullest sense who we are, we can rest assured that we belong to God.

As *imago Dei*, we are responsible not only for ourselves and our own lives, but are innately connected to the lives and suffering of others. We cannot exist as atomistic individuals, separate from any real connection to one another. We are never fully human unless we are human in relationship. And this necessitates an ethic of responsibility for and openness to the well-being of others, particularly those who are pushed to the edges of society, whose own humanity has been called into question or stripped from them entirely.

For this reason, an emphasis on human dignity is at the heart of the Christian moral life. It is an expression of the responsibility that we share for one another and the obligations we have to ensure that the image of God in each of us is preserved and defended. To be grounded in our personhood in the triune being of God necessitates preserving the rights of every other human being to live fully human lives—to be free from injustice, oppression, and violence. This provides a practical grounding for political systems designed to protect the worth of each individual person.

To say that personhood is socially constituted, however, leads directly to the question of the kind of society that most fully reflects the kind of persons who can live in the embrace of agapic love. This is the subject of the next chapter.

5

"Its Gates Will Never Be Shut"

The Kingdom of God and the Vision of a World For All

In the depths of winter, I finally learned that within me there lay an invincible summer.

—Albert Camus, *Personal Writings*[1]

INTRODUCTION

To speak of human persons in the image of God, as we argued in the previous chapter, is to speak of human identity as inescapably socially constituted. Contrary to the perspective common in modern political theory, as exemplified by Hobbes, Rousseau, and Locke, that we are first and foremost atomized individuals in the state of nature, who come together in communities for the sake of safety and convenience, the truth of the matter is that we are incapable of becoming individuals except insofar as we are embedded within communities and cultures to begin with.[2] It is only from that starting point that we begin to differentiate ourselves from our social context, accepting or rejecting those dimensions of selfhood

1. Camus, *Personal Writings*, 181–82.

2. On the politics of atomic individualism, see MacPherson, *Political Theory of Possessive Individualism.*

that are imposed upon us from without and taking some form of ownership over our own sense of identity.

What Christian theology adds to this picture is the recognition that the primordial relationship within which every human being comes into existence is with the God who is, in the essence of the divine being, communal and relational. Our own personhood is thus an echo of the triune personhood of the one God.

The question before us now is how this conception of identity can offer resources to confront the challenges to human dignity and democratic governance that continue to grow on a global scale. The purpose of this chapter is to provide an outline of some of those resources, with an eye to developing a public theological response to the resurgent authoritarianism with the United States and around the world. Central to my argument in this chapter is the idea that the kingdom of God provides the governing metaphor through which Christians can construct a defense of human rights and democratic governance where those ideas are under threat. Further, the church must become the champion of these ideas as a community grounded in the anticipation of the coming kingdom of God.

THE KINGDOM OF GOD AS CULTURAL CRITIQUE

Christian theological reflection on public life is necessarily grounded in the life and teaching of Jesus Christ, and Christ's teaching is in turn grounded in the idea of the kingdom of God (or, in Matthew's terminology, the kingdom of heaven). There is a massive body of exegetical and theological literature on how this idea should be interpreted, and it is well beyond the scope of this project to offer any kind of exhaustive account. However, as a concept it is crucial for creating a bridge between the "theological" dimension of public theology and the "public" dimension.

It is important to note that the very word "kingdom" in English may not offer the best translation of the text. The Greek word *basileía* may be better translated as "realm" or "rule." The word conveys not simply the idea of authoritarian monarchical power, but rather of the sovereign presence of a king within the world. Throughout his preaching, Christ emphasizes the kingdom coming, not as an overpowering imposition of divine compulsion, but rather as something growing organically in the midst of human experience, as in the parable of the sower (Matt 13:1–9) or the mustard seed (Matt 13:31–32); or else he describes it as something that we discover unexpectedly, as in the parable of the hidden treasure

(Matt 13:44) or the pearl of great price (Matt 13:45–46). What these parables convey is the idea that, unlike the worldly kingdoms with which his hearers were familiar, the presence God's kingdom was to be sought and discovered rather than coercively imposed.

As Douglas John Hall argues, the kingdom (or "reign" in his preferred terminology) may be best understood by what it is not. First, it is not a "plan of action, a strategy for change."[3] He continues: "The whole point of Jesus's communication of the coming reign of God is surely to acquire participants. Yet the participants are neither the initiators of this new and decisive form of God's earthly sovereignty nor is it to be achieved through their efforts. . . . If they do not heed the call to involvement others will; it will occur, regardless of their individual responses."[4] Just as the yeast leavens the dough regardless of our own desires or wishes, the reign of God emerges within the world with or without us.

He continues by noting, second, that it is not "an ideal or utopian vision." "The *basiliea* whose advent he proclaims is for him not only a vision but a reality; it is to be inaugurated—has already been inaugurated—quietly and without the fanfare, tumult, and self-righteousness of revolutionaries."[5] To say that it is not a utopian vision does not mean that it is fully present and apparent within the world. It remains ahead of us even as it grows within our midst. Yet it remains present and grounded within the lives and experiences of those who heed Christ's call to come and follow him.

Third, Hall argues, it is not merely a personal or spiritual transformation, a "subjective state" or a "*metanoia* of the heart."[6] He notes that the King James translation of Luke 17:21 as "the kingdom of God is *within you*" has created a misleading understanding among English-speaking, particularly North American Christians, who read it to mean that it is a matter of individual transformation. The Revised Standard Version's translation—"the kingdom of God is *in the midst of you*"—better conveys the sense that the God's reign is coming to be within the world and among the people of God, rather than only within the hearts of individual believers.[7]

3. Hall, *Confessing the Faith*, 460.

4. Hall, *Confessing the Faith*, 460.

5. Hall, *Confessing the Faith*, 460.

6. Hall, *Confessing the Faith*, 461.

7. The New Revised Standard Version makes the point even more explicitly, stating "the kingdom of God is *among you*" (italics added).

This opens up the recognition that the kingdom, realm, or reign of God should be understood as a form of social and cultural critique, a vantage point from which to judge the insufficiency of existing social and political arrangements and a means by which to call into question the given political and civic structures that we inhabit. Hall expresses skepticism toward the idea that the *basileia tou Theou* can be understood primarily in terms of its social and political implications, lest it be reduced to a political ideology. Nevertheless, it serves an essential role in criticizing the inadequacy of any and all existing social arrangements:

> In my judgment . . . *basiliea tou Theou*, if it is to function as biblical faith intends, ought not to be heard as an overtly political category, or as an open invitation to invest it with specific political content. Rather, it must be kept free to be a vantage point of truth, justice, and courage from which any and every system and regime may be watched and assessed. Since every human "kingdom" creates its victims, the "kingdom of God" is above all the sovereignty of one who identifies with the excluded; and every political ideology and agenda excludes someone.[8]

This said, however, it cannot be the case that the kingdom of God simply exists as the negative space, the shadow of the existing kingdoms of this world. If it is indeed growing in the midst of the world, then the green shoots of its presence should be detectable and comprehensible within our own experience. Hall acknowledges that this is the case, recognizing that the Decalogue, the prophetic books of the Bible, and the Sermon on the Mount offer us positive imagery from which we can infer the kind of a society that would be consonant with God's reign: "If we are speaking about *God's* reign, then we are speaking about a sovereignty that is continuous with the whole character and intention of God as these are presented in the continuity of the Testaments; and as Christians, we are speaking in particular about Jesus, the supreme exemplar and representative both of the divine sovereign and of human obedience."[9]

Nevertheless, Hall almost immediately reverts to the negative in describing the social implications of a commitment to God's reign:

> This testimony to the positive content of the symbol is not inconsiderable. There is at least enough here for us to realize that certain systems, practices, and events are *not* acceptable to those

8. Hall, *Confessing the Faith*, 461.

9. Hall, *Confessing the Faith*, 462. Italics in original.

> whose perspective on the world can be associated with this symbol. The reign of God is *not* compatible with tyranny, gross economic disparity, the degradation of the earth and of human beings because of their skin pigmentation, or their gender, or their sexual orientation. It is *not* compatible with violence, war, slavery, "ethnic cleansing," indifference to those in need, personal greed and acquisitiveness, and so on and so on. Such things may surely be said straightforwardly by anyone with only a slight knowledge of the background of Jesus' use of this term and his own exemplification of its meaning.[10]

Hall is understandably reluctant to offer any detailed analysis of what the positive image of society that corresponds to this negative analysis might be. Yet, the image of a prospective social agenda can be seen within the space defined by the *nots* Hall enumerates—tyranny should be met by a commitment to democracy; economic disparity with a dedication to economic equality. If the realm of God is incompatible with the degradation of other human beings, then it must be committed to the radical inclusion of all. A rejection of violence, war, and slavery requires a commitment to a positive ethic of peace, nonviolence, and liberation.

Hall's legitimate fear is that these commitments too quickly devolve into ideology. And yet, it is necessary that Christian theology move continually within the dialectical relationship between the positive affirmation of the values that the kingdom of God embodies and the critical recognition that every temporal realm must inevitably fall short of the full embodiment of those values. The *via negativa* must be matched with the *via positivia* while at the same time acknowledging that it is only together that we begin to form an adequate understanding of God's kingdom and its implications for social life. The place where this dialectical process is embodied and practiced is the church.

THE CHURCH AND THE FORMATION OF IDENTITY

Throughout this project, we have seen the way in which identity is neither fixed nor innate, but is the product of both our personal self-understanding and the context in which that self-understanding comes about—the *habitus* through which we encounter the possibilities of selfhood to which we have access. While our *habitus* does not determine our identity, it exercises a strong influence on how our identity is defined, and how

10. Hall, *Confessing the Faith*, 462. Italics in original.

broad the options are for us. As James K. A. Smith notes, "I learn how to constitute my world from others, but I learn how to constitute *my* world. The 'I' that perceives is already a 'we.' My perception is communal, a debt I owe."[11] Within a medieval village, the options for defining one's identity may have been relatively narrowly construed, whereas in a globalized and digitally connected world, the options often seem limitless. Yet those options are always both intertwined with the context from which we have emerged and our own appropriation, or refusal to appropriate, those communal contributions in terms of our own self-identification. We are, Smith notes, both constrained by our *habitus* and yet at the same time free (to a degree) in relation to it.

Yet, even within such a world, we still operate and dwell within communities that shape how we perceive those options. Within the Christian context, it is the church that is, or ought to be, the key setting within which questions of identity are negotiated. To be grounded in the church is to understand that one's identity is neither a matter of complete and unfettered individual choice, as atomized individualist accounts of the self might suggest, nor is it wholly externally determined, as collectivist or authoritarian accounts of the self might suggest. Rather, our self-understanding emerges within a community whose own sense of self is governed by a reliance on God's grace as a core commitment, and the incarnation of Christ as its guiding norm.

This is not to suggest, however, that the relationship between how we conceive of ourselves and our relationship to the church as a community is not complex and often troubled. To be related to the church does not mean to be subsumed within or dominated by the church. To borrow a turn of phrase from David Tracy, the church functions within our personal lives as well as our public lives as a "generalized other"—a community that we forge our identities in reference to, but not necessarily in submission to. As this generalized other, the church becomes the setting in which we see ourselves reflected back upon ourselves, for better, and often for worse. At its best, it provides us with a space within which we can come to an understanding of our identity, in whatever way we may define it as a reflection of the divine grace and Christlike love that the community is called to embody.

Alas, the church is seldom at its best, and far too many people have been injured by forms of the church in which they are not affirmed as

11. Smith, *Imagining the Kingdom*, 84. Italics in original.

beloved children of God.[12] This is particularly so for LGBTQ+ Christians, who are often, and forcefully, rejected by churches who deny those forms of identity. Here, the church's role as generalized other can take on a toxic and damaging character. At the same time, these communities do not exhaust the available options. More supportive and inclusive communities, which embrace and celebrate queer identities, do exist. What's more, to say that any community serves as a generalized other does not imply that the acceptance of these communities is necessary or required for the formation of one's identity, any more than it is necessary, in Tracy's analysis, for the construction of a public theology. Our identities are formed in relation to it, but not determined by it. And when a church's reflection of ourselves becomes a funhouse mirror distortion of who we are, we may be called upon to reject it.

At the same time, the church is not solely a generalized other in Tracy's sense. For Christians, the church is also a formational community, through which we establish habits of thought and practice that contribute, often inchoately, to our sense of identity. This is certainly clear among those who have been injured by the church in various ways, and who yet find their Christian habits of mind and sense of identity indelibly imprinted on their consciousness long after they have rejected Christianity as a set of institutions, practices, and ideas.

Smith argues that the institutions in which we participate form us, not primarily through what they tell us about the world and our place in it, but through the practices that they embody, and how those practices shape our desires. Smith's focus is on the Christian university, but for that reason is also grounded in the life of the church.[13] He notes that the real

12. As Paul Tillich notes: "The churches which represent the Kingdom of God in its fight against the forces of profanation and demonization are themselves subject to the ambiguities of religion and are open to profanation and demonization. How, then can that which is itself demonized represent the fight against the demonic and the which is profanized represent the fight against the profane? The answer was given in the chapter on the paradox of the churches: they are profane and sublime, demonic and divine, in a paradoxical unity. The expression of this paradox is the prophetic criticism of the churches by the churches" (Tillich, *Systematic Theology*, 3:377).

13. Smith's location at Calvin University, a church-affiliated Protestant university, makes the connection between school and church explicit. And yet, it must be said, much of what he argues about the Christian university does not apply equally to a Catholic setting. While Catholic universities, at least in the United States, have a diverse set of relationships to the institutional church, for many of them, the particularly *Roman Catholic* aspects of their identities are not pedagogically front-and-center. Some dimensions of Catholic identity are highlighted, but the formational dimension of Chistian higher education that is central to Smith's argument is often downplayed, though again, there is tremendous variation from institution to institution.

lessons that are imbued within these settings have little to do with the cognitive content of what is taught or preached, but in the cultural norms that are absorbed through constant exposure. Referencing George Orwell's *Road to Wigan Pier*, Smith writes: "The information that the public schools provided—like Latin and Greek—didn't really take root. What did get inscribed into the pupils, however, was an entire comportment to the world and society, a training in 'snobbishness' that could not be easily overturned or undone by new facts or data or information."[14]

The church, like the university, forms our identity through the formation of our desires. We are, Smith argues, innately desiring creatures; but what we desire is not predetermined, rather it is shaped by what we are taught is *desirable*. This instruction, however, comes from *how* we are taught to desire, which is to say, how we are taught to love: "To be human is to love, and it is what we love that defines who we are. Our (ultimate) love is constitutive of our identity."[15]

He goes on to argue that the object of our desire is, in sum, the object of our worship, and the practice of worship, the liturgies that we undertake in order to express that love, are the means by which we are formed as loving, desiring creatures. The fundamental moral and spiritual question of human, and particularly Christian, life, then becomes what it is that we are being formed to desire, which we learn through the act of worship. Within the community of worship we are taught what it is for which we should strive, and what it means for us to be the kinds of human beings for which such striving is comprehensible. In other words, worship shapes the *telos* of our desire by embodying that desire in liturgical practices:

> The *telos* to which our love is aimed is not a list of ideas or propositions or doctrines; it is not a list of abstract, disembodied concepts or values. Rather, the reason that this vision of the good life moves us is because it is a more affective, sensible, even aesthetic *picture* of what the good life looks like. A vision of the good life captures our hearts and imaginations not by providing a set of rules or ideas, but by painting a picture of what it looks like for us to flourish and live well. This is why such pictures are communicated most powerfully in stories, legends, myths, plays, novels, and films rather than in dissertations, messages, and monographs. Because we are affective before we are

14. Smith, *Desiring the Kingdom*, 30.

15. Smith, *Desiring the Kingdom*, 51.

> cognitive (and even *while* we are cognitive), visions of the good get inscribed in us by means that are commensurate with our primarily affective, imaginative nature.[16]

We are, he argues, habituated through these symbolic forms to desire a particular vision of the world and of our place within it. We "desire the kingdom," he argues, but the nature of the kingdom is not predetermined. Rather, "every one of us is on a kind of Arthurian quest for 'the Holy Grail,' that hoped-for, longed-for, dreamed-of picture of the good life—the realm of human flourishing—that we pursue without ceasing."[17]

But if this is so, then it matters crucially that we belong to communities that form us to desire the right *kind* of kingdom—the kingdom of God—and that our values are shaped by the right *kind* of desires—those that are identifiable with *basileía tou Theou* described in the life and teaching of Jesus Christ.[18] The tragedy of American Christianity is how thoroughly the Christian community stands in opposition to the reign of God embodied by Christ. If this was not made clear at the founding of the nation, when Christianity and slavery were seen to be compatible with one another, it was at least well-articulated by H. Richard Niebuhr's description of American Christianity as the belief that "a God without wrath brought men without sin into a kingdom without judgement through the ministrations of a Christ without a cross."[19]

Yet, if the church cannot simply absent itself from the public life of the society to which it belongs, then it is crucial that Christians be formed as the kinds of people who can participate fruitfully as citizens within that society. The church forms us then, or should do so, not only as desiring persons, but also as *public* persons, capable of exercising responsibility within the political and civil spheres central to the creation of a just and equitable shared community. The church forms us as civic actors precisely in offering us a setting through which we can develop the skills of public participation.

16. Smith, *Desiring the Kingdom*, 53, Italics in original.

17. Smith, *Desiring the Kingdom*, 54.

18. For Stanley Hauerwas, this commitment to a particular set of virtues grounded within the Christian community and exemplifying the Christian story required an unqualified commitment to an ethic of nonviolence. The harder question, which I hope to approach throughout this project, is what it means to embody the values of the kingdom in the midst of a society which refuses to acknowledge either the values or the narrative on which those values are based. See Hauerwas, *Peaceable Kingdom*.

19. Niebuhr, *Kingdom of God in America*, 193.

William Everett argues that, by understanding the nature of the self as being, in its public representation, a kind of "performer," we can develop a useful model for conceiving of how institutions within civil society, particularly, I would argue, the church, form us as public citizens. Under this model, he argues, "the self appears as an actor situated in a story performed before various audiences in some worldly scene."[20] These scenes in which we perform as participants within the private and civic spheres shape us in ways that overflow into our participation within public space. They function, he argues, as "theaterolas," literally "little theaters," within which we rehearse the practices of public responsibility:

> Private spheres are the little stages of our lives. To draw on the old distinction between the ecclesia and the ecclesiola (the big church and the little church within), they are the "theaterolas" of our life. They are arenas of presentation, as Erving Goffman has so richly pointed out. They are studios relatively detached from the larger, more public arenas. These theaterolas occur not only in family settings but in all intimate relationships.[21]

To press the metaphor further, we experience these little theaters not only within family and intimate spaces, but also within all of the institutional spaces that stand between our individual selves and the state—schools, unions, civic organizations, and other forms of associational life as well as the church. Because we are, as persons, involved in many such associations, we are multiply formed by those associations. We are never subject to only one formational setting, but are shaped by how we come to understand ourselves as students among other students, activists among other activists, athletes among other athletes. As in our relations to the church, what we discover (or create) of ourselves in these settings requires us to embrace some of the demands made on us by them, and

20. Everett, *God's Federal Republic*, 155. Everett's larger project in this volume involves a reconception of symbols such as "kingdom" and "king" in terms that are more amenable to the political context of a democratic republic. More broadly, he offers a way of understanding what it means for Christians to be publicly involved as citizens within such a polity. This is a subject to which I hope to return in the third volume of this project.

21. Everett, *God's Federal Republic*, 155–56. I will note one difference that I have with Everett's approach is in his description of these spheres as "private." As I argued in *Exodus Church and Civil Society*, the distinction between "public" and "private" in our conception of society is too simple a model for the complexity of human institutional life. Civil society, as an intermediate space between public and private, which includes those institutions through which we as individuals come to learn the skills of public participation, is a crucial concept for a sufficiently rich conception of society.

to reject others. I am never *only* who I am in the classroom or on the basketball court, but I discover who I am in part by what I experience there. To return to Hannah Arendt's idea of the public as a "space of appearance," distinct from the state, as we are formed by the institutions within which we participate, we operate within the space of appearance created by our interactions with others. The church then *becomes* public precisely because we participate as public persons within it.

In this respect, the church serves a uniquely identity-forming role (once more, both positively and negatively). As noted, even if one rejects the institution of the church and the label of Christian, the church can wield a powerful role in defining who we understand ourselves to be. Within the church we occupy the space of appearance formed by the values and priorities identified within that community. But the community itself is not bound to embrace one specific and exclusive set of values, precisely because the church is not simply a single community. Because Christian churches exist within myriad cultures and are made up of individuals with widely diverse understandings of themselves and their identities, the values embraced by particular local Christian communities express their Christian self-conception with respect to those local values. The gospel stands in critical relation to those values—not necessarily wholly affirming nor wholly denying them, but placing those values under the scrutiny of the kingdom of God.

To speak of the church as identity-forming is to recognize, on the one hand, the way in which one's participation within it shapes core aspects of one's self-conception, and on the other, how that participation shapes us as participants within the context of public life. As Christian identity is grounded in the self-emptying of God in Christ and the divination of human existence in the incarnation, Christian identity necessarily acknowledges the innate dignity of all human beings in their struggle for recognition. The kingdom of God, in this respect, should be understood as that realm within which that dignity is recognized and honored, and in which the particular identities of each unique human being are seen as a reflection of the *imago Dei*.

When the church fails to do so, and seeks to diminish the dignity of individuals and groups on the basis of their identity, or when it violates that sense of dignity by excluding human beings from participation within the community of grace established in Christ, it fails to reflect the reign of God to which it claims to have allegiance.[22] The agapic love of the triune God represents the moral core of the church, and provides the plumb line according to which Christian action toward other human beings should be judged. Our communities should seek to form us as public persons such that our primary motivation within society is to exemplify that love toward our neighbors, and even our enemies.

More broadly, however, it should seek to make us into the kind of people who respect and embrace democratic practices in political life, and who value the kind of "rooted cosmopolitanism" described by Appiah, which reaches beyond the narrow confines of our local and particular communities toward a sense of global responsibility, while at the same time remaining grounded by and within those communities.

ROOTED COSMOPOLITANISM, THE CHURCH, AND THE KINGDOM OF GOD

Recall that, for Appiah, the idea of a "rooted cosmopolitanism" was an antidote to, on the one hand, forms of nationalism that constrain our sense of loyalty and our understanding of identity to the narrow confines of state and ethnicity, and on the other, to the kind of cosmopolitan ideology that refuses to acknowledge any connection to community, culture, or history. This form of cosmopolitanism is, he writes "an aery nothing," which imposes no sense of connection or loyalty on those who claim it.[23] By the same token, a "ruthless cosmopolitanism" that seeks to impose a singular, utopian view upon the world would be equally intolerable.

What Appiah argues for instead is, as he puts it, a "wishy-washy version of cosmopolitanism," which "doesn't seek to destroy patriotism, or separate out 'real' from 'unreal' loyalties."[24] Rather, as we discussed in

22. There is an obvious, though I think largely specious, objection to this line of argument, which is that there are human practices and forms of identity that stand contrary to anything that the church ought to affirm. Yet, to speak of Christian identity in the sense that I mean it, is to speak of an identity grounded in the self-giving love of Jesus Christ, a love that is contrary to acts of violence, abuse or exploitation. Such practices, I would certainly agree, are contrary to anything that might be associated with the reign of God or the sense of an identity formed by a Christian community. Yet, it seems that the objection is seldom lodged against the large-scale violence and exploitation of military, political, or economic institutions or their leaders, while focusing particularly on the sex lives of consenting adults.

23. Appiah, *Ethics of Identity*, 214.

24. Appiah, *Ethics of Identity*, 222.

chapter 3, "a tenable cosmopolitanism, in the first instance, must take seriously the value of human life, and the value of particular human lives, the lives people have made for themselves, with the communities that help lend significance to those lives."[25] In other words such a view recognizes that the wide embrace of social and cultural difference sought within a cosmopolitan ethos can only be effectively grounded in values and relationships that are local and contextually grounded, in other words, "rooted."

It is here that I want to take Appiah's essentially secular philosophical idea and apply it within the context of the idea of church I have been engaging throughout this chapter. It is within the church that Christians find *both* the universal cosmopolitan horizon of values Appiah discusses *and* the local, rooted community grounded in relationships of care and responsibility. This is precisely how the church functions as a theaterola for the development of public persons.

In the first instance, we do not participate in church in the abstract. Rather, the church is always the local expression of a global phenomenon. As the body of Christ, each local church community and each participant within that community participates as a distinct and gifted individual tasked with particular roles within that community. As we find and fulfill those roles through our participation, we undergo the identity-forming process of being formed in the image of Christ. As Paul puts it in Romans, this is the setting within which Christians are "transformed by the renewing of [our] minds" (Rom 12:2).

Yet, the first part of that verse is no less important to understanding the kind of formation that takes place within the church, for Paul begins with the admonition to "not be conformed to this age" (Rom 12:2). For Paul, the contrast is between the hierarchies and divisions that defined relations within Roman society and the egalitarian and grace-bound values of the *ekklesia* so that, as he continues, we "may discern what is the will of God—what is good and acceptable and perfect" (v. 2). The transformation of which Paul speaks (in the Greek, literally a "metamorphosis") is one through which we are freed from the values of "this age" and given the power to rightly discern God's intentions for ourselves and the world.

At the same time, the concrete local expression of the church through which we undertake that transformation is itself an expression of a cosmopolitan community, one not limited by national borders or

25. Appiah, *Ethics of Identity*, 222–23.

ethnic identity, but one that recognizes a common kinship with all humanity, seeing in each human being the image and likeness of the God of Jesus Christ, to whose body we belong as members of the church. Yet, as Douglas John Hall insists, this church only fully realizes its identity as the body of Christ in the act of *confession*, that is to say, a commitment to the world and its wellbeing as the beloved creation of that same God.

The church, Hall insists, does not confess itself, nor does it confess on its own behalf. Rather, he argues, drawing on Barth, the church witnesses to the Word of God made incarnate in Jesus Christ, without whom there is nothing for the church to confess. There is a threefold dimension to this confession. First, the church's witness must be addressed outward, to the world, rather than becoming an inward and insular conversation addressed only to itself. He continues: "the biblical God is from the beginning to end a world-oriented God, a geo- and anthropocentric God who will not abandon the world 'prematurely' (Bonhoeffer) as the religious so regularly do!"[26]

Second, he notes, the church's confession is oriented toward the correction and ongoing reformation of the church itself. However, this does not imply a fossilized orthodoxy, or even unity, which makes the mistake of crystalizing the church within an unchangeable expression, rather than remaining open to the leading of the Holy Spirit. "When the confession of faith devolves into a concern for orthodoxy, order, or uniformity, or even unity within the church itself, such internal preciousness displaces the only legitimate rational for theological vigilance, which is 'that the world may believe.'"[27]

Rather, the church's confession is always done within a particular context and setting. "The reason that the church is a 'confessing church' is that its confession has always to be discovered, grasped, and framed anew. . . . The mere repetition of the confessions of yesteryear—the Apostle's Creed, the Nicene Creed, Heidelberg, Barmen—does not constitute confession."[28] It is only when we engage faithfully with those confessions, applying their lessons within our own contexts, that they take on life for the contemporary world.

Yet, to say that the church's confession is to and for its contemporary setting does not imply that the church is bound by that setting. To say that the church is "in the world but not of it" (see John 16:10–18) is to say

26. Hall, *Confessing the Faith*, 37.

27. Hall, *Confessing the Faith*, 37.

28. Hall, *Confessing the Faith*, 38.

that the church confesses within its own particular context, but that its confession necessarily challenges and is in turn challenged by that context. It "stands under . . . the questions, dilemmas, anxieties and longings of the world for which the confession is intended."[29] The confession of the church is thus always a public act:

> All of this is to say that which the Scriptures say in so many direct and indirect ways: that the confessing "people of God" which can only confess the faith if it is not "of" the world, must nevertheless be very decisively "in" it. They must be in the world, not only physically and factually (where else could they be?) but also spiritually and intellectually. That is, they must know the problems, anxieties, longings, and frustrations of their historical moment from the inside—as their own problems, anxieties, longings, and frustrations. Therefore they will understand, when they are *denied* answers and pushed over to the side of doubt and disbelief, that this is not only owing to their own weakness but that it belongs to the economy of God. They are being made participants in the world's questions so that they may listen anew for the answers that come from beyond both the church and the world's storehouse of answers. And in this—precisely this!—they are being conformed to Jesus Christ, who was emptied and humbled in order that his name could be the source of exaltation for others."[30]

Thus, the act of confession pushes Christians out into the world, not with a playbook of pat answers, but in order to encounter and respond to the world's questions in faith. Yet, this move to worldliness, to publicity, is not a move out of or away from the church, but rather the very expression of the church's orientation toward the world, the whole of the world, the cosmopolitan world. As Graham Ward states: "Whatever action the church undertakes, whatever proclamations it makes, is located in the world's times and spaces, its histories, its societies, its cultures, its languages, and its ideologies."[31] However, this is only possible to the degree that we are rooted within the community of the church and prepared, formed, and transformed, in order to confess the meaning of the church's witness within our own context. "Insofar as the church is a public and material manifestation of that which transcends the world—the operations

29. Hall, *Confessing the Faith*, 39.

30. Hall, *Confessing the Faith*, 41, Italics in original.

31. Ward, *Politics of Discipleship*, 24.

of God in Christ with respect to redemption—the church's actions and speech address the world from a point beyond it."[32]

The kind of rooted cosmopolitanism compatible with this call to Christian witness is one that is grounded in an understanding of the kingdom of God as the *telos* of human social life, and thus calls Christians to act in ways that anticipate the values and norms of God's reign within their public lives. What such an anticipatory approach would look like is by no means obvious, but as noted above, it is not only possible, but I believe necessary to at least speak in broad terms about how that way of life would appear.

For Smith, this remains grounded in the idea of worship, which, he argues, "narrates an understanding of public life *internal* to its practice."[33] The public task of the church is simply "to make explicit that which is already implicit in the liturgy."[34] This implies that the church's public work is to be found in its proclamation of the gospel within the Christian community, for the sake of the world. Thus, he argues:

> The church's worship does not "become" political when it is translated into policy or hooked to partisan agendas. The politics of worship is tied to the renewal of moral agency of the people of God, who are formed to be sent. In this sense, the very fact of Christian worship is a twofold political act involving the formation of political agents and the proclamation *to* legislators and lawmakers that the created order of culture is subject to a higher law.[35]

The challenge of such a proclamation, as distinct I would argue from the confession of which Hall speaks, is the recognition that the character of a pluralistic democratic polity means that public life is determined, not only by the Christian understanding of what such a higher law might imply, but by the many other, non-Christian, participants within that polity. Smith believes that the church can account for pluralism to the degree that it becomes a locus for the cultivation of "virtues like patience, long-suffering, and above all, love."[36] Drawing on the neo-Calvinist tradition of Abraham Kuyper, Herman Bavinck, and Herman Dooyeweerd, Smith

32. Ward, *Politics of Discipleship*, 24.
33. Smith, *Awaiting the King*, 56. Italics in original.
34. Smith, *Awaiting the King*, 56.
35. Smith, *Awaiting the King*, 60. Italics in original.
36. Smith, *Awaiting the King*, 132.

argues in favor of a "principled pluralism" in society, which recognizes that pluralism has structural, cultural, and directional dimensions. Directional pluralism, as described by Smith, goes to the heart of why one should be cautious about attempts to impose a uniform conception of Christian society, in the manner of Christian nationalism or integralism. Smith suggests that Christians should offer "two cheers for pluralism: a normative 'celebration' of pluralism with respect to structural and cultural plurality, while directional/confessional plurality is descriptively recognized and constructively addressed but not normatively celebrated."[37]

Yet, an understanding of the confessional approach to Christian public life of the kind advocated by Hall seems to offer a bit more humility on this front than the neo-Calvinist approach would allow. However many "cheers" one may offer for pluralism, particularly of the directional sort, it is precisely in the struggle to articulate a moral vision for society that can be embraced across religious traditions that the Christian conception of public action can be better understood within the Christian tradition itself, and articulated in a way that need not be confined within the particular cultural forms of expression of the Christian community. This is, I take it, the implication of Hall's recognition that the church may be *denied* answers and pushed toward doubt and disbelief in its engagement with the wider public of which it is a part. The Christian expression of its directional preferences for public life are by no means inherently sounder than the preferences expressed by other groups, and Christianity may need to listen and learn at least as much as teach within a pluralistic and democratic setting.

Even so, it is the task of the church to be fully engaged within the discourse around public goods, and to articulate and advocate for an understanding of God's reign that can be made manifest within such a society. The values and norms symbolized within the idea of the kingdom of God can't help but serve as the foundation for a Christian social ethic to the degree that the church remains faithful to its calling. At the same time, the particular application of those norms is always articulated within and in response to the particular circumstances in which Christians find themselves.

One model for the articulation of such a "kingdom ethic" is offered by David Gushee and Glen Stassen in their book of that title. For them, public theology is rooted in the claim that "Jesus taught that participation

37. Smith, *Awaiting the King*, 137.

in God's reign requires the disciplined practices of a Christ-following countercultural community that obeys God in its inner communal life and by publicly engaging in works of love, justice, and protection of the dignity and sacred worth of human life."[38] The Christian life of discipleship is motivated by the command to act as salt and light in the midst of the world through actions that reflect the light of God's reign within the world. In this respect, their claim is similar to that of H. Richard Niebuhr, who argued that the moral task to which we are called "is not that of building utopias but that of eliminating weeds and tilling the soil too that the kingdom of God can grow."[39]

To "follow Jesus" in the manner Gushee and Stassen advocate requires that Christians engage thoughtfully in the complex moral debates around such issues as the death penalty, divorce, economic and ecological justice, and the realities of racism, homophobia, and bigotry. They stress that Christian ethics is not merely about ideals, but concrete practices, "practices that are actually and regularly done, embodied in action."[40] As we embody these practices through our actions, we demonstrate the meaning and importance of the kingdom of God within the public spaces that we occupy. This is how Christians serve as salt and light in the world and, they emphasize, "bring glory to God and advance God's reign," which "is the deepest meaning and purpose of kingdom ethics."[41]

If the church is the locus through which our understanding of God's reign is presented and in light of whose values we are formed as public persons and rooted cosmopolitans, the next pressing question to be addressed is what this requires of us in the context of rising authoritarianism and the crisis of democracy. This, in turn, requires an understanding of the relationship between the idea of God's reign and the troubled democratic political context we currently confront.

DEMOCRATIC PLURALISM AND THE KINGDOM OF GOD

As the first two chapters of this project attempted to establish, democracy in the United States and around the world is in a state of crisis.[42] Forms of

38. Gushee and Stassen, *Kingdom Ethics*, 195.

39. Niebuhr, "Communication," 447.

40. Gushee and Stassen, *Kingdom Ethics*, 445.

41. Gushee and Stassen, *Kingdom Ethics*, 448.

42. To be precise, the form of government in most of the countries where it is under threat is some form of democratic republicanism. Many on the right have made a great

authoritarian religious and ethnic nationalism have become a prevalent threat within most of the world's major democratic countries, from Germany, France, and Poland, to India, Brazil, and the Philippines, to the United States. While not all these forms of authoritarianism are directly grounded within religious ideologies, religion does play a prominent role in many of them, and certainly within American Christian nationalism.

David Gushee has offered an analysis of the way in which those forms of what he refers to as "authoritarian reactionary Christianity" have emerged in several of these nations.[43] Defined as "support for or indifference to democratic backsliding," he offers it as an alternative to terms such as "Christian nationalism" on the grounds that it "may offer a broader historical and cultural framework to name and understand what we are seeing in much of the world today."[44] He notes that the imperfections of democracy have frequently led Christians to be cynical or skeptical about the value of democracy as a form of government. And yet, along with Reinhold Niebuhr, he affirms the principle that "man's capacity for justice makes democracy possible; but man's inclination to injustice makes democracy necessary."[45]

It is certainly true that democratic societies and those who participate in them are replete with flaws. Yet, the value of democracy as a form of government is grounded in the recognition that those flaws are not diminished by the concentration of power into one or a few sets of hands. What makes the resurgent forms of authoritarianism rising throughout the world particularly dangerous is the failure, or in many cases, refusal,

---

deal out of this distinction, claiming that it is wrong to call these countries "democracies." To a large degree, this is simply disingenuous pettifoggery. What makes these political structures unique is their *democratic* character, in which the population at large expresses its will through the election of representatives, as opposed to through direct deliberation. To act as though this somehow renders them un- or anti-democratic is to fundamentally misunderstand or misrepresent the issues at stake in these definitions. I will use democracy to indicate those forms of government in which the will of the people as expressed through a democratic process.

43. Gushee, *Defending Democracy from Its Christian Enemies.*

44. Gushee, *Defending Democracy from Its Christian Enemies*, 43–44.

45. Gushee, *Defending Democracy from Its Christian Enemies*, 7. This widely-quoted line comes from Niebuhr's *The Children of Light and the Children of Darkness*, which Niebuhr subtitled "A Vindication of Democracy and a Critique of Its Traditional Defense." Both aspects of this subtitle are important to understanding Niebuhr's argument, insofar as he wants to insist on democracy as an indispensable element of modern political life while at the same time recognizing that its value is not grounded in superior human virtue or reason, but, as the quote suggests, precisely because of the limitations it places on the human propensity for self-interest and injustice.

to acknowledge the often self-evident flaws demonstrated by the leaders of those movements. This is, of course, nowhere more true than in the case of Donald Trump.

In *The Dark Charisma of Donald Trump*, Dustin Byrd offers a "political psychology" of Trump and the role that he plays within the MAGA movement. At the core of his analysis is the intensely narcissistic and self-directed nature of everything Trump does. Trump "routinely reminded his audience that no one knew the dangers facing the nation better than him; no one knew the incompetence and criminality of the political establishment better than him; no one knew the economic unjustness of the system better than him since he, the billionaire, had benefited from that unjustness."[46] This claim to superior insight allowed him to claim, as he did during the 2016 campaign that "I alone can fix it!"[47]

To those who looked at Trump and saw, not a failed businessman and professional fraud, but a leader who would shake up the government and tip the scales in their favor against immigrants, women, and egg-headed intellectuals, he was a leader onto whom they could project their deepest desires and most passionate resentments:

> Trump would be their national chieftain, and as their model, they too could unleash their pussy-grabbing, woman-fucking, take-no-shit-from-liberals worldview. The national chieftain was powerful, demanding, and unapologetic; no one could limit him and his will-to-power. As such, Trump was the sole individual who could not only transform Washington, D.C., but also change the very culture of America, which they believe had gone off track through the feminization of American men, especially liberals and progressives. The fear of gynocracy was [palpable] in the Trump movement, and he benefitted greatly from it.[48]

It is precisely this assumption of unilateral competence and unconstrained power as manifested in Trump that poses a direct danger to democracy. In the early weeks of the current administration, he declared that "he who saves his country violates no law" (a quote widely attributed to Napoleon).[49]

46. Byrd, *Dark Charisma of Donald Trump*, 354.
47. Applebaum, "I Alone Can Fix It."
48. Byrd, *Dark Charisma of Donald Trump*, 255.
49. Haberman et al., "Trump Suggests No Laws Are Broken."

Trump's elections of course expose the dangers of democracy no less than authoritarianism. The fact that Trump was able to prevail in not one, but two democratic elections demonstrates precisely the democratic imperfections to which Gushee refers. There is nothing inherent to democratic systems of government that ensures the election of talented, or even competent, leaders. And it is often the case that authoritarian leaders come to power through democratic means.

Luke Bretherton makes this point in distinguishing between democracy as a practice versus democracy as a form of government, writing:

> Democratic politics can be distinguished from democracy as a mode of statecraft (e.g., voting systems, parliamentary forms of government, etc.) even as it is a way of determining and disciplining the use of unilateral power. Democratic politics names a set of practices for generating nonviolent forms of relational power and cooperation through various kinds of shared speech and action (e.g., community organizing, unions, cooperatives, demonstrations, etc.). Democratic politics in this sense means not just participation in decision making but also the capacity of ordinary people to act collectively to reconstitute their common life through shared speech and action.[50]

Bretherton goes on to elaborate several presuppositions that guide his understanding of what constitutes genuinely democratic politics: the capacity to build relationships with those with whom we differ, the capacity to listen across those differences, and the capacity to extend grace to those with whom we differ while also recognizing the flaws and limitations of those with whom we agree. "I assume," he writes, "that democratic politics is premised on the recognition that love and sin are political realities."[51]

I understand Bretherton to be arguing, correctly, for democracy not only as a set of political structures and procedures, but as a set of principles, values, and practices, informed both by a theological perspective (e.g., the coexistence of love and sin within human life and community) and our own individual and collective experiences. Democracy in this sense is incompatible with authoritarianism precisely on the level of morality. It does not validate an authoritarian leader if they have come to power via democratic means, but neither does it invalidate democracy. It does, however, expose the kinds of limits and flaws inherent to any political morality. The remedy for this is the articulation of democracy's

50. Bretherton, *Christ and the Common Life*, 445–46.

51. Bretherton, *Christ and the Common Life*, 446.

moral foundation, which, in the context of Christian ethics, also requires further reflection on the conjunction between democratic norms and the values of the kingdom of God.

Even taking into account Hall's understanding of kingdom language as a form of critique of existing systems—the recognition that God does not fully reign within the historical context, and the values of God's kingdom are not fully manifested within the systems and structures by which we are governed—the tension between the idea of "kingdom" and that of democracy remains. Christian nationalists and integralists attempt to resolve the tension by insisting that the kind of democratic structures they are willing to tolerate are open only to those who are recognized and certified as among the saved, sanctified and ratified by church authorities to participate in public life. They openly reject the idea of democracy as an intentionally pluralistic, and necessarily secular, political system, only seeing as valid systems of government in which the "godly" alone are allowed to rule. Others are, at best, tolerated.

To speak of democracy as a set of values is to assert that it embodies a set of substantive moral principles that reflect a genuine expression of the human good. It is not, in that sense, simply one possible expression of human political organization among others, but is grounded in an understanding of both the possibilities and limitations of human social organization, superior to autocratic or oligarchic governments precisely in the ways we have already described—by amalgamating diverse understandings of how society should operate and allowing for the contention of those understandings in a public forum. It is not the vision of one or a few that prevails, but the collective vision of society as expressed through the act of public participation, primarily voting, but also forms of speech and assembly through which citizens give voice to the diversity of opinions about the goods society should pursue.

Democracy in the sense I am describing depends upon and embraces a pluralism of views, cultures, ideologies, and moralities. "Democratic politics entails the radical extension of who is considered capable and worthy of being political agents, aiming as it does to form a common life through ensuring that political agency is distributed as widely as possible."[52] In this way it remains open to the new possibilities inherent in mass public deliberation. It also allows for all citizens to be included within that deliberation. At the same time, this pluralism of worldviews

52. Bretherton, *Christ and the Common Life*, 445.

also guards against the risks inherent in autocratic systems in that, while democracies can, and often do, err in their collective wisdom, they also provide the basis for correction—as one approach tries and fails, other approaches are available, and the democratic process, when it is properly functioning, does not allow for flawed policies to remain in place indefinitely.

It is in precisely this sense that democratic political systems become a reflection of the reign of God emerging within the historical setting. It is a mistake to think of the kingdom of God autocratically or heteronomously. Rather, as Paul Tillich argued, we encounter God theonomously through the meeting of our own consciousness with that of the divine.[53] God's will is not imposed upon us from without, but rather emerges from our experience of God as our ground of being. The kingdom of God is an ideal within history through our discernment of the *kairos* immanent in the particularity of our situation.[54] And yet, because it is interpreted and applied through our fallible human action, there is no guarantee that we will understand and apply it faithfully. The democratic process ensures that our discernment takes place in and through the common life of the community rather than through authoritarian imposition.

The Bible repeatedly reminds the church that it is in and through the power of the Holy Spirit, manifested within the Christian community, that God's reign becomes visible within history. Divine action occurs in and through the deliberation of the community of faith, and that divine action is not limited only to those who are members of the church or profess to be Christian. Divine action takes place always and everywhere in those settings where God chooses to be present, including secular social and political structures. As Karl Barth puts it: "God may speak to us through Russian Communism, a flute concerto, a blossoming shrub, or a dead dog."[55]

Barth rightly insisted that the church could not be reduced to an apparatus of the state, and nor could the state be subordinated to the church. Rather "the Christian community has a task of which the civil community can never relieve it and which it can never pursue in the forms peculiar to the civil community."[56] That task is to "proclaim the

53. Tillich, *Systematic Theology*, 3:249.

54. Tillich, *Socialist Decision*, 132.

55. Barth, *Church Dogmatics* I/1, 55–56.

56. Barth, *Community, Church, and State*, 157.

rule of Christ and the hope for the Kingdom of God."[57] The fundamental flaw in Christian nationalisms of all kinds is the failure to recognize this core distinction. The state, in whatever form, cannot fulfill the church's task of proclaiming God's reign. The church does not have a superior position within society compared with other faiths or communities. Rather "the Christian community shares common interests with the world and its task is to give resolute practical expression to this community of interest. The Christian community prays for the civil community."[58]

Nevertheless, the Christian community participates in the civil community according to the norm established in Jesus Christ, alongside and often in collaboration with non-Christians. But the purpose of that participation is not to force the state into submission to Christian principles and priorities, but rather to serve as a witness to the reign of Christ and the kingdom of God as participants in what Barth understands to be a fundamentally secular (or as he puts it, "pagan") setting.[59] "The Christian community within the State does know about the Kingdom of God . . . and brings it to man's attention."[60] The church, he states, "subordinates" itself to the civil community in accordance with Paul's words in Rom 13. However, Barth is at pains to note what this means:

> The last thing this instruction implies is that the Christian community and the Christian should offer the blindest possible obedience to the civil community and its officials. What is meant is (Romans 13:6f) that Christians should carry out what is required of them for the establishment, preservation, and maintenance of the civil community and for the execution of its task, because, although they are Christians and, as such,

57. Barth, *Community, Church, and State*, 158.

58. Barth, *Community, Church, and State*, 159.

59. This is not to imply, Barth insists, that the state, any more than any other aspect of creation, is free from the sovereign rule of God. Rather, "however much human error and human tyranny may be involved in it, the State is not a product of sin but one of the constants of the divine Providence and government of the world in its action against human sin: it is therefore an instrument of divine grace. The civil community shares both a common origin and a common centre with the Christian community" (*Community, Church, and State*, 156).

60. Barth, *Community, Church, and State*, 167. Elsewhere he writes, "The Church is not the Kingdom of God, but it has knowledge of it; it hopes for it; it believes in it; it prays in the name of Jesus Christ, and it preaches His Name as the Name above all others. . . . If the Church takes up its share of political responsibility, it must mean that it is taking that human initiative which the State cannot take: it is giving the State the impulse which it cannot give itself; it is reminding the State of those things of which it is unable to remind itself" (170).

> have their home elsewhere, they also live in this outer circle. Jesus Christ is still its centre: they too, are therefore responsible for its stability. "Subordination" means the carrying out of this joint responsibility in which Christians apply themselves to the same task with non-Christians and submit themselves to the same rule. The subordination accrues to the good of the civil community. . . . The "subordination" will be an expression of the obedience of a free heart which the Christian offers to God in the civil sphere as in the sphere of the Church—although with a different purpose (he renders to Caesar what is Caesar's and to God what is God's—Matthew 22:21).[61]

Thus the work of participation in public life is one that Christians undertake in obedience to God and alongside those of very different faiths and ideologies. In this way Barth acknowledges the pluralistic dimension of public life.

At the same time, he also argues that the Christian community is not indifferent to the form or structure of the state in which it participates, nor of the values for which it advocates. On the contrary, Christian faith requires support for movements and parties that advocate for social justice and democracy: "The Church must concentrate first on the lower and lowest levels of human society. The poor, the socially and economically weak and threatened, will always be the object of its primary and particular concern, and it will always insist on the state's special responsibility for these weaker members of society. . . . It will always choose the movement from which it can expect the greatest measure of social justice."[62]

A genuinely Christian political commitment, he notes, "betrays a striking tendency to the side of what is generally called the 'democratic' State," while at the same time remaining free of any commitment to a particular, and necessarily partial form of democratic governance. As with Gushee and Bretherton, Barth recognizes that whatever the democratic tendencies within Christianity may be, democracy as actually practiced is subject to the reality of human fallibility: "No democracy as such is protected from failing in many or all the points we have enumerated and

61. Barth, *Community, Church, and State*, 159–60.

62. Barth, *Community, Church, and State*, 173. For Barth, this entailed a clear commitment to Christian socialism. See Hunsinger, *Karl Barth and Radical Politics*.

degenerating not only into anarchy but also into tyranny and thereby becoming a bad state."[63]

To speak of Christian commitment to democracy does not entail a commitment to a particular Christian party or explicitly identified Christian political movement. "Can there be any other 'Christian' party in the State but the Christian fellowship itself, with its special mission and purpose?"[64] The Christian community is not partisan in this sense, as the existence of a "Christian party" implies that all other parties in some way represent interests opposed to Christianity. Rather, "the Church's supreme interest must be rather that Christians shall not mass together in a special party, since their task is to defend and proclaim, in decisions based on it, the Christian gospel that concerns all men."[65]

The kingdom of God then serves as the norm and limiting principle for Christian participation in society and advocacy for democratic values. It is, as Barth argues, the task of the church to "remind" the world of the kingdom of God.[66] But the kingdom itself always remains above and beyond any temporal form of civil government. No political organization can "anticipate" the kingdom of God, but it is the task of Christians within society to constantly point to God's reign as the *telos* of all human community.[67] At most, the state can function as "an allegory, as a correspondence and an analogue to the kingdom of God which the church preaches and believes in."[68] And the way in which that correspondence takes place is through the Christian participation within a pluralistic and democratic civil community.

"THE HOME OF GOD IS AMONG MORTALS": ESCHATOLOGY AS NORMATIVE ETHICS

Throughout this chapter I have been making the case for a Christian public theology grounded in the symbol of the kingdom of God. Yet, God's reign is an eschatological, not a temporal hope. As I noted above, it exists above and beyond the historical situation in which we exist, and so there

63. Barth, *Community, Church, and State*, 181.
64. Barth, *Community, Church, and State*, 182.
65. Barth, *Community, Church, and State*, 183.
66. Barth, *Community, Church, and State*, 162.
67. Barth, *Community, Church, and State*, 168.
68. Barth, *Community, Church, and State*, 169.

remains a valid question as to how it might function as a norm or guide in public life. Here I would like to develop the idea of God's kingdom as the starting point for a normative Christian ethic that can guide our public participation by examining the vision of the new heaven and earth as described in Revelation 21.

This chapter takes place after passages describing the persecution of the church, the war of the Lamb of God against the dragon and its armies, and the final judgment. It concludes the book by promising a "new heaven and a new earth" with a new Jerusalem at its center, "prepared as a bride adorned for her husband" (vv. 1–2). The author then goes on to describe a voice declaring: "See, the home of God is among mortals. He will dwell with them; they will be his peoples, and God himself will be with them and be their God; he will wipe every tear from their eyes. Death will be no more; mourning and crying and pain will be no more, for the first things have passed away" (vv. 3–4). The section concludes by declaring "See, I am making all things new" (v. 5).

Taken as a whole, this passage offers a vision of a world transformed through the nonviolent triumph of the Lamb over the dragon and the purging of sin and evil from the world. It presents an eschatological end-state, a genuine end of history as opposed to the ersatz one advocated by Hegel and Fukuyama, in which God is fully present among God's people, and the forces of death and destruction have been wholly and completely defeated.

Richard Bauckham notes the two symbolic forerunners of the heavenly Jerusalem in Revelation—on the one hand, the earthly Jerusalem, which is to be completed and fulfilled in its heavenly counterpart, and Babylon, the symbol for the earthly regimes that oppose the Lamb of God. He continues:

> We recall that part of the strategy of Revelation, in creating a symbolic world for its readers to enter, was to redirect their imaginative response to the world. If they were to dissociate themselves from Babylon and its corrupting influence on their own cities, they needed not only to be shown Roman civilization in a different light from the way its own propaganda portrayed it; they also needed an alternative. . . . Since Babylon is the great city that rules over the kings of the earth (17:18), even over the earthly Jerusalem, this alternative could belong only to the eschatological future. It is God's alternative city: the New

> Jerusalem that comes down from heaven. It belongs to the future, but through John's vision it exercises its attraction already.[69]

This is a point that Jürgen Moltmann makes as well. The future does not pacify us by proclaiming a future fulfillment of our hopes (as the old Wobbly organizing song would have it: "pie in the sky when you die, by and by"). Rather, hope for the future exercises power in the present, both in providing assurance that present suffering is neither absolute nor inevitable, and more significantly, by providing an eschatological norm for present human action. "The believer does not simply take the day as it comes but looks beyond the day to the things which according to the promise of him who is the *creator ex nihilo* and raiser of the dead are still to come."[70]

It is the faith in the promise which makes present moral action possible in light of God's coming future. The present moment becomes the reflection of the future reign of God insofar as those committed to the crucified and resurrected Christ act according to the promises inherent in that reign, seeking a righteousness beyond history, by striving to bring it to a semblance of historical realization. In Moltmann's words: "To believe means to cross in hope and anticipation the bounds that have been penetrated by the raising of the crucified."[71]

Anticipation in Moltmann's sense is not quite the same as the understanding of anticipation rejected by Barth. By "anticipation" Barth seems to mean "presumption," that is, usurping the work of God by seeking to build the reign of God through purely human means. This was the same condemnation that Reinhold Niebuhr made of the Social Gospel movement in the 1930s and 1940s. But Moltmann recognizes that the kingdom of God is an eschatological hope, not a human possibility. It is by living in and through a hope beyond history that human beings are motivated to generate new moral possibilities within history. These possibilities foreshadow the new Jerusalem descending upon earth proclaimed by Revelation 21.

What then does this passage promise? The central promise of this passage is that God will be fully present among God's people: "He will dwell with them; they will be his peoples, and God himself will be with them and be their God" (21:3). In the divine presence, death, mourning,

69. Bauckham, *Theology of the Book of Revelation*, 129.

70. Moltmann, *Theology of Hope*, 32.

71. Moltmann, *Theology of Hope*, 20–21.

and weeping will be abolished in the renewal of creation. Those who dwell within the new Jerusalem will drink the water of life. At the same time, all those things that are associated with the image of Babylon will not dwell within that city—no immorality, no deception, no violence or exploitation (vv. 3–8).

Charles Talbert views the overriding message of Revelation to be a warning against assimilation to the values and practices that the author associates with Babylon.

> John's message is that assimilation is not a possible avenue of action for Christians, because the ethos of statist society and the ethos of Christian community are, at base, incompatible. Statist society, taken to its logical outcome, represents an alternate religion. Those who fail to worship with statist society's religious framework will experience the full force of that society's sanctions against them.[72]

This would seem to imply that Christians must divest themselves from all involvement in temporal matters in order to avoid contamination by the values of Babylon. However, I think that this overreads Revelation in a sectarian and separatist fashion. Read this way, it would suggest that the public world in which Christians dwell is a matter of indifference, and perhaps even an object of hostility. If the world as it exists holds nothing for Christians beyond the worship of the beast and assimilation to the reign of Babylon, then it is best avoided. But the applicability of Revelation to a faithfully Christian public theology requires a more complex reading.

The Babylon of which Revelation speaks refers to the beast of John's own time—Rome. The symbol of Babylon refers to any worldly kingdom that stands against the reign of the Lamb, and the warning against assimilation refers to the same kinds of practices, regardless of what historical empire represents them. As Bauckham argues: "Since the evil of these cities was echoed and surpassed by Rome, how much more must God's judgement on them fall also on Rome. The city which the prophetic cap fits must wear it."[73]

But within history there is no neat division between Babylon and the New Jerusalem, between the Roman Empire and the kingdom of God. Rather, we dwell within the public sphere both as Christians and as

72. Talbert, *Apocalypse*, 111.

73. Bauckham, *Theology of the Book of Revelation*, 153.

citizens, both as faithful followers of Christ and those called upon to act with responsibility to our neighbors in the context of temporal life. The challenge for Christians has always been in how one can be *both* faithful *and* responsible. This is the key error of those who would advocate for a Christian withdrawal from public life, becoming "resident aliens" or seeking to live in "Benedict communities" instead of facing the ambiguity of social and political action in the midst of fallen institutional structures (as though the church itself is not a fallen institution, comprised of fallen people). As Bauckham writes:

> Revelation does not respond to the dominant ideology by promoting Christian withdrawal into a sectarian enclave that leaves the world to its judgement while consoling itself with millennial dreams. Since this is the standard caricature of the apocalyptic mentality, it must be strongly emphasized that it is the opposite of Revelation's outlook, which is oriented to the coming of God's kingdom in the whole world and calls Christians to active participation in this coming of the kingdom. . . . It is in the public, political world that Christians are to witness for the sake of God's kingdom. Worship, which is so prominent in the theocentric vision of Revelation, has nothing to do with pietistic retreat from the public world. It is the source of resistance to the idolatries of the public world.[74]

The real question is how Christianity can stand for the values of God's reign in the midst of the ambiguity of public life, and it is here that a commitment to democratic pluralism is central to Christian public theology, precisely because it grounds the idea of public participation as a nonviolent engagement with those with whom we may disagree vehemently, but with whom we are bound to act with love and respect. It is the ideology of violence, deception, and exploitation that Christians are called to resist, the ideology of Babylon, Rome, and—far too often—the United States, which certainly seems to "wear the prophetic cap" of empire in the modern world.

When the worldly cities in which Christians dwell reflect not the values of the Lamb, but the vices of Babylon, Christians are called, as Bauckham notes, to witness publicly on behalf of the new Jerusalem, the kingdom of God, and the reign of Christ, as a form of resistance. And the culminating vision of Revelation tells us that, for those who embrace the Lamb of God, and the values for which he stands—love, grace,

74. Bauckham, *Theology of the Book of Revelation*, 161.

nonviolence, and respect for persons as made in the *imago Dei*—the new Jerusalem awaits. As the chapter concludes, we glimpse something of what this looks like: "The nations will walk by its light, and the kings of the earth will bring their glory into it. Its gates will never be shut by day—and there will be no night there. People will bring into it the glory and honor of the nations" (vv. 24–26).

This is a vision of the presence of divinity permeating the whole of creation and the whole of human society, such that there is no longer any corruption or division among the peoples of earth. The heavenly city has gates, but John notes that they are never shut, and the kings and people of *all* nations come through it in order to mingle in its glory. It is notable that they are not melded into one singular identity within the new Jerusalem, but continue to be uniquely themselves, bearing God's glory while also contributing their own. "The nations and the kings will enjoy their own glory—all the goods of human culture—the more though dedicating it to God's glory."[75]

Yet, here again we note that the reign of God is not one of hierarchical domination. That is the way of Babylon and of the beast. Rather, through God's immanent presence within all of creation, God becomes "all in all" (1 Cor 15:28):

> As for the image of God's rule in the eschatological kingdom, what is most notable is the fact that all implication of distance between "the One who sits on the throne" and the world over which he rules has disappeared. His kingdom turns out to be quite unlike the beast's. It finds its fulfilment not in the subjection of God's "servants" (22:3) to his rule, but their reigning with him (22:5). The point is not that they reign over anyone: the point is that God's rule over them is for them a participation in his rule. The image expresses the eschatological reconciliation of God's rule and human freedom.[76]

Thus the eschatological vision of Revelation provides a moral grounding for Christian public participation in light of the hope of God's coming kingdom. This does not imply, as Christian nationalism mistakenly asserts, the seizure of political power by a putatively "Christian" faction in order to rule as it sees fit. Rather, it implies a participation in public life alongside others as a witness to the hope that motivates our public action. And, at the same time, it requires active resistance to those movements

75. Bauckham, *Theology of the Book of Revelation*, 141.

76. Bauckham, *Theology of the Book of Revelation*, 142.

and ideologies grounded in violence and exploitation, in light of the vision of a future world free of those things. The war of the Lamb that Revelation describes is, as Walter Wink has argued, not a struggle between the violence of God and the violence of the Beast, but a celebration of the Lamb's nonviolent victory over the rule of Babylon and the beast.[77]

77. Wink, *Engaging the Powers.*

Conclusion

We return to where we started, with the apocalyptic moment in which we are living, and what this moment unveils about ourselves and the social context within which we are striving to live out our faith. Throughout this project, I have been concerned to articulate the way in which questions of identity are at the forefront of the social, political, and theological questions that have brought us to this point, and as I come to the conclusion, I want to highlight key aspects of the argument for readers.

American democracy, as I argued at the outset, relies on often-competing symbolic frameworks, which provide the basis for contradictory visions of what the United States is, and crucially, whom it is for. For a long time, the aspirational myth of an inclusive America was in ascendance. We looked at the history of the country and its many failures to become a country for all of those who dwell here, and sought to do better—to become more inclusive, more egalitarian, and to open up the prospect for a better life to more and more people. We took the declaration on the pedestal of the Statue of Liberty seriously, understanding the United States as a place where one could come from anywhere on Earth and be welcome. Of course, this aspirational myth was never something we fully achieved, as we continued to struggle with our national legacy of slavery, oppression, and genocide. Yet there was, implicitly and often explicitly, a desire to become more like the country we wished ourselves to be, a country that genuinely welcomed the tired, the poor, and the huddled masses yearning to breathe free.

And yet, this aspirational myth was always in competition with another version of the United States, one that emphasized particularity and exclusion rather than the universalism and inclusion represented by the aspirational myth. This version of the American story grounds what has risen to prominence in the past decade under the general heading of

"Christian nationalism." Robert P. Jones connects this tradition explicitly with white supremacism, labeling it "white Christian nationalism,"[1] while David Gushee emphasizes the threat it poses to democracy, terming it "authoritarian reactionary Christianity."[2]

Here again, it must be noted, these two traditions did not arise as wholly separate, competing streams of thought in American history, but arose together, often intertwining and diverging in unexpected ways. There is no unambiguously righteous tradition of political identity in the United States. It has always been a project of taking that which is best from the deeply ambiguous history of the United States and crafting an aspirational identity from it. It is the ideological equivalent of panning for gold.

What has become apparent over the last ten years is that the exclusionary and particularist account of American identity has become increasingly prominent, and this is nowhere more clearly the case than in the Make America Great Again movement and the presidencies of Donald Trump. It is here that we can see the converging streams of nationalism, authoritarianism, isolationism, and white supremacy coming together to illuminate the thinly veiled cracks within the American body politic. Yet neither Trump the man nor MAGA the movement exist apart from the emerging wave of religious authoritarianism and conspiracism within American society.

In order to understand how we have gotten here, we need a fuller understanding, not only of those social and political forces, but of how identities are formed and constituted. No one has a singular identity; our identities are the product of the various claims that are made upon us by the overlapping communities within which we live our lives. It is when one of those identities seeks to make an exclusive claim upon our loyalty that we experience the inherent tensions among those overlapping claims. The struggle for recognition and dignity within society contributes to the conflicts that arise over questions of identity, often leading to violence.

At the same time, we cannot wholly replace the strong claims of particular identities with broadly universalist appeals to the weak ties of general humanity. National, ethnic, sexual, gender, and other identities remain fundamental dimensions of how we understand ourselves in the context of a much larger world, and the particularity of the communities in which those identities are expressed are crucial to establishing and

1. Jones, *Hidden Roots of White Supremacy*, 5.

2. Gushee, *Defending Democracy From Its Christian Enemies*, 43.

maintaining our sense of self in a world that would otherwise be too encompassing for us to manage. The appeal to universal and cosmopolitan values needs to take place within the recognition of their relationship to our particularity. This is what Kwame Anthony Appiah refers to as "rooted cosmopolitanism."[3]

Christian identity, however, goes further than these general insights about the tensions between the universal and particular, recognizing that our identities are ultimately grounded in our status as the beloved children of God, created in the divine image. God knows who we are more intimately than even we do ourselves, in all of our complexity and in recognition of all of the multifarious cross-pressures that constitute our understanding of who we are. We are not permitted to place other, exclusive, identities above our understanding of ourselves as created in the divine image.

In Christ we have the fullest possible expression of what it means to be human—to possess a particular identity and yet to be universally related to the whole of humanity. This creates a context for the responsibilities that we have for one another—responsibilities to care for and respect the dignity of one another solely on the basis of our common humanity. Yet, those responsibilities are always mediated and interpreted in light of our particularity. Ultimately, it means taking the risk of descending, as Christ did, into the realm of non-identity, breaking bread with and standing on the side of the poor, the outcast and the marginalized, putting their needs and concerns first and holding institutions accountable when they thrive on suffering and oppression.

Within the church, we develop the skills for participation within a diverse and pluralistic society, and it is through the development of those skills that we come to understand the centrality of standing on behalf of justice and democratic government, precisely because the church is, in principle if not always in fact, the community that embodies the demand for justice on behalf of all those created in the image of God. Democratic values follow naturally from the recognition that every human being is an equal participant in the divine life, and possesses both the privilege and the obligation of acting with moral responsibility in the world.

At the heart of Christian public theology is the acknowledgement that no worldly nation can fully embody the values of the kingdom of God, and thus the horizon of Christian public responsibility always extends beyond our present situation and into the future of God's coming

3. See Appiah, *Ethics of Identity*, 222–23.

reign. The image of the new Jerusalem in the book of Revelation provides a powerful metaphor for the society Christians anticipate in their public engagement—one in which particularity is not diminished or destroyed but is taken up within the cosmopolitan and universal realm that God is establishing on earth as it is in heaven. This is a vision of a society in which all of those things that stand against God's self-giving love have been eliminated, and all human beings can fully and freely embrace their identities as children of God and sisters and brothers of Christ.

This offers a moral basis for political action on behalf of the principles of democratic pluralism. Such principles are not merely formal or pragmatic, but reflect the deep moral core of Christian faith, grounded in our origin and our destination, our creation as *imago Dei* and our consummation as citizens of God's realm. None of this is to suggest that there are not genuine problems with democracy as it is actually practiced, but it is to insist that those problems, rooted in our fallen condition, are deviations from a fully realized embrace of democratic pluralism, one that genuinely respects the diversity of identities that contribute to a healthy and sustainable public life. In the end, however, the vision of God's kingdom on earth as it is in heaven is a pledge and a promise, that for all the faults and failures of human public life, for all our all-too-human inability to fully embody its values, it stands as the plumb line according to which our public action should be judged.

This project has been an attempt to offer an analysis of the current state of American public life using the tools of public theology. There is of course much more that should be said, and I make no claims to have offered a comprehensive account either of the issues facing American public life or the possible solutions. I hope that others will find this account useful as a contribution to the ongoing discussions about Christian public responsibility in the face of rising authoritarianism, both in the United States and globally.

The second volume of this project, *Christianity and Political Economy*, will examine questions of economic ethics and the Christian call to equality and social justice. While the question of identity was a necessary starting point for the larger social analysis I hope to continue throughout this project, addressing the material conditions that define many of the relations through which individuals come into contact with and address one another in public life is a further step toward a more comprehensive account of public life from the perspective of public theology, which I hope to offer in the third volume of this project.

Afterword

"Hell is empty, and all the devils are here!"
—William Shakespeare, *The Tempest*, Act 1, Scene 2

THIS IS MY THIRD attempt at writing this afterword. The first was written in the immediate aftermath of Donald Trump's 2024 election, while the second was written shortly after his inauguration. The ongoing process of editing this project has meant that events continued to outstrip my attempts to document them. It will no doubt be the case that anything I write here will also have been outstripped by further outrages before this book is in print. Nevertheless, it is important to state a few things here.

I began this project shortly after the first election of Donald Trump in 2016, and the bulk of it was completed prior to the 2024 election. As it neared completion, I had assumed, foolishly, that the material on Donald Trump would mostly be of retrospective interest. As I write, several months into the second Trump administration, I realize that it may have more contemporary relevance than I had realized. This thought gives me no comfort.

We already have ample evidence that Donald Trump's second term in office will exceed his first in corruption, lawlessness, and authoritarianism. During his first term, there were at least some minimal guardrails in place to prevent his abuses of power from becoming too excessive. And yet, even then, we saw attempts to ban Muslims from the United States, as well as a family separation policy at the US/Mexico border that resulted in children being taken from their parents, and in some cases, never reunited. We saw astounding levels of government corruption, much with the explicit purpose of putting money into the pockets of the Trump family. We saw collaboration between Donald Trump and foreign adversaries such as Russia. The maladministration eventually culminated in the botched response to the COVID-19 pandemic. There is no reason to believe a second Trump administration will not find ways of topping even the most egregious of his past abuses. As Steven Levitsky and Lucan Way write:

> The country's vaunted constitutional checks are failing. Trump violated the cardinal rule of democracy when he attempted to overturn the results of an election and block a peaceful transfer of power. Yet neither Congress nor the judiciary held him accountable, and the Republican Party—coup attempt notwithstanding—renominated him for president. Trump ran an openly authoritarian campaign in 2024, pledging to prosecute his rivals, punish critical media, and deploy the army to repress protest. He won, and thanks to an extraordinary Supreme Court decision, he will enjoy broad presidential immunity during his second term.[1]

And yet, Trump not only recaptured control of the Republican Party and won the nomination without more than token opposition; he retook the presidency, not, as in 2016, simply through the quirks of the American Electoral College, but with a majority of the popular vote. More people, of every background—white, black, Latino, suburban, rural, urban, red state, blue state—voted for Trump in 2024 than in 2016.

The reasons this was so have already led to a great deal of analysis and introspection, which will no doubt continue in the months and years to come. There were recriminations against Kamala Harris, the Democratic Party, and progressive political factions in the United States. And there may be elements of blame in all those areas. But at least part of the answer must address issues of identity.

On the one hand, the Trump campaign leveraged controversies around so-called "identity politics" in order to motivate voters concerned about questions of sexuality and gender, as well as immigration and nationality, to support him. Even absurd smears against (it must be said legal) Haitian immigrants found traction. Similarly, Trump was able to appeal to the perception in some circles that the Democratic Party had become captive to an array of identity-based constituencies who did not reflect the concerns of average Americans.

On the other hand, Trump was able to make inroads within groups that had been widely assumed to belong to the Democratic Party, largely

1. Levitsky and Way, "Path to American Authoritarianism," para. 3.

on the basis of identity. Latino voters, for example, voted for Trump 42 percent to 57 percent, a huge gain over previous elections.[2] This suggests that the liberal political assumptions about how racial and ethnic categories affected voting patterns were, at best, outmoded. This seems to have been the case, even taking into account the explicitly racist dimensions of Trump's campaign.

Then there was the question of Kamala Harris's identity. As a woman, she faced headwinds in the form of an entrenched misogyny among many Americans (both men and women) who could not envision a woman as president. Then there were the attempts made to suggest that, because she had never given birth to a child, she was somehow paradoxically "less" of a woman, regardless of the work she did mothering her stepchildren. Lest we forget, there was Trump's attempt to suggest that she was somehow not "really" black because her mother was Indian. From every angle, Harris's identity, in all of its dimensions, was made into campaign fodder by her opponents.

Added to this, from the outset, the Trump administration has targeted Diversity, Equity, and Inclusion programs (which, as I argued in chapter 3, are hardly immune to criticism) across the entire federal government and within higher education. Once again, at stake is the question of how complex issues of identity are navigated, and how the diversity of ways in which identity is constructed and described are (or increasingly are not) validated within the public realm. The cruel revocation of all recognition of transgender identity on the part of the government is just one example of how a very specific conception of identity is being imposed from above by the new administration.

On the level of policy, it is unclear to what extent the well-publicized Project 2025 will actually provide a guide for the administration, although all indications suggest that it offers the comprehensive foundation for the administration's policy actions.[3] Other right-wing organizations, such

2. Gerbaud et al., "How Latinos Voted in the 2024 Election," para. 1.

3. It is notable that the president of the Heritage Foundation, which published the project, Kevin Roberts, delayed the release of his new book, *By Dawn's Early Light*, for which Vice President J. D. Vance wrote the foreword, in order to avoid drawing adverse attention to the Trump campaign. According to a review in *The New Republic*, "Most of the book's 11 chapters each single out a usual suspect: public schools, China, godlessness, regulation, and so on. But the overall goal here is a much more widespread destruction of any number of cultural and governmental institutions, only a few of which are enumerated in the opening pages: 'Every Ivy League college, the FBI, the New York Times, the National Institute of Allergy and Infectious Diseases, the Department of Education, 80 percent of "Catholic" higher education, BlackRock, the Loudoun County

as the America First Policy Institute, have proposed their own agendas.[4] But whichever of the competing plans predominates, the net effect will be similar—there will be potentially severe restrictions on reproductive freedom, crackdowns on immigration (legal or illegal), increased discrimination against the LGBTQ+ community, and cuts to education and social services, accompanied by large tax breaks for the ultra-wealthy.[5]

Given Republican Party control of both houses of Congress in addition to the presidency and its current dominance over the federal judiciary, the United States can look forward to a more authoritarian, more centralized government that will undermine the rule of law, the separation of powers, and the separation of church and state.

At the heart of the policy program in a second Trump administration will clearly be the issues of identity that have motivated white Christian nationalism for the past several years—racial grievance, religious intolerance, and the attempt to recover the status and privilege that they believe has been thwarted by a more diverse, pluralistic, and cosmopolitan ideology over the past several decades.

All of this has serious implications for the future of a democratic society. It remains to be seen whether a second Trump administration will launch a full-scale attack on democracy as such, though already in the early weeks of the administration, the forecast looks grim. Even if the Trump administration isn't able to effectuate a wholesale abandonment of democracy, it will certainly contribute to an erosion of it. Many of the ideological leaders of contemporary conservatism take their cues from Victor Orbán's "illiberal democracy" in Hungary—in which the formal structures of democratic society remain, but in an attenuated form. The erosion of an independent judiciary and legislature, already well underway in the United States, allow for the concentration of greater power within the executive branch, and thus a greater risk of autocracy. But as long as those formal democratic structures continue to benefit the autocracy, they will be left in place, as a kind of fig leaf over the regime's abuses.

But then again, this assessment may be overly optimistic (if "optimism" is even the right word here). It will remain the case that many

---

Public School System, the Boy Scouts of America, the Bill & Melinda Gates Foundation, the World Economic Forum, the Chinese Communist Party, and the National Endowment for Democracy'" (Dickey, "Voters Have a Right to Know").

4. See https://americafirstpolicy.com.

5. The connections between Project 2025 and the Trump administration are well documented. See, for example, Shao and Wu, "Many Links."

people will be harmed by an unrestrained Trump administration—certainly immigrants, both documented and undocumented, Muslims, LGBTQ+ citizens, and those who rely on government infrastructure for everything from health care and education to housing assistance. Abetted by a supine Congress and the vast authority bequeathed by the Supreme Court, the administration has little to prevent it from executing whatever policy choices it cares to.

Unless this administration is stopped through active resistance by the public and through the reclamation of their constitutional responsibilities as co-equal branches of government by Congress and the courts, we can expect further examples of authoritarianism, lawlessness, violence, cruelty, intolerance, and corruption. Unless there is a sustained public outcry, we can expect the democratic values of the United States to be replaced by an increasing oligarchy. The process is well underway, even mere months into the administration. The deportation of migrants without due process, and in defiance of the courts, is only one of the most egregious examples of encroaching tyranny. The administration's purging of career federal officials and the targeting of universities and independent institutions offers additional evidence. The question is not whether the administration will attempt to go further; the question is who will stop them.

Public theology can serve to describe, as H. Richard Niebuhr put it, "what's going on"[6] in the world, interpret it according to the texts and traditions of the Christian church, and offer some resources for constructive theological engagement on behalf of the Christian community. But these can only be offered as resources for the church. It is for Christians, activated by their passion for the gospel and their hope for the kingdom of God, to organize and engage in the struggle to preserve democracy, however imperfect and flawed it may be, for the sake of creating a more just, equal, and open society for all people, whether or not they call themselves Christian.

In the final analysis though, the fact remains that, as Christians, we are always simultaneously citizens of two realms—this world with its particular nation-states and political arrangements, and the particular identities that we claim and that claim us, and the kingdom of God. Yet, our values derive from, and our ultimately loyalty belongs to, God. Christian nationalism defines loyalty to God in terms of loyalty to the state.

6. Niebuhr, *Responsible Self*, 60.

But a morally grounded public theology recognizes that no state, and no nation, can fully embody the values of God's kingdom. It always stands in contradiction to even our highest human achievements, and yet its values govern how we act as citizens of these other realms. And in the face of violence and autocracy, this demands that we stand in resistance.

May 4, 2025

Bibliography

Adorno, Theodor. *Aspects of the New Right-Wing Extremism*. Translated by Wieland Hoban. Cambridge: Polity, 2020.

———. "The Meaning of Working Through the Past." In *Critical Models: Interventions and Catchwords*, 295–306. New York: Columbia University Press, 1998.

Adorno, Theodor, et al. *The Authoritarian Personality*. Hoboken, NJ: John Wiley and Sons, 1950.

Ahmari, Sohrab. "Against David-French-ism." *First Things*, May 29, 2019. https://www.firstthings.com/web-exclusives/2019/05/against-david-french-ism.

———. *Tyranny, Inc.* New York: Forum, 2023.

Ahmari, Sohrab, et al. "Against the Dead Consensus." *First Things*, March 21, 2019. https://www.firstthings.com/web-exclusives/2019/03/against-the-dead-consensus.

Ahmed, Akbar. *Jinnah, Pakistan, and Islamic Identity: The Search for Saladin*. London: Routledge, 1997.

America First Policy Institute. "The America First Agenda." https://americafirstpolicy.com/.

Anderson, Carol. *White Rage: The Unspoken Truth of Our Racial Divide*. New York: Bloomsbury, 2016.

Anton, Michael, et al. "National Conservatism: A Statement of Principles." https://nationalconservatism.org/national-conservatism-a-statement-of-principles/.

Appiah, Kwame Anthony. *Cosmopolitanism: Ethics in a World of Strangers*. New York: W. W. Norton, 2006.

———. *The Ethics of Identity*. Princeton, NJ: Princeton University Press, 2007.

———. *The Lies That Bind: Rethinking Identity*. London: Profile Books, 2018.

Applebaum, Ann. *Twilight of Democracy: The Seductive Lure of Authoritarianism*. New York: Doubleday, 2020.

Applebaum, Yoni. "I Alone Can Fix It." *The Atlantic*, July 21, 2016. https://www.theatlantic.com/politics/archive/2016/07/trump-rnc-speech-alone-fix-it/492557/.

Arendt, Hannah. *The Human Condition*. 2nd ed. Chicago: University of Chicago Press, 1998.

———. *The Origins of Totalitarianism*. New York: Anchor, 1968.

Aslan, Reza. *Beyond Fundamentalism: Confronting Religious Extremism in the Age of Globalization*. New York: Random House, 2010.

———. *How to Win a Cosmic War: God, Globalization, and the End of the War on Terror.* New York: Random House, 2009.

Augustine. *On Christian Doctrine*. Garden City, NY: Dover, 2009.
Bailie, Gil. *Violence Unveiled: Humanity at the Crossroads*. St. Louis: Crossroad, 1995.
Barber, Benjamin. *Jihad vs. McWorld: Terrorism's Challenge to Democracy*. New York: Ballantine Books, 1995, rev. 2001.
Barth, Karl. *Church Dogmatics*. 4 vols. New York: T. & T. Clark, 2009.
———. *Community, Church, and State*. Gloucester, MA: Peter Smith, 1960.
Bauckham, Richard. *The Theology of the Book of Revelation*. Cambridge: Cambridge University Press, 1993.
Bayne, Nicholas. "Why Did Seattle Fail: Globalization and the Politics of Trade." *Government and Opposition* 35 (2000) 131–51.
Berman, Marshall. *All That Is Solid Melts into Air: The Experience of Modernity*. New York: Penguin, 1988.
Berman, Paul. *Terror and Liberalism*. New York: W. W. Norton, 2003.
Bethge, Eberhard. *Dietrich Bonhoeffer: A Life*. Rev. ed. Minneapolis: Fortress, 2000.
Billington, Michael. "Dennis Potter: There Is a Nostalgic, Right-Wing Impulse in Britain." *The Guardian*, May 15, 2015. https://www.theguardian.com/stage/2015/may/15/dennis-potter-nostalgic-rightwing-england
Bivins, Jason C. *The Religion of Fear: The Politics of Horror in Conservative Evangelicalism*. Oxford: Oxford University Press, 2008.
Bonhoeffer, Dietrich. "The Church and the Jewish Question, April 1933." In *Behind Valkyrie: German Resistance to Hitler, Documents*, edited by Peter Hoffmann, 137–55. Montreal: McGill-Queen's University Press, 2011.
———. *Ethics*. Minneapolis: Fortress, 2005.
———. *Letters and Papers from Prison*. New York: Touchstone, 1971.
Bottici, Chiara, and Benoît Challand. *The Myth of the Clash of Civilizations*. London: Routledge, 2010.
Bretherton, Luke. *Christ and the Common Life*. Grand Rapids: Eerdmans, 2019.
Breitenberg, Hal. "To Tell the Truth: Will the Real Public Theology Please Stand Up?" *Journal of the Society of Christian Ethics* 23 (2003) 55–96.
———. "What Is Public Theology?" In *Public Theology for a Global Society: Essays in Honor of Max L. Stackhouse*, edited by Deirdre Hainsworth and Scott Paeth, 3–17. Grand Rapids: Eerdmans, 2010.
Brokaw, Tom. *The Greatest Generation*. New York: Random House, 2001.
Brunner, Emil. *The Divine Imperative*. Cambridge: Lutterworth, 1941.
Buchanan, Patrick. "Culture War Speech: Address to the Republican National Convention." August 17, 1992. https://voicesofdemocracy.umd.edu/buchanan-culture-war-speech-speech-text/.
Bump, Philip. "Another Night at the Garden: How Trump's Rally Echoed on in 1939." *The Washington Post*, October, 28, 2024. https://www.washingtonpost.com/politics/2024/10/28/trump-rally-madison-square-garden/.
Byrd, Dustin J. *The Dark Charisma of Donald Trump: Political Psychology and the MAGA Movement*. Kalamazoo, MI: Ekpyriosis, 2023.
Calvin, John. *Institutes of the Christian Religion*. Louisville, KY: Westminster, 1960.
Camus, Albert. *Personal Writings*. New York: Vintage, 2020.
Capehart, Jonathan. "The Damage Rachel Dolezal Has Done." *The Washington Post*, June 12, 2015. https://www.washingtonpost.com/blogs/post-partisan/wp/2015/06/12/the-damage-rachel-dolezal-has-done/.

Carbine, Rosemary P. *Nevertheless, We Persist: A Feminist Public Theology*. Maryknoll, NY: Orbis, 2023.

Carroll, Jordan S. *Speculative Whiteness: Science Fiction and the Alt-Right*. Minneapolis: University of Minnesota Press, 2024.

Carter, Bill. "ABC to End 'Politically Incorrect.'" *The New York Times*, May 14, 2002. https://www.nytimes.com/2002/05/14/business/abc-to-end-politically-incorrect.html.

Carter, J. Kameron. *Race: A Theological Account*. Oxford: Oxford University Press, 2008.

Cartledge, Mark J. *The Holy Spirit and Public Life: Empowering Ecclesial Praxis*. Minneapolis: Fortress, 2022.

Chambers, Whittaker. "Faith for a Lenten Age." *Time*, March 8, 1948. https://whittakerchambers.org/articles/time-c/religion-faith-for-a-lenten-age/.

Chamberlain, Will, et al. "National Conservatism: A Statement of Principles" https://nationalconservatism.org/national-conservatism-a-statement-of-principles/.

Coates, Ta-Nahisi. "The Case for Reparations." *The Atlantic*, June 2014. https://www.theatlantic.com/magazine/archive/2014/06/the-case-for-reparations/361631/.

Cohen, Stanley. *Folk Devils and Moral Panics*. London: Routledge, 2011.

Cone, James. *A Black Theology of Liberation*. Maryknoll: Orbis, 1990.

———. *The God of the Oppressed*. New York: HarperCollins, 1975.

Cooper, Clint. "Fort Oglethorpe Billboard Picturing Trump with Messianic Words Is Wrong-Headed." *Chattanooga Times Free Press*, September 14, 2021. https://www.timesfreepress.com/news/2021/sep/14/cooper-fort-oglethorpe-billboard/.

Cooper-White, Pamela. *The Psychology of Christian Nationalism: Why People Are Drawn in and How to Talk Across the Divide*. Minneapolis: Fortress, 2022.

Crean, Thomas, and Alan Fimister. *Integralism: A Manual of Political Philosophy*. Neunkirchen-Seelscheid: Editiones Scholasticae, 2020.

Crossman, Richard H., and David C. Engerman. *The God that Failed*. New York: Columbia University Press, 2001.

Cunningham, David S. *These Three Are One*. Oxford: Blackwell, 1998.

D'Angelo, Robin. *White Fragility: Why Is It So Hard for White People to Talk About Racism*. Boston: Beacon, 2018.

Daub, Adrian. *The Cancel Culture Panic: How an American Obsession Went Global*. Redwood City, CA: Stanford University Press, 2024.

Denker, Angela. *Red State Christians: Understanding the Voters Who Elected Donald Trump*. Minneapolis: Broadleaf, 2022.

Devi, Faisal. *Muslim Zion: Pakistan as a Political Idea*. Cambridge, MA: Harvard University Press, 2013.

Dickey, Colin. "Voters Have a Right to Know What Kevin Roberts's Disturbing Book Says." *The New Republic*, August 9, 2024. https://newrepublic.com/article/184651/voters-right-know-kevin-robertss-disturbing-book-says-j-d-vance-project-2025.

Dreher, Rod. *The Benedict Option*. New York: Sentinal, 2018.

Du Mez, Kristin Kobes. *Jesus and John Wayne*. New York: Liveright, 2020.

Edwards, Jonathan. *Observations Concerning the Scripture Oeconomy of the Trinity and Covenant of Redemption*. Hungerford: Legare Street, 2022.

Eco, Umberto. *Interpretation and Overinterpretation*. Cambridge: Cambridge University Press, 1992.

———. *Inventing the Enemy*. London: Vintage, 2013.

———. *The Role of the Reader*. Bloomington: Indiana University Press, 1979.

Ellison, Harlan. *Greatest Hits*. New York: Union Square & Co., 2024.

Ellison, Ralph. *Invisible Man*. New York: Penguin, 2007.

Everett, William Johnson. *God's Federal Republic: Reconstructing Our Governing Symbol*. Mahway, NJ: Paulist, 1988.

Francis, Leslie J., and Hans-Georg Ziebertz. *The Public Significance of Religion*. Leiden: Brill, 2011.

Friedman, Thomas. *The World Is Flat*. New York: Picador, 2005.

FitzGerald, Francis. *The Evangelicals: The Struggle to Shape America*. New York: Simon & Schuster, 2018.

Flegenheimer, Matt. "How J. D. Vance Thinks About Power." *The New York Times*, August 3, 2024. https://www.nytimes.com/2024/08/03/us/politics/jd-vance-donald-trump-2024-campaign.html.

Fukuyama, Francis. *The End of History and the Last Man*. Florence, MA: Free Press, 2006.

———. *Identity: The Demand for Dignity and the Politics of Resentment*. New York: Picador, 2018.

Gabriel, Trip. "Trump Escalates Anti-Immigrant Rhetoric With 'Poisoning the Blood' Comment." *The New York Times*, October 5, 2023. https://www.nytimes.com/2023/10/05/us/politics/trump-immigration-rhetoric.html.

Ganz, John. "The Year the Clock Broke." *The Baffler*, November 2018. https://thebaffler.com/salvos/the-year-the-clock-broke-ganz.

———. *When the Clock Broke: Con Men, Conspiracists, and How America Cracked Up in the Early 1990s*. New York: Farrar, Strauss, and Giroux, 2024.

Ganz, John, and Steven Klein. "A Serious Man: On Jordan Peterson." *The Baffler*, February 7, 2018. https://thebaffler.com/latest/peterson-ganz-klein.

Gerbaud, Gladys, et al. "How Latinos Voted in the 2024 Election." AS/COA, November 6, 2024. https://www.as-coa.org/articles/how-latinos-voted-2024-us-presidential-election.

Ghemawat, Pankaj. *World 3.0: Global Prosperity and How to Achieve It*. Boston: Harvard Business Review, 2011.

Ghosh, Partha S. *BJP and the Evolution of Hindu Nationalism*. New Delhi: Manohar, 2000.

Gírard, Rene. *The Scapegoat*. Baltimore: Johns Hopkins University Press, 1986.

———. *Violence and the Sacred*. Baltimore: Johns Hopkins University Press, 1972.

Goldman, Samuel. *After Nationalism: Being American in an Age of Division*. Philadelphia: University of Pennsylvania Press, 2021.

Gorski, Philip, et al. *The Flag and the Cross: White Christian Nationalism and the Threat to American Democracy*. Oxford: Oxford University Press, 2022.

Graham, Elaine. *Between a Rock and a Hard Place: Public Theology in a Post-Secular Age*. London: SCM, 2013.

Greene, Graham. *The Quiet American*. New York: Penguin, 2004.

Gushee, David. *Defending Democracy from Its Christian Enemies*. Grand Rapids: Eerdmans, 2023.

Gushee, David P., and Glen H. Stassen. *Kingdom Ethics: Follow Jesus in Contemporary Context*. 2nd ed. Grand Rapids: Eerdmans, 2016.

Gustafson, James. *Ethics from a Theocentric Perspective*. Chicago: University of Chicago Press, 1984.

Haberman, Maggie, et al. "Trump Suggests No Laws Are Broken If He's 'Saving His Country.'" *The New York Times*, February 15, 2025. https://www.nytimes.com/2025/02/15/us/politics/trump-saves-country-quote.html.

Habermas, Jürgen. *Moral Consciousness and Communicative Action*. Cambridge, MA: MIT Press, 1990.

———. *The Theory of Communicative Action*. 2 vols. Boston: Beacon, 1984, 1987.

Haidt, Jonathan. *The Righteous Mind*. New York: Pantheon, 2012.

Hall, Douglas John. *Confessing the Faith*. Minneapolis: Fortress, 1998.

Hansen, Len, ed. *Christian in Public: Aims, Methodologies, and Issues in Public Theology*. Stellenbosch: African SUN Media, 2007.

Hart, David Bentley. "A Person You Flee at Parties: Donald and the Devil." *First Things*, May 6, 2011. https://www.firstthings.com/web-exclusives/2011/05/a-person-you-flee-at-parties.

Hasic, Albinko. "'The Gates of the Wall Stand Open Wide': What Happened the Day the Berlin Wall Fell." *Time*, November 7, 2019. https://time.com/5720386/berlin-wall-fall/.

Hauerwas, Stanley. *In Good Company: The Polis as Church*. Notre Dame: University of Notre Dame Press, 1995.

———. *The Peaceable Kingdom: A Primal in Christian Ethics*. Notre Dame, IN: Notre Dame University Press, 1983.

Hauerwas, Stanley, and William Willamon. *Resident Aliens: Life in the Christian Colony*. Nashville: Abingdon, 2014.

Hate Ali, Mohanad. *Nationalism, Transnationalism, and Political Islam: Hizbullah's Institutional Identity*. London: Palgrave Macmillan, 2018.

Hazony, Yoram. *The Jewish State: The Struggle for Israel's Soul*. Boston: Basic, 2009.

———. *The Virtue of Nationalism*. Boston: Basic, 2018.

Hegel, G. W. F. *Hegel's Phenomenology of Spirit*. Oxford: Oxford University Press, 1977.

Held, David, and Anthony McGrew. *Globalization/Anti-Globalization*. Cambridge: Polity, 2002.

The Heritage Foundation. *A Mandate for Leadership: The Conservative Promise*. Washington, DC: The Heritage Foundation, 2023.

Holpuch, Amanda. "Rachel Dolezal Identifying as African American Is Highly Unusual, Experts Say." *The Guardian*, June 13, 2105. https://www.theguardian.com/us-news/2015/jun/13/rachel-dolezal-african-american-naacp-spokane.

Hoppe, Hans-Hermann. *Democracy—the God that Failed: The Economics and Politics of Monarchy, Democracy, and the Natural Order*. London: Routledge, 2001.

Huber, Wolfgang. *Violence: The Unrelenting Assault on Human Dignity*. Minneapolis: Fortress, 1993.

Hui, Yuk. "On the Unhappy Consciousness of Neoreactionaries." *Eflux Journal* 81 (2017) 1–12. https://www.e-flux.com/journal/81/125815/on-the-unhappy-consciousness-of-neoreactionaries/.

Hume, David. *An Enquiry Concerning the Principles of Morals: A Critical Edition*. Edited by Tom L. Beauchamp. Oxford: Clarendon, 1998.

———. *A Treatise of Human Nature*. Oxford: Oxford University Press, 2000.

Hunsinger, George. *Karl Barth and Radical Politics*. Philadelphia: Westminster, 1976.

Huntington, Samuel P. *The Clash of Civilizations and the Remaking of the World Order*. New York: Simon & Schuster, 2011.

Ignatiev, Noel. *How the Irish Became White*. London: Routledge, 2008.

Jardina, Ashley. *White Identity Politics*. Cambridge: Cambridge University Press, 2019.

Jensen, Michael A., and Sheehan Kane. "QAnon-Inspired Violence in the United States: An Empirical Assessment of a Misunderstood Threat." *Behavioral Sciences of Terrorism and Political Aggression* 16 (2024) 65–83.

Jensen, Robert. *The Triune Identity: God According to the Gospel*. Minneapolis: Fortress, 1982.

Johnson, Chalmers. *Blowback: The Costs and Consequences of American Empire*. 2nd ed. New York: Henry Holt, 2004.

Jones, Robert P. *The End of White Christian America*. New York: Simon & Schuster, 2016.

———. *The Hidden Roots of White Supremacy*. New York: Simon and Schuster, 2023.

———. *White Too Long: The Legacy of White Supremacy in American Christianity*. New York: Simon & Schuster, 2020.

Jones, Tony. *Did God Kill Jesus: Searching for Love in History's Most Famous Execution*. New York: HarperCollins, 2015.

Jung, Carl. *Answer to Job*. Princeton, NJ: Princeton University Press, 2010.

Kang, Jay Caspian. "Identity Crisis." *The New Yorker*, March 4, 2024. https://www.newyorker.com/magazine/2024/03/04/a-professor-claimed-to-be-native-american-did-she-know-she-wasnt.

Kantorowicz, Ernst. *The King's Two Bodies: A Study in Medieval Political Theology*. Princeton, NJ: Princeton University Press, 2016.

Karni, Annie, et al. "Trump Plays on Racist Fears of Terrorized Suburbs to Court White Voters." *The New York Times*, July 28, 2020. https://www.nytimes.com/2020/07/29/us/politics/trump-suburbs-housing-white-voters.html?.

Kaplan, Eran. *The Jewish Radical Right: Revisionist Zionism and Its Ideological Legacy*. Madison: University of Wisconsin Press, 2005.

Kendi, Ibram X. *How to Be an Antiracist*. London: One World, 2019.

Kim, Sebastian, and Katie Day, eds. *The Companion to Public Theology*. Leiden: Brill, 2017.

King, Martin Luther, Jr. "I Have A Dream." In *A Testament of Hope: The Essential Writings and Speeches*, edited by James M. Washington, 217–20. San Francisco: HarperOne, 2003.

Kirkpatrick, Jeanne. *Dictatorships and Double Standards: Rationalism and Reason in Politics*. New York: Simon & Schuster, 1982.

Klein, Naomi. *This Changes Everything: Capitalism vs. the Climate*. New York: Simon & Schuster, 2014.

Kojeve, Alexandre. *Introduction to the Reading of Hegel: Lectures on the Phenomenology of Spirit*. Ithaca: Cornell University Press, 1969.

Kostko, Adam. *What Is Theology?* New York: Fordham University Press, 2021.

Kramer, Katherine J. *The Politics of Resentment: Rural Consciousness and the Rise of Scott Walker*. Chicago: University of Chicago Press, 2016.

LaCugna, Catherine. *God For Us: The Trinity and Christian Life*. New York: HarperCollins, 1973.

Lee, Sang Hyun. *The Philosophical Theology of Jonathan Edwards: Expanded Edition*. Princeton, NJ: Princeton University Press, 2000.

Levi, Margaret. "Coalitions of Contention: The Case of the WTO Protests in Seattle." *Political Studies* 54 (2006) 651–70.

Levitsky, Steven, and Lucan A. Way. "The Path to American Authoritarianism: What Comes After Democratic Breakdown." *Foreign Affairs*, February 11, 2025. https://www.foreignaffairs.com/united-states/path-american-authoritarianism-trump.

Littlejohn, Bradford. "Ahmari Among the Protestants." *American Reformer*, February 25, 2022. https://americanreformer.org/2022/02/ahmari-among-the-protestants/.

Linker, Damon. *The Theocons: Secular America Under Siege*. New York: Anchor, 2006.

Livius, Titus. *The History of Rome*. Loeb Classical Library. Cambridge, MA: Harvard University Press, 1919.

MacPherson, C. B. *The Political Theory of Possessive Individualism*. Oxford: Oxford University Press, 2011.

Marti, Gerardo. *American Blindspot: Race, Class, Religion and the Trump Presidency*. Lanham: Rowman & Littlefield, 2020.

Marx, Karl, and Freidrich Engels. *The Marx-Engels Reader*. New York: W. W. Norton, 1978.

Matthewes, Charles. *A Theology of Public Life*. Cambridge: Cambridge University Press, 2007.

Maximus, Valerius. *Facta et Dicta Memorabilia Volume 1: Books 1–5*. Loeb Classical Library. Cambridge, MA: Harvard University Press, 2000.

McManus, Matt. "Yarvin's Case Against Democracy." *Commonweal*, January 27, 2023. https://www.commonwealmagazine.org/curtis-yarvin-thiel-carlyle-monarchism-reactionary.

Menon, Kalyani Devaki. *Everyday Nationalism: Women of the Hindu Right in India*. Philadelphia: University of Pennsylvania Press, 2012.

Migliore, Daniel. *Faith Seeking Understanding*. 4th ed. Grand Rapids: Eerdmans, 2023.

Milbank, John. *Theology and Social Theory*. Oxford: Blackwell, 1993.

Moltmann, Jürgen. *The Church in the Power of the Spirit*. Minneapolis: Fortress, 1993.

———. *The Crucified God: The Cross as the Foundation and Criticism of Christian Theology*. New York: HarperCollins, 1991.

———. *On Human Dignity: Political Theology and Ethics*. Minneapolis: Fortress, 1984.

———. *The Open Church: Invitation to a Messianic Lifestyle*. London: SCM, 1978.

———. *The Spirit of Life*. Minneapolis: Fortress, 1992.

———. *Theology of Hope*. New York: HarperCollins, 1991.

———. *The Way of Jesus Christ: Christology in Messianic Dimensions*. Minneapolis: Fortress: 1993.

Mounk, Yascha. *The Identity Trap: A Story of Ideas and Power in Our Time*. New York: Penguin, 2023.

Neuhaus, Richard John. *The Naked Public Square*. Grand Rapids: Eerdmans, 1984.

Niebuhr, H. Richard. "A Communication: The Only Way Into the Kingdom of God." *The Christian Century*, March 30, 1932.

———. *The Kingdom of God in America*. Middletown, CT: Wesleyan University Press, 1988.

———. *The Responsible Self*. Louisville, KY: Westminster John Knox, 1999.

Niebuhr, Reinhold. *The Irony of American History*. Chicago: University of Chicago Press, 2008.

———. *Moral Man and Immoral Society*. New York: Charles Scribner's Sons, 1932.

———. *The Self and the Dramas of History*. New York: Charles Scrivner's Sons, 1955.

Novak, Michael. *Unmeltable Ethnics: Politics and Culture in American Life*. 2nd ed. London: Routledge, 1995.

Orbán, Victor. "Prime Minister Viktor Orbán's Speech at the 25th Bálványos Summer Free University and Student Camp." https://2015-2019.kormany.hu/en/the-prime-minister/the-prime-minister-s-speeches/prime-minister-viktor-orban-s-speech-at-the-25th-balvanyos-summer-free-university-and-student-camp.

———. "Full Text of Viktor Orbán's Speech at Băile Tuşnad (Tusnádfürdő) of 26 July 2014." https://www.almendron.com/tribuna/wp-content/uploads/2016/01/discurso-viktor-orban.pdf.

Paeth, Scott. *Exodus Church and Civil Society: Public Theology and Social Theory in the Work of Jurgen Moltmann*. London: Routledge, 2008.

———. "Globalization, Global Ethics, and the Common Good." In *Multi-Religious Perspectives on a 'Global Ethic': In Search of a Common Morality*, edited by William Schweiker and Myriam Renaud, 119–36. London: Routledge, 2020.

———. "The Great Recession: Some Niebuhrian Reflections." *Soundings* 95 (2012) 389–410.

———. "Jürgen Moltmann's Public Theology." *Political Theology* 6 (2005) 215–34.

———. "Jürgen Moltmann and the 'New Political Theology.'" In *The Companion to Political Theology*, edited by Rubén Rosario-Rodriguez, 211–24. London: T. & T. Clark, 2019.

———. "Public Theology in the Context of Globalization." In *The Companion to Public Theology*, edited by Sebastian Kim and Katie Day, 185–219. Leiden: Brill, 2017.

———. "Whose Public? Which Theology? Signposts on the Way to a 21st Century Christian Ethic." *The International Journal of Public Theology* 10 (2016) 461–85.

Parents Involved in Community Schools v. Seattle School Dist. No. 1. 551 U.S. 701 (2007).

Patrick, Gnana. *Public Theology: Indian Concerns, Perspectives, and Themes*. Minneapolis: Fortress, 2020.

Paul VI, Pope. *Dignitatis Humanae*. Vatican City, December 7, 1965. https://www.vatican.va/archive/hist_councils/ii_vatican_council/documents/vat-ii_decl_19651207_dignitatis-humanae_en.html.

Philips, Emo. "The Best God Joke Ever—And It's Mine!" *The Guardian*, September 29, 2005. https://www.theguardian.com/stage/2005/sep/29/comedy.religion.

Placher, William. *The Triune God: An Essay in Postliberal Theology*. Louisville, KY: Westminster John Knox, 2007.

Plato. *Symposium*. Translated by Alexander Nehamas and Paul Woodruff. Indianapolis: Hackett, 1989.

Potter, Dennis. *Brimstone and Treacle: A Play*. London: S. French, 1978.

Public Religion Research Institute, *A Christian Nation? Understanding the Threat of Christian Nationalism to American Democracy and Culture*. Washington, DC: PRRI/Brookings Institute, 2023.

Rahner, Karl. *The Trinity*. St. Louis: Crossroad, 1997.

Rasmussen, Larry. "There's No Place to Hide in the Anthropocene." *Sojourners*, April 2023. https://sojo.net/magazine/april-2023/theres-no-place-hide-anthropocene.

Reilly, Katie. "Here Are All the Times Donald Trump Insulted Mexico." *Time*, August 31, 2016. https://time.com/4473972/donald-trump-mexico-meeting-insult/.

Ritchie, Michael, dir. *The Candidate*. Burbank, CA: Warner Bros., 1972.

Roberts, Kevin. *By Dawn's Early Light: Taking Back Washington to Save America*. New York: HarperCollins, 2024.

Roediger, David. *Working Toward Whiteness: How America's Immigrants Became White*. New York: Basic, 2018.

Rothschild, Mike. *The Storm Is Upon Us: How QAnon Became a Movement, Culture, and Conspiracy Theory of Everything*. Brooklyn: Melville House, 2021.

Rusch, William. *The Trinitarian Controversy*. Minneapolis: Fortress, 1980.

Said, Edward. "The Clash of Ignorance." *The Nation*, October 2001. https://www.thenation.com/article/archive/clash-ignorance/.

Sandifer, Elizabeth. *Neo-Reaction a Basilisk: Essays Around the Alt-Right*. New York: Eruditorum.

Sartre, Jean Paul. *Antisemite and Jew: An Exploration of the Etiology of Hate*. New York: Shocken, 1995.

———. *Existentialism and Human Emotions*. New York: Citadel, 1985.

Schmitt, Carl. *The Concept of the Political*. Chicago: University of Chicago Press, 1996.

———. *Political Theology*. Chicago: University of Chicago Press, 2006.

Schopenhauer, Arthur. *The World as Will and Idea*. London: Everyman, 1995.

Seidel, Andrew L. *The Founding Myth: Why Christian Nationalism Is Un-American*. New York: Union Square & Co., 2019.

Sen, Amartya. "Democracy as a Universal Value." *Journal of Democracy* 10 (1999) 3–17.

———. *Development as Freedom*. Milwaukee: Anchor, 2000.

———. *Identity and Violence: The Illusion of Destiny*. New York: W. W. Norton, 2006.

Shao, Elena, and Ashley Wu. "The Many Links Between Project 2025 and Trump's World." *The New York Times*, October 22, 2024. https://www.nytimes.com/interactive/2024/10/22/us/politics/project-2025-trump-heritage-foundation.html.

Sharlet, Jeff. *The Undertow: Scenes from a Slow Civil War*. New York: W. W. Norton, 2023.

Shaw, George Bernard. "Music in London." *The World*, November 15, 1893.

Sherwin-White, A. N. *The Roman Citizenship*. Oxford: Oxford University Press, 1980.

Shin, Allen K., and Larry Benfield, eds. *The Crisis of Christian Nationalism*. New York: Church Publishing, 2024.

Sider, Ronald. *The Spiritual Danger of Donald Trump: 30 Evangelical Christians on Justice, Truth, and Moral Integrity*. Eugene, OR: Cascade, 2020.

Sides, John, et al. *The Bitter End: The 2020 Presidential Campaign and the Challenge to American Democracy*. Princeton, NJ: Princeton University Press, 2022.

Simpson, Gary M. "Theologia Crucis and the Forensically Fraught World: Engaging Helmut Peukert and Jürgen Habermas." In *Habermas, Modernity, and Public Theology*, edited by Don Browning and Francis Schussler Fiorenza, 173–205. Spring Valley, NY: Crossroad, 1992.

Smallwood, Teresa L. *Public Theology and Violent Rhetoric Examined in a Queer Womanist Critical Ethnography*. London: T. & T. Clark, 2025.

Smith, James K. A. *Awaiting the King*. Ada, MI: Baker Academic, 2017.

———. *Desiring the Kingdom: Worship, Worldview, and Cultural Formation*. Ada, MI: Baker Academic: 2009.

———. *Imagining the Kingdom: How Worship Works*. Ada, MI: Baker Academic, 2013.

Sommer, Will. *Trust the Plan*. New York: HarperCollins, 2023.

Stern, Fritz. *The Politics of Cultural Despair*. Oakland: University of California Press, 1974.

Stewart, Katherine. *The Power Worshipers: Inside the Dangerous Rise of Religious Nationalism*. London: Bloomsbury, 2020.

Stackhouse, Max, et al. *The Local Church in a Global Era*. Grand Rapids: Eerdmans, 2000.

Stigliz, Joseph. *Fair Trade for All*. Oxford: Oxford University Press, 2005.

———. *Globalization and Its Discontents Revisited: Anti-Globalization in the Era of Trump*. New York: W. W. Norton, 2017.

Szelényi, Zsuzsanna. *Tainted Democracy: Viktor Orbán and the Subversion of Hungary*. London: Hurst Publishers, 2023.

Tait, Joshua. "Mencius Goldbug and Neoreaction." In *Key Thinkers of the Radical Right: Behind the New Threat to Liberal Democracy*, edited by Mark Sedgwick, 187–203. Oxford: Oxford University Press, 2019.

Táíwò, Olúfémi. *Elite Capture: How the Powerful Took Over Identity Politics (And Everything Else)*. Chicago: Haymarket, 2022.

Talbert, Charles. *The Apocalypse: A Reading of the Revelation of John*. Louisville, KY: Westminster John Knox, 1994.

Taylor, Charles. *Sources of the Self*. Cambridge, MA: Harvard University Press, 1989.

Theil, Peter. "The Education of a Libertarian." *Cato Unbound: A Journal of Debate*, April 13, 2009. https://www.cato-unbound.org/2009/04/13/peter-thiel/education-libertarian/.

Tillich, Paul. *Against the Third Reich: Paul Tillich's Wartime Broadcasts into Nazi Germany*. Louisville, KY: Westminster/John Knox Press, 1998.

———. *The Religious Situation*. New York: World, 1963.

———. *The Socialist Decision*. New York: Harper & Row, 1977.

———. *Systematic Theology*. 3 vols. Chicago: University of Chicago Press, 1963.

Tolstoy, Leo. *The Kingdom of God Is Within You*. Lincoln: University of Nebraska Press, 1984.

Toobin, Jeffrey. *Homegrown: Timothy McVeigh and the Rise of Right-Wing Extremism*. New York: Simon & Schuster, 2023.

Toor, Saadia. *The State of Islam: Culture and Cold War Politics in Pakistan*. London: Pluto, 2011.

Tore Flåten, Lars. *Hindu Nationalism, History and Identity in India: Narrating a Hindu Past Under the BJP*. London: Routledge, 2016.

Tracy, David. *The Analogical Imagination*. London: Crossroad, 1998.

Trans Legislation Tracker. "2024 Anti-Trans Bill Tracker." https://translegislation.com/bills/2024.

Tuvel, Rebecca. "In Defense of Transracialism." *Hypatia* 32 (2017) 263–78.

Uddin, Sufia M. *Constructing Bangladesh: Religion, Ethnicity, and Language in an Islamic Nation*. Chapel Hill, NC: University of North Carolina Press, 2006.

United States Catholic Bishops. *Economic Justice For All*. United States Catholic Conference, 1997.

Van Der Veer, Peter. *Religious Nationalism: Hindus and Muslims in India*. Oakland: University of California Press, 1994.

Vance, J. D. *Hillbilly Elegy: A Memoir of a Family and Culture in Crisis*. New York: Harper 2018.

Volf, Miroslav. *After Our Likeness: The Church as the Image of the Trinity*. Grand Rapids: Eerdmans, 1998.

Waldsten, P. Edmund, ed. *Integralism and the Common Good: Essays from The Josias. Volume 2: The Two Powers*. Brooklyn: Angelico, 2022.

Walzer, Michael. *Just and Unjust Wars*. New York: Basic, 1977.

Ward, Graham. *The Politics of Discipleship: Becoming Postmaterial Citizens*. Ada, MI: Baker Academic, 2009.

Weber, Max. "Politics as a Vocation." In *From Max Weber: Essays in Sociology*, 77–128. London: Routledge, 1970.

Weinberg, Justin. "Philosopher's Article On Transracialism Sparks Controversy (Updated with response from author)." *Daily Nous*, May 1, 2017. https://dailynous.com/2017/05/01/philosophers-article-transracialism-sparks-controversy/

Weiss, Volker. "Afterword." In *Aspects of the New Right-Wing Extremism*, by Theodor Adorno et al., 42–64. London: Polity, 2020.

Whitehead, Andrew L., and Samuel L. Perry. *Taking America Back for God*. Oxford: Oxford University Press.

Williams, Daniel K. "What Really Happens When Americans Stop Going to Church." *The Atlantic*, September 3, 3023. https://www.theatlantic.com/ideas/archive/2023/09/christianity-religion-america-church-polarization/675215/.

Wills, Gary. *Nixon Agonistes: The Crisis of the Self-Made Man*. New York: Mariner, 2002.

Wink, Walter. *Engaging the Powers*. Minneapolis: Fortress, 1992.

Winthrop, John. *A Model of Christian Charity*. New York: Cosimo Classics, 2020.

Wolfe, Stephen. *The Case for Christian Nationalism*. Moscow, ID: Canon, 2022.

Yarvin, Curtis. "A Gentle Introduction to Unqualified Reservations." Self-Published under the pseudonym "Mencius Moldbug," 2009.

Yarvin, Curtis. *An Open Letter to Open-Minded Progressives*. N.d.: Unqualified Reservations, 2015.

Žižek, Slavoj. *Living in the End Times*. New York: Verso, 2011.

Index

www.ingramcontent.com/pod-product-compliance
Lightning Source LLC
LaVergne TN
LVHW091129080826
845145LV00008B/2092